12/13
36.00

Anytime,
Anywhere

Anytime, Anywhere

*Student-Centered Learning
for Schools and Teachers*

Edited by

Rebecca E. Wolfe
Adria Steinberg
Nancy Hoffman

HARVARD EDUCATION PRESS
CAMBRIDGE, MASSACHUSETTS

Library of Congress Control Number 2012954832

Paperback ISBN 978-1-61250-569-5
Library Edition ISBN 978-1-61250-570-1

Published by Harvard Education Press,
an imprint of the Harvard Education Publishing Group

Harvard Education Press
8 Story Street
Cambridge, MA 02138

Cover Design: Joel Gendron
Cover Photo: © Rob Lewine/Tetra Images/Corbis

The typefaces used in this book are Minion and Christiana.

Contents

Foreword

The greatest opportunity facing our country today is that of sustaining and growing a flourishing society in the context of a fast-changing world. The days are gone when basic schooling coupled with ingenuity and hard work was sufficient for America to maintain a strong global economic position. The acceleration of technology, hyperconnectivity, and knowledge development requires a similar update to the skills individuals will need to support their families and build successful communities—and for the progress of our nation.

Our adequate preparation as a society for a fruitful future depends on increasing the skill and knowledge levels of each and every young person, which in turn depends on a lifetime of access to high-quality, developmentally appropriate and equitable learning opportunities. Yet instead, in the United States, we currently find ourselves in conditions of growing inequality, stagnant educational outcomes, and tightening school budgets.

Is it time to renovate our systems of education as one might renovate an old home? Can we just slap on a new coat of paint—or do we need to challenge assumptions about where, when, and with whom learning occurs?

At the Nellie Mae Education Foundation, we think it is the latter. To reach this goal for the coming decades, we are working to remodel systems with a set of principles that define *student-centered approaches* to learning. We believe these approaches and the systems necessary to nurture and manage them constitute the most promising route to achieving equity and excellence for all students, especially those who are underserved.

More specifically, we support movement from the current one-size-fits-all system, which is now overwhelmingly driven by time, to a more tailored approach, where the primary driver is learning, to meet students where they are. While we must set the same high standards of achievement, we must also provide different routes, environments, and pacing for each learner to get there. For secondary education, which is the focus of our grant making, this means:

- Seat time, as defined by Carnegie units, is no longer the best indicator of whether a student has mastered skills and knowledge.
- Students are not expected to learn the same curricula in the same way at the exact same pace.
- Students are not tracked based on generalized notions of ability, but rather get the support that they need to master each standard or competency.
- Students have multiple opportunities to deepen their understanding of concepts through application and practice, in school, in the community, in workplaces, and through online experiences.
- Responsibility for learning becomes a shared effort, as students understand what they need to learn, where they stand, and how to move forward.

To encourage this transformation, we are investing in four related strategies: research and evaluation, policy change, practice, and public understanding and demand. Our resources support states, districts, and communities across New England as they implement, sustain, and build demand for student-centered approaches that foster deeper learning for every student. These strategies are guided by recent research on motivation and the learning sciences to better prepare students to thrive in work and life. All of our grant programs promote new student-centered models of schooling that offer a path away from a one-size-fits-all approach to more personalized learning for all students. More specifically, our District Level Systems Change Initiative includes long-term investment in districts with a commitment to simultaneously "raise the bar" and "close the gaps."

Effective student-centered learning in a school is complex; spreading this approach through and across schools and districts requires a paradigm shift. Technology is already beginning to drive some of this redesign, and increasing interest from policymakers at all levels—including the priority of "personalization" identified in the federal government's District Race to the Top grants—will result in increasing the speed of change.

As a result of our interest in student-centered learning, in early 2010 the Nellie Mae Education Foundation embarked on a long-term, significant investment in expanding the knowledge base and the field by partnering with Boston-based Jobs for the Future (JFF) to commission a set of research papers that has resulted in this book for educators. JFF brings a set of attributes uniquely suited to this task: a sophisticated, rigorous research capacity grounded in decades of experience in educational practice, combined with deep understanding of the challenges facing underserved students. We couldn't have asked for a better partner in bringing together existing knowledge to bear on the emerging field of student-centered learning to answer a fundamental question: *What do we know?* This volume is the fruits of months of labor, combining streams of knowledge as varied as the development of motivation in adolescent learners and sustainable systems change in school districts.

We are painfully aware that support for an educational approach is no guarantee that it is implemented effectively or equitably. This edited volume focuses particularly on those students who have not been well served by our educational system in the past. There is no question that race- and income-related achievement gaps are overwhelmingly a result and reflection of the inequities in our society. That is why we need an approach that focuses on the real needs of students, whatever their starting point, rather than some imaginary "average" student who faces none of these challenges.

What does it take to achieve this transformation? There are many necessary steps and parallel pathways to navigate. This volume addresses a few key drivers that we need to better understand in order to create sustained systems change. One persistent theme focuses on the advancement of pedagogy and curriculum built on *how* people learn, as well as how children and adolescents develop. Another is to adjust, amend, and/or rescind policies that promote an assembly-line, batch-processing approach to secondary schooling. Rather, we need to frame it as an orchestra with learners at the center and all parts of the system working in concert to play in tune from a common sheet of music.

However, there is another dimension or set of participants in this picture: the "audience." The advancement of an orchestra-like system of learning versus an assembly-line system of schools also depends on the continued enlistment and support of the community and the public.

Perennially tighter school budgets, rapid technological development, and openness to new ideas in an era of growing recognition that we have reached the limits of progress resulting from test-based accountability are all converging to create a spirit of innovation. Development of the Common Core State Standards is a step in the right direction, and creates opportunity for a new conversation framed by student-centered approaches. However, we recognize the need to carefully evaluate the results of this work, whether supported by the Foundation or others, because not every approach will be equally successful.

In our era, the search is on for effective, affordable approaches to ensuring that all students meet higher learning targets than ever before—and that those who are currently the most underserved have the opportunity to receive an education that allows them to thrive. *Anytime, Anywhere* suggests that such a path is available—and while not easy, it will lead to greater opportunity and equity for all students as they prepare for success in college and beyond.

When we began our collaboration with JFF, we couldn't have anticipated the development of a powerful learning community between the authors of the chapters, who codeveloped outlines, reviewed one another's manuscripts, challenged one another's thinking, consulted regularly over the course of the project, and presented the papers publicly in dialogue with one another's ideas. Sometimes there is a stereotype of researchers as academics far removed from the application of their work, but in fact, the authors were just the opposite—energized to drive a movement forward and constantly searching for ways to do this, both in their own work and as a group. They not only informed us, but also inspired us with their deep commitment to educational change.

We realize that we are stretching across a gap—building on the strongest evidence available even while acknowledging the need to create new, innovative solutions and develop the technology that makes them widely available. Much more knowledge is needed before we have the demonstrated proof to articulate just what this means for our educational system and how we should move forward to achieve the values of equality and progress that we share, but have not yet enacted, as a nation, such as:

- A better understanding of the architecture of new governance, finance, and management systems that the implementation of student-centered approaches demand
- The evidence base to show that creative and varied approaches to learning work, especially for students who need them most
- Knowledge about how to rebuild public understanding of education systems that meet not only economic and job demands, but that strengthen our democracy and culture
- A better understanding of systems that adapt to change approaches as new demands and opportunities arise

However, at Nellie Mae, we believe that there is simply too much knowledge already in hand supporting student-centered learning approaches for readers to come away from this book unconvinced. There are myriad proof points, whether found in schools, cognitive sciences, or the growing number of evaluations. The overarching theme that arises within this volume is: change is possible. The brain is plastic, shaped by experience over time—and motivation, the key to effective learning, can be developed through well-structured opportunities to master rigorous material. Maybe the system can change and adapt as well.

In education we talk a lot about evidence, yet our systems—from teacher preparation to accountability—rarely reflect what the research tells us. In supporting the expansion of the knowledge base for student-centered learning, our goal is to be both thorough and transparent. We don't want to overstate these results—there is still much to be learned. But I challenge you to read these chapters and ignore the accumulation of convincing research: student-centered learning is an idea whose time has come, and it is possible to achieve the kind of deep change we need.

Nicholas C. Donohue
President and CEO
Nellie Mae Education Foundation

Acknowledgments

The Jobs for the Future team is grateful to the many people who have supported and guided the Students at the Center project as it became a book. First and foremost, we are grateful to the researchers who did the hard work of synthesizing complex bodies of knowledge, enduring multiple rounds of edits. The authors are the joy and the power inside this book—along with the teachers, students, and committed scholars whose voices they bring to life on behalf of better educational outcomes for all young people. The JFF team would also like to thank the JFF communications staff, Marc S. Miller and Sophie Besl, for editorial contributions and especially Carol Gerwin, our consulting editor, for her keen ear and insights in helping us create a comprehensive, accessible book for educators working in schools. We are also grateful to our program officers at the Nellie Mae Education Foundation, Beth Miller and Eve Goldberg, for conceptualizing this project and serving as engaged partners at each step of the way; and also to Nicholas Donohue, NMEF President, for his vision and tenacity in putting student-centered learning at the core of the Foundation's work. Finally, we thank the Harvard Education Press for their encouragement, responsiveness, and gentle advice.

—Rebecca E. Wolfe, Adria Steinberg, and Nancy Hoffman

Introduction

Rebecca E. Wolfe, Adria Steinberg,
and Nancy Hoffman

VISIT A HIGH SCHOOL in any U.S. city or town and you will see vastly different approaches to teaching and learning. Entering some classrooms, you may recognize the education of your childhood: the teacher stands in front of the room, reviewing material from the textbook while students sit at their desks, expected to take notes quietly and raise their hands only to respond to questions the teacher poses. A written test comes at the end of each unit.

Other classrooms will present a striking contrast. Stepping inside, you see a dynamic learning environment that may remind you of a workplace in the digital age: students confer in small teams or work individually on laptops or smartphones as the teacher checks in with groups or meets with students one at a time. Whether planning PowerPoint presentations, creating videos, or writing blog posts, the young people are, each in their own way, pursuing a multistep project that both deepens their learning and demonstrates it both inside and outside the classroom, during the school day and after. Peers and teachers critique these efforts as part of a continuous improvement process. Later, a panel of experts from outside the school will assess their mastery of the subject in a public exhibition.

If you observe many classrooms, you will see that learning environments today often share elements of both instructional models. A growing number of teachers are beginning to venture into the more dynamic and individualized instructional modes. Students may do some work in groups; they may share papers for peer comment; some units may end with a project of their own choosing. Yet the old-fashioned, teacher-directed style predominates, especially in urban districts that focus tightly on raising basic literacy and math skills to meet improvement goals on state standardized tests. This kind of classroom is a version of the industrial or factory model of education prevalent since early in the twentieth century: schools move students along much like cars on an assembly line, with different pieces of information getting "attached" to them in each classroom, each quarter, each grade level.

The industrial model has long had its critics. In fact, since the middle of the nineteenth century, respected theorists have offered compelling arguments for more student-centered approaches that change the relationship between the teacher, learner, and curriculum in ways that put the young person at the center and enable the student to shape his or her own learning.

The writings of Horace Mann and John Dewey, Paulo Freire and Theodore Sizer, and many other educators have inspired generations of teachers to break out of the industrial mold. Some whole-school experiments are examples of student-centered models as well—the University of Chicago Laboratory Schools, Big Picture Learning's Met schools, Expeditionary Learning schools, early college high schools, and newer, technology-based schools such as Quest to Learn and the School of One, among others. Many public schools have joined numerous private progressive schools in practicing student-centered approaches to teaching and learning, just as more mainstream education reforms have incorporated elements of student-centered practices (e.g., reading and writing workshops and inquiry-based science curricula).

Still, the scale of such experiments remains small. The divergence of student-centered approaches from long-accepted notions of schooling, the bureaucratic and political difficulties of changing standard operating procedures, and the challenges for teachers of implementing such practices effectively have conspired against their more widespread adoption. Furthermore, an unintended consequence of the rise of standardized testing has been to reinforce the notion that all students must learn the same material in the same way.

GROWING INTEREST IN STUDENT-CENTERED LEARNING

All the contributors to *Anytime, Anywhere* start from the recognition that interest in student-centered approaches to learning is growing despite long-standing barriers. Fueling this renewed interest are important developments in brain science, technology, and educational policy.

Perhaps most compelling to teachers are findings emerging from research on how students learn and what makes them eager to learn. For example, neuroscientists have shown that the abilities of students are far from fixed. In fact, the brain changes continually as learning experiences shape its very architecture. Moreover, the neural changes that underlie lasting learning occur when experiences are active, not passive. Neuroscientists have also shown that learning and emotion work together in the brain: while the brain tags some experiences as positive and worth approaching, it designates others as negative and to be avoided.

Considered in the context of this expanding neuroscience knowledge base, student-centered approaches to teaching and learning make a great deal of sense. Teachers can see how the research on mind, brain, and education aligns closely with many student-centered practices: active learning when students are up, out of their chairs, "doing"; the fostering of positive relationships with teachers and other adults; frequent formative assessments to help students track their own progress and own their goals; and the exploration of topics students perceive as relevant to their lives and goals, to name just some of the most common.

Teachers are also becoming increasingly cognizant of how advances in educational technology make it more feasible for them to implement student-centered practices, even in classrooms of students with a wide range of learning differences. As any good teacher will tell you, individual students have a complex profile of strengths and limitations and learn best through experiences tailored to their own needs and interests. Increasingly, the challenges of achieving such differentiated, customized instruction are being mitigated by multimedia learning technologies, social media, and learning management systems that make it easier to individualize learning and to keep track of the multiplicity of assignments, projects, and assessments in a single classroom. And, of course, today's young people have grown up with the new media: they find technology not only a compelling, but also a natural way to inquire about the world.

The third impetus behind the growing interest in student-centered approaches to learning is the agreement of forty-six states and the District of Columbia to adopt the Common Core State Standards, which raise the bar for education excellence. Developed with the recognition that global social and economic imperatives create a new urgency for a better-educated workforce and citizenry, the Common Core standards are pegged to college and career readiness for all students.

Teachers know all too well how difficult it is to help the full range of students—who enter their classrooms at vastly different levels of literacy and numeracy—to attain these standards. Since the beginning of the standards movement in the early 1990s, teaching and learning have too frequently taken a back seat to isolating and assessing a narrow band of knowledge and skills. The Common Core holds new promise, but only if it is coupled with close attention to rethinking the learning environment in both in-school and out-of-school settings, and the instructional core—that vital interconnection of teacher, student, and curriculum.

While the Common Core does not specify particular pedagogical approaches, its underlying assumptions differ from the standards of the past. Woven into its fabric is the importance of active learning; applying knowledge, not just acquiring it; and using multiple ways of solving problems. The knowledge base on student-centered learning assembled in this volume offers teachers many of the entry points they will need to engage adolescents in the deeper learning the Common Core requires. The authors speak directly to what is known about how to achieve the level of intellectual engagement and social and emotional development that will be necessary if all students are to reach the promised outcomes of college and career readiness. The practices they describe represent a way to not only to meet the demands of the Common Core but, even more important, to achieve its promise.

THE ORIGINS OF THIS BOOK

Despite the wide interest in and need for student-centered approaches to learning, educators have scant access to a comprehensive accounting of its key components. To build the knowledge base and momentum for this emerging field, Jobs for the Future (JFF), a national education and workforce nonprofit based in Boston, created the Students at the Center project with funding from the Nellie Mae Education Foundation. The first phase of the project involved commissioning papers from nine teams of noted researchers, seven of which are included as chapters in the book; the other two are available online. Determining and shaping the papers was done with an eye to what the research and education community needed to better understand in order to build the field. Wherever applicable, authors were asked to place an explicit focus on secondary education. Because of the project's larger goals, JFF did not simply identify writers and sign them on to write in isolation. The research teams committed to becoming a "learning community," and they outlined, refined, and revised their papers in deep, engaged conversation with one another. Along with participating in regular phone calls before and during the writing process, the writers came together in three face-to-face sessions: during the kickoff of the project, when only paragraphs and outlines of the papers existed; when the papers were nearing final form, to participate in outlining the introduction to the collection; and a third time, as the presenters and centerpieces of a symposium in April 2012 with over 150 researchers, practitioners, policy makers, and funders in attendance.

Building on the momentum begun with the research and symposium, Students at the Center is developing tools and materials and working with educators to translate the research to practice. Despite growing interest in and the need for a more student-centered approach to learning, educators—particularly at the high school level—too rarely have enough access to rich descriptions of what it looks like in practice. Nor do they have ready access to the theory and research that explain its power and support its expansion. The authors in *Anytime, Anywhere* address that challenge. They paint a picture of student-centered learning in the hands of excellent schools and teachers. They identify four essential features that define this burgeoning field; namely, that student-centered approaches to learning:

- Embrace the student's experience and identity as a key starting point of education
- Allow for pacing and advancement based on demonstration of proficiency
- Expand and reshape the role of the educator
- Harness the full range of learning experiences anytime, anywhere

Further, they delve into how these approaches could start to address seemingly intractable achievement gap issues and draw deeply on recent research to support the case for spreading student-centered learning practices throughout our schools.

HOW THE BOOK IS ORGANIZED

This volume is intended to present a comprehensive overview of student-centered learning and the practices and research supporting them for schools and teachers. It is organized in three parts, beginning with current practices and assessment.

The chapters in part 1 provide a bounty of present-day examples of what student-centered teaching, classrooms, schools, and assessment look like in the United States. Part 1 poses and answers the questions: *What does student-centered teaching and learning look like in schools today? How are teachers using assessment both to enhance the learning process and to keep track of its effectiveness?* In answer to the first question, Barbara Cervone and Kathleen Cushman identify eight elements of student-centered practices in chapter 1. In addition, they examine subsequent changes to the role of the teacher who delivers these elements. Some (e.g., strong relationships; supporting social and emotional growth) may feel familiar to those acquainted with good teaching practices and recent beliefs in what constitutes effective teaching. Others (e.g., anywhere, anytime learning; personalization; and choice in curricular tasks) reflect newer reforms and are closely linked to technological advances and what they have made possible. Whether describing a familiar or new practice, Cervone and Cushman demonstrate the impact of having all eight core elements in place consistently across all classrooms at student-centered schools. They also discuss what teaching in these settings looks like as educators become facilitators of knowledge who are themselves perpetual learners.

In chapter 2, Heidi Andrade, Kristen Huff, and Georgia Brooke answer the second question, concerning assessment, arguing in favor of a balanced system of assessment that includes formative, interim, and summative measures. They then define five qualities of student-centered assessments—individualized, promote learning and growth, help students manage their own learning, motivating, and useful to a variety of audiences—and use these to examine a variety of formative, interim, and summative assessments from the classroom through the national level. While formative assessments most embody these qualities, the authors also discuss ways that systematized assessments, even though they usually are geared to very broad audiences, could be more student-centered.

Part 2 offers educators a look at some practices that hold promise for better education experiences and outcomes particularly for underserved populations, while ultimately improving education for all. Specifically, these chapters focus on student-centered approaches that support the reading and math engagement and achievement of special needs, black, African American, and Latino/a students.[1] This part of the book poses and answers the questions: *How can teachers use student-centered approaches to create positive learning environments in which increasingly diverse learners thrive and develop? Specifically, how do advances in digital media allow us to move away from the myth of the average learner? How can educators use cultural and social identities to enhance literacy and mathematics instruction for black, African American and Latino/a students?*

In chapter 3, David H. Rose and Jenna W. Gravel argue that neuroscience and the promise of technology point toward both the need and the ability to customize curricula to individual learners, while providing scaffolds to help all learners to reach high standards. They explain how the principles of universal design for learning (UDL) provide guideposts for this customization in the classrooms to ensure that all students have access to information and the means for learning. Rose and Gravel merge science, technology, and learning theory to portray invigorating alternatives to use in serving students with disabilities and in so doing, optimizing curriculum for all. In chapter 4, Alfred W. Tatum presents a compelling case that to advance the literacy of African American male adolescents, educators must pay close attention to the historical role that literacy has played for African American males. Doing so, he says, shifts the focus of literacy education from short-term test gains to the broader goals of instilling the desire and skills for lifelong learning and a positive relationship to literature. As Tatum explains, instruction does African American adolescent males a disservice when it addresses only the fundamentals of literacy (e.g., decoding, writing mechanics) and not the reader's own social, cultural, and personal identity. His comprehensive framework for reading instruction conceptualizes four sets of vital signs that teachers must address in moving toward genuine, significant improvements in literacy outcomes: reading, the reader, reading and writing instruction, and educator's approaches.

Similarly, in chapter 5, Rochelle Gutiérrez and Sonya E. Irving explore the learning of Latino/a and black students in another vital area of the curriculum—mathematics—focusing on the critical importance of context. The authors describe the many ways that diverse cultures use mathematics and how learners demonstrate proficiency in a multitude of settings—none of which necessarily translate to sanctioned practices tested in U.S. classrooms. Gutiérrez and Irving argue that paying attention to the student's identity, emotional reactions, and motivation toward learning mathematics makes a difference in the eventual acquisition of skills. For this reason, small-group and out-of-school settings are often more effective in teaching mathematics to Latino/a and black students. The authors also present examples of how educators could address Latino/a and black students' mathematics achievement by integrating motivational structures and opportunities for students to engage with mathematics more contextually within more traditional settings. These observations and examples are drawn from the authors' investigation of research fields within mathematics education.

Part 3 looks to the future by synthesizing the ongoing research in learning theory and science that underlies all the topics in this volume. These chapters provide a strong support for the kinds of practices, classrooms, schools, and systems envisioned by *Anytime, Anywhere* and the Students at the Center project. Part 3 poses and answers the questions: *What do advances in the emerging field of mind, brain, and education tell us about how people learn? What roles do agency, motivation, and engagement play in learning? Given the diversity of students in a classroom and the unique ways each one learns, how can educators understand the variety of motivations and provide a range of growth opportunities that motivate and engage students, both collectively and individually?*

Authors Christina Hinton, Kurt W. Fischer, and Catherine Glennon begin this part by elucidating the alignment of developments in brain science with student-centered approaches. In chapter 6, they describe significant recent advances in our understanding of how humans learn, made possible by new, powerful imaging tools that for the first time can study the learning brain in action. Similarly, they discuss the role of new genetics technologies that explore complex gene-environment interactions and innovative cognitive science methods for analyzing learning that track alternative learning pathways. As a result of these new developments in science, we know that: students' abilities are not fixed but rather always developing; learning occurs in both formal and informal contexts when the brain is actively engaged; and students each have a complex profile of strengths and limitations and learn best through experiences tailored to their individual needs and interests. The authors present strong research underpinnings for the practices and approaches described in previous chapters covering literacy, language, and mathematics acquisition and implications for underserved populations. They also lay out the neurological groundwork for the critical interactions between emotion, motivation, and relationships and learning taken up in greater detail by in the final chapter.

In chapter 7, Eric Toshalis and Michael J. Nakkula look across the large bodies of research and theory relevant to three interrelated topics—motivation, engagement, and student voice—to explore how learners can progress along the trajectory from novice to expert and how teachers can motivate students to become engaged learners. Toshalis and Nakkula explain the critical importance of self-regulation in student-centered learning and discuss the powerful role of student voice and agency for motivating and engaging students.

HOW TO USE THIS BOOK

We envision several audiences for *Anytime, Anywhere*. First and foremost, these chapters are designed for teachers and instructional leaders, many of whom have used some of the practices described here for years. For them, the value of the book lies in its solid research grounding and evidence for what so many of them have long known intuitively about "what works" with their students. In addition, the book and the companion resources on the Students at the Center website (www.studentsatthecenter.org) provide these and less-seasoned educators with numerous examples and tools they can adapt and apply to deepen their practice. (See "Resources on the Web.") Readers with interests in more specific applications of student-centered approaches may want to dip into particular chapters for insight into cognitive science, literacy, mathematics, assessment, serving

RESOURCES ON THE WEB

Some key topics are beyond the scope of the book but vital to the success of student-centered approaches to learning and teaching. Chief among these are investigations of the kinds of precertification and professional development training teachers need to implement—in a cohesive way—the kinds of practices illustrated throughout, along with the financial, structural, or policy conditions necessary to support this work. We encourage readers to look at the Students at the Center website (www.studentsatthecenter.org) for resources on a number of these topics, as well as additional resources for practitioners, researchers, and policy makers:

- Nine white papers prepared for the 2012 Students at the Center Research Symposium. These include extended versions of the book chapters and additional papers on personalization in schools and district-level supports for student-centered learning.

- Extensive bibliographies and executive summaries for the nine white papers.

- Audio and video clips of the classrooms described and students discussing their experiences in student-centered schools, blogs written by chapter authors and project staff, additional articles, and video commentaries.

- A searchable database of tools and resources to help educators implement the student-centered approaches to teaching and learning.

underserved populations, special education, diverse learners, education technology, and social and emotional supports.

The book also offers school leaders and administrators a solid grounding and provocative text from which to lead professional development, with companion tools for doing so on the website. Administrators can use the entire volume or selections from it to expand department or whole-school understanding of the school structures, culture, and practices that best support how their students—and their teachers—think and learn.

Finally, schools of education and precertification programs will find the collection applicable to courses on as diverse topics as cognitive science, learning and teaching; school reform policy and practice; urban education; addressing achievement differences; and leadership.

ENERGY, CURIOSITY, AND JOY

The interest today in student-centered approaches to learning is not simply another swing of the pendulum. Our opportunity—and challenge—is to encourage more schools and teachers to take advantage of advances in educational theory and practice, learning methods, and new technologies to implement student-centered learning. Too many of our classrooms are stuck in the early twentieth century, while the tools for creating a twenty-first-century education are being invented around them. No one yet knows the impact of the exponential increase in technology platforms and applications designed to both personalize instruction and make it more powerful and cost-effective. None of these platforms or applications has been implemented at a large scale, and it will be some time before research evidence will be broad and deep enough to give a reliable indication of impact. But as experimentation and improvement go forward in multiple modes, it is essential for all educators to have a baseline understanding of how young people learn best.

In the face of continuing failures to raise U.S. educational achievement and education attainment levels significantly, and the inability to close persistent race and income gaps, an increasing number of educational thinkers and activists are deciding to harness what is known about how students learn and what engages them in learning. The contributors to this volume provide a strong research and theoretical grounding for those who seek to reinvigorate and reinvent education, and especially for teachers who seek to infuse classrooms every day with energy, curiosity, and joy.

PART ONE

The Starting Point

What does student-centered teaching and learning look like in schools today? How are teachers using assessment both to enhance the learning process and to keep track of its effectiveness?

Student-centered approaches to learning shift the educational paradigm regarding when, where, and how learning takes place; how learning is measured; and who plays the various roles that teachers assume every day. Part 1 examines what the day-to-day business of student-centered education looks like when that shift happens. Although students are at the heart of every chapter, authors in this section shine a spotlight on teachers, teaching, and how to assess learning from a student-centered perspective.

CHAPTER 1

Learning from the Leaders

Core Practices of Six Schools

Barbara Cervone and Kathleen Cushman

FOR ALMOST FORTY YEARS, the two of us have championed high schools that put students at the center. Through interviews and observations of teachers, students, and administrators—in classrooms, teams, exhibitions, and the community—we have found that student-centered learning environments vary, emerging from specific local conditions and priorities. At the same time, all such learning environments share a common foundation of practices. These begin with teachers supporting each student in developing a new relationship to learning, one involving considerable choice and responsibility. Consequently, this kind of setting demands an approach to teaching that involves facilitating and coaching more than direct instruction. Student-centered teachers thus also develop a fresh relationship to their craft, playing multiple roles at each moment and always learning new skills.

15

In recent visits to six exemplars of student-centered learning, we observed a range of proven models for enacting such learning that are raising achievement for underserved populations. We found that:

• Student-centered teachers support each student in developing a new relationship to learning, defined by ever more complex challenges, increasing autonomy, and expanding awareness of connections of one's own work to that of others in the larger world.
• Student-centered teaching practices share eight common core elements: strong relationships with students; personalization and choice in curricular and instructional tasks; appropriate challenge levels for each learner; support for students' social and emotional growth and identity development; anytime, anywhere and real-world learning; technology that is integral to teaching and learning; clear, timely assessment and support; and practices that foster autonomy and lifelong learning.
• Student-centered teachers forge a new relationship to teaching, one in which the teacher constantly shifts among multiple roles, from curriculum planner and classroom facilitator, to assessor, adviser, and community connector.

THE RESEARCH SITES AND THEIR
STUDENT-CENTERED DESIGNS

In choosing our research sites, we looked for a range of models known for effectively enacting student-centered practices.[1] The schools we selected embrace the following designs: Big Picture schools, which individualize student learning via their internship experiences; early college high schools, which challenge and support students to begin college coursework in high school; Internationals Network For Public Schools with its touted approach to teaching English language learners; "hybrid" schools that enlarge students' academic choices by integrating computer-based instruction into the curriculum; and schools with long track records of putting into action the principles of the Coalition of Essential Schools.[2] (See "The Research Schools: Six Exemplars of Everyday Practice.")

THE RESEARCH SCHOOLS:
SIX EXEMPLARS OF EVERYDAY PRACTICE

This study looked at six high schools, representing a range of models for enacting student-centered learning:

Alief Early College High School: A partnership with Houston Community College in Texas, Alief is one of 270 early college high schools nationally. Without paying any college tuition, students can earn an associate's degree and a high school diploma in five years. All students take four years of AVID (Advancement Via Individual Determination) academic enrichment and support classes, which focus on inquiry, critical thinking, and other key college skills.

Bronx International High School: Bronx International High School, in New York City, is part of the Internationals Network For Public Schools. It serves primarily immigrants and non-native English speakers from the nation's poorest congressional district. It embraces the core beliefs of International schools, including heterogeneous classrooms, experiential learning, and language and content integration.

The Dayton Early College Academy: The Dayton Early College Academy, or DECA, located on the campus of the University of Dayton in Ohio, is part of the Early College High School Initiative, managed by Jobs for the Future. It began as a public school and reorganized four years later as a charter. DECA students graduate by completing a series of six "gateways" in which they demonstrate college preparatory skills, personal growth, community service, job shadows, and internships.

MetWest: One of sixty Big Picture Learning schools, MetWest is part of the Oakland (California) Unified School District. MetWest holds that learning must be based on the interests and goals of each student and relevant to the "real world." Working with mentors at successive community internships of their own choosing forms the core of all students' individualized learning plans.

NYC iSchool: NYC iSchool, a flagship for the New York City Department of Education's new Innovation Zone, is a collaboration with Cisco Systems. Access to technology is ubiquitous, with many online courses, curricula posted on shared sites, and constant e-mail exchanges with teachers. Students satisfy state standards in core courses but also learn through outside internships, and interdisciplinary "challenge-based modules" on the problems of twenty-first-century society.

Noble High School: A rural comprehensive high school in southern Maine, Noble High School is part of the Coalition of Essential Schools. All but 5 percent of the thousand students are white, but they reflect a diverse mix of rural, working-class, and low-income families. Its practices—including heterogeneous grouping, interdisciplinary teams, block scheduling, and exhibitions—are rare among large rural comprehensive high schools.

We simultaneously targeted schools where almost all of the students were low-income and minority, or rural (in one of our six choices). In every school in our study, most students would be the first in their families to attend college. Only Noble has more than five hundred students.

It is no accident that five of our research sites are small high schools, with fewer than five hundred students. Data from a variety of studies show that, especially for students from low socioeconomic backgrounds, smaller school size is conducive to effective student-centered practice.[3] With notable exceptions—including one school in this study—teachers in small schools are more likely to know their students well, focus on their individual strengths and needs, focus on student work over time, and collaborate on instructional strategies that help students engage with rigorous work.[4]

CORE ELEMENTS OF TEACHING PRACTICE IN STUDENT-CENTERED LEARNING

What does teaching look like when it centers on students' learning needs? In our interviews and observations, eight core elements rose to the fore, working together to give rise to deep adolescent learning:[5]

- Strong relationships with students
- Personalization and choice in curricular and instructional tasks
- Appropriate challenge levels for each learner
- Support for students' social and emotional growth and identity development
- Anytime, anywhere and real-world learning
- Technology that is integral to teaching and learning
- Clear, timely assessment and support
- Practices that foster autonomy and lifelong learning

While many engaging practices are apparent in the six schools, we chose these elements for their prevalence and, in some cases, their inventiveness. The foundation of every element is supporting every student in developing a new relationship to learning—defined by ever more complex challenges, increasing autonomy in addressing those challenges, and expanding awareness of the connections of the learner's work to the larger world.

The core elements (see figure 1.1) exist not as discrete functions but in a dynamic relationship, affecting and contributing to one another. Student-centered teaching does not come about as schools cherry-pick its elements one by one. Instead, it is a cultural shift involving virtually every aspect of what goes on in a school.

ELEMENT 1: STRONG RELATIONSHIPS WITH STUDENTS

Teachers who take the time to know their students well can create trusting, respectful relationships that support learning. Acting as coaches and facilitators as well as the suppliers of information, they often develop

FIGURE 1.1   Core elements of teaching student-centered learning

Strong relationships with students	Anytime, anywhere, and real-world learning
• Teacher-student advisement • Norms of trust, respect, and inclusiveness • Easy contact between students and teachers • Reaching out to families • Connecting students with community mentors	• Flexible schedules • Community service and internships • Curricular projects that engage the world outside school
Personalization and choice in curricular tasks	**Technology that is integral to teaching and learning**
• Personal learning plans • Substantial choice in curricular tasks • Opportunities to demonstrate mastery in varied ways • Independent projects that build on special interests	• Online learning adapted to individual student needs • Online tools that promote student collaboration • E-mail
Appropriate challenge levels for each learner	**Clear, timely assessment and support**
• Scaffolding • Differentiated instruction • Supporting students with special needs • Focusing on practice and revision habits so that students push themselves	• "Just in time" feedback • Gateways and exhibitions • Customized assessments • Student feedback on curriculum and instruction
Supporting social and emotional growth	**Fostering autonomy and lifelong learning**
• Knowing students well and educating the "whole child" • Student reflection • Engaging peers • Coaching students on how to present themselves publicly	• Building capacity to self-regulate • Learning about learning

students' academic knowledge and skills through collaborative interaction. Such connections enable adults to better understand and meet their students' individual needs, whether in the form of extra academic help, accommodation to personal circumstances, or intervention in times of stress. Students recognize and appreciate "a teacher who cares" and will try hard for that person.[6] Many other adults also become involved, inside and outside school.

In the schools we visited, several structures and practices stand out for their contributions to building strong relationships with students: teacher-student advisement; norms of trust, respect, and inclusiveness; easy contact between teachers and students; reaching out to families as an extension of building relationships with students; and connecting students with community mentors.

Teacher-Student Advisement

Adults in schools advise students in many ways, of course, but by far the best-known structure for that is the advisory group (known as *advisory*), in which a small group of students meets regularly with an adult who keeps a close eye on their social, emotional, and academic development. Every school studied includes such advisement. In practice, advisory takes many shapes, ranging from daily sessions to weekly meetings, one-on-one or in groups.

At MetWest (as at all Big Picture schools), the advisory displaces conventional instruction as the central structure of the school, and students learn through internships and mentorships as well as in more formal tutorials and high school or college courses. All teaching adults are known as *advisers*. Each supervises and coordinates the learning and assessment of a group of twenty students for at least two years, in every academic subject and internship. This radical restructuring of the teacher's role reflects Big Picture's conviction that adults at school should chiefly guide and facilitate the adolescent's self-directed path of discovery. Greg Cluster, who has worked at MetWest almost since its inception in 2002, says: "You need to teach students how to take initiative to pursue learning, and that's it, and that's all that matters."[7]

Alief Early College High School has created a hybrid design for advisement. Each student is assigned two staff members—one academic support teacher and one mentor. All students take four years of academic enrichment and support classes (part of the school's AVID program), which focus on inquiry, critical thinking, and other key college skills. Each AVID teacher guides cross-disciplinary academic development for a group of twenty-five to twenty-eight ninth- and tenth-grade students. At the same time, every single staff member—including the school secretary and custodian—mentors twelve students, one on one, in a program called Knights Friends Forever (after the school mascot). "Their AVID class is very much a family," said Terri Guidry, who directed the school in its first two years, "But we feel like the more supports we give [our students], the more successful they're going to be. We say, 'If you need anything, if you feel frustrated, if you get stressed out, if you need help, come see me. I'm your person to help guide your way through this program.'"

Norms of Trust, Respect, and Inclusiveness

Establishing norms of mutual trust and respect between adults and students is essential for learning. At every level, from course assignments to dress codes, all six schools we studied work hard to create a culture where young people are taken seriously and treated fairly. Students told us that they respond positively to teachers who demonstrate these convictions, whether or not they like a teacher personally. If they believe their teachers will do their jobs competently and without bias, they are willing to fulfill their part of the deal: pay attention, do the work, and play by the rules.[8]

Teachers create that climate through their attitudes and actions. At the NYC iSchool, all new teachers learn about classroom management and classroom structures at the beginning of each year. But this goes far beyond traditional talks about controlling unruly behavior, noted principal Alisa Berger: "We spend time on . . . how you support student learning, how you talk to kids in a way that they feel loved and supported and encouraged . . . where they feel safe and free to take risks, make mistakes, knowing that we love them no matter what. You can't learn unless that's in place."

When students violate behavioral norms at the schools we visited, interventions take learning, rather than punishment, as their goal. Terri Guidry, who was Alief Early College High School's first leader, came from a background in school counseling. "We don't do punishment," she explained: "It's more: 'I expect more of you. That's not college-going behavior. We have to get you ready to go over to the college, and so that takes mature behavior.' Ultimately, teachers want the students to be responsible for their own behavior and regulate themselves. After a while, students start to remind their peers. A lot of times we don't have to correct behavior—the students will correct other students. Especially the tenth-graders, they'll be like, 'Stop acting like you're silly! Stop it! We need to get to work!'"

Easy Contact Between Teachers and Students

The small enrollment and small facilities of five of the schools we visited encourage a culture of informal, as-needed contact between all players. Teachers and teens frequently strike up impromptu conversations about student growth and learning—in hallways, in computer labs, in lunchrooms.

The large high school, Noble, accomplishes this more deliberately through vertical learning academies and pods. The vertical learning academies place ninth- and tenth-graders in learning teams of eighty students with five teachers; the pods are designed so that each team has its own common space with adjoining classrooms. Thus, Noble meshes its structural and physical layout to maximize regular contact between teachers and students.

In addition, basic technology provides the circuitry for anytime, anywhere communication between Noble's students and teachers, all of whom carry their laptops everywhere. In school and out, they use e-mail to check in, keep on top of assignments, turn in work, ask and answer questions, and share information. Their unofficial rule: keep it short; reply ASAP. Julie Gagnon, a math teacher, acknowledged that having a laptop puts teachers "on call," but she said there's no question the additional work beats the alternative of "missed assignments and deadlines, wondering what's happened to a student, students not getting the feedback they need to revise and improve." All the back-and-forth may even save time, she said: "You can settle something in a quick e-mail exchange right then and there, instead of having to track each other down and then it's too late . . . We've only had the laptops for a year, but I can't imagine the school functioning without them."

Reaching Out to Families

All six schools regard parents and guardians, and often other family members, as partners. They expect parents to be active members of the school community, joining in family nights and school celebrations and attending the exhibitions that mark their children's progress. Most important, they view parent participation as integral to building strong relationships with students—even, sometimes, as an opportunity to ameliorate a student's strained relationship with a parent.

Frequent, effective communication is crucial, teachers said. Given everyone's busy and often difficult lives, many teachers rely on the ease of e-mail to answer parents' questions or resolve problems.

Some schools set up more formal structures. At Dayton Early College Academy, teachers visit the homes of their advisees before school starts each fall. They also host monthly meetings where parents and teachers exchange concerns, and the teachers readily contact parents with questions. "Not a day passes without my exchanging information with parents—either at their instigation or mine," teacher Jessica Austin said.

The teachers we interviewed know well that their outreach efforts are complicated by estrangement, language barriers, parents working multiple jobs, homelessness, students moving from one caregiver to another, the emotional safety of the student—not to mention the adolescent predilection to keep parents or guardians out of their lives. They also acknowledge the parental expectations, often shaped by previous experience, that communication from school only spells trouble. "We do everything we can to indicate it's not about 'gotcha,' about telling parents where their child has screwed up—or maybe where the parent has screwed up," said Noble language arts teacher Jennifer England. "It's about engaging parents as partners, in good times and bad."

Connecting Students with Community Mentors

All of the schools in our study, to varying degrees, count on community mentors as part of the critical web of adult-student relationships. Marge Mott, a longtime DECA faculty member, explained why outside-of-school connections are so important: "If there's one thing this school recognizes for sure, it's that students at this school need every adult on deck. It's our job to connect them with writing mentors who can help with their essays, college students who can serve as tutors and role models, a lifetime reader who can share her passion for books."

In Alief's ubiquitous AVID classes, student volunteers from the adjacent Houston Community College work as tutors and informal mentors. Trained to coach students in asking high-level questions, they bring to their groups a distinct sense of the outside world, whether it comes from a first-generation college youth who has made it through rough waters to get there or a retiree with business experience.

At MetWest, almost all of the structures and practices revolve around the school's robust commitment to learning through community internships, with mentors at the core. Students learn specific job skills, general workplace skills, habits of professionalism, and how to build relationships with adults, said Greg Cluster, who coordinates the school's internship program. "They learn to see adults as resources for learning what you want to learn in the world . . . not just as authority figures, to either obey, if you're a 'good kid,' or disobey, if you're a 'bad kid.'"

In turn, MetWest puts enormous energy into identifying, coaching, and supporting its field-based mentors, who often come to them through the personal networks of teacher-advisers or the initiative of students themselves. The school keeps a database of some four hundred organizations and businesses that have taken its students in the past and the individuals who have stood out as strong mentors. Teacher-advisers visit mentors regularly to collaboratively plan and assess the student's work and progress and to coach the mentor on what learning outcomes they expect.

ELEMENT 2: PERSONALIZATION AND CHOICE IN CURRICULAR AND INSTRUCTIONAL TASKS

Adolescents put a high value on taking charge of their own lives, and when they initiate and have a say in learning activities, they invest in them more. (Chapter 7 discusses this in depth.) For this reason, student-centered teaching encourages a high degree of choice and personalization in how students approach their learning targets. Teachers who support and facilitate these approaches are building on students' innate drive toward self-determination.[9] The schools we visited expected students to create and review their own personal learning plans; exercise substantial choice in assignments, readings, and topics when completing course tasks; demonstrate mastery in different forms and media; and pursue independent projects and extended learning opportunities that built on special interests.

Personal Learning Plans

The practice in U.S. public schools of creating an "individualized educational program" to match each student's needs began when the Individuals with Disabilities Education Act mandated it in federal legislation designed to protect the rights of children with disabilities. Whether or not they formalize such a process, the schools we visited all display a commitment to teaching whose substance and pace matches each student's developmental needs.

However, each had its own way of carrying out this ambitious idea. At the NYC iSchool, all ninth-graders create their own plans for learning at school and beyond, following a quarter-long "challenge-based module" on the psychology and neuroscience of learning. With a growing understanding of mind and brain, the students reflect on how they themselves learn best and incorporate these strategies into their plans. The course, according to its co-teachers Susan Herzog (science) and Jennifer Rygalski (humanities), reflects a founding principle of the school: students must understand their own learning styles in order to make responsible educational choices.

At the end of each quarter, students each lead a twenty-minute conference with their parents and adviser to review their work and decide on personal and academic goals for the next quarter. At the end of tenth grade, iSchool students personalize their learning plans even further, choosing an academic focus area (English, history, math, science, psychology, business, the arts, or technology) to explore in increasing depth in the two years before graduation.

At Dayton Early College Academy, the six gateways required for graduation feed, mark, and alter learning plans. The steps in each plan are cumulative, requiring students to demonstrate and reflect on the progress they have made since their previous gateway and to look ahead, deepening their strengths and addressing their weaknesses. Just as important, students proceed through their gateways at their own pace; the timing becomes, in effect, part of the personal learning plan. "We have students who will go a year and a half without completing a gateway, and then finish two in six months," DECA's Marge Mott explained.

Substantial Choice in Curricular Tasks

Teachers at our study schools routinely build student choice into the school day, believing intuitively that students who have a say in their learning invest in it more. Dante, a senior at DECA, could not agree more: "One of the things they tell you here is to do what you love and love what you do," he said. "Having choices helps make that happen, even if it's just choosing the side you'll take in a classroom debate." Another student added, "It's more important that the choices are constant than big." At Noble High School, one teacher reflected, students may end a day having made more than a dozen decisions about what they would do: which book to read during the sustained silent reading required of all students every day; which from among the week's assignments to tackle that day in algebra; which essay topic to pick—or devise—in a language arts unit on personal narrative; which team to join in researching the pre–Civil War South; which practice set (from among a list of ten) to focus on in a class on study skills. "We can't imagine classrooms where the choices given students can be counted on just one hand," the teacher said.

Students exercise choice in other forums, too. NYC iSchool principal Alisa Berger used the example of learning about the parts of the circulatory system for an online biology course in preparation for the state Regents exam. "Kids can choose how they engage with it," she said, noting that they can listen to a lecture, play a game, or watch a video of blood working its way through the system: "You make the choices, and when you feel like you have mastered the content you take the quiz, which our teachers make up using sample questions from old Regents exams. If you don't feel ready, you go back and do the online work again, this time maybe making a different choice for how to learn the content."

Opportunities to Demonstrate Mastery in Different Forms and Media

How students at our study schools demonstrate their grasp of challenging material has changed markedly from the time when the chief options were a research paper or a pencil-and-paper test. Each school has opened avenues for students to exhibit conceptual mastery more dynamically— for example, by creating videos and mixed-media presentations, inventing and then building products, conducting experiments and surveys, debating and performing dramatic role-plays, and designing interactive games and Web sites. Inviting parents, students from other classrooms, and the broader community to view student work is common. The schools see public demonstrations of proficiency as integral to learning: students must not only know important content but also be able to communicate it effectively to others.

At Bronx International, the goal of communicating in English goes hand in hand with mastering intellectual material. Teacher Dolan Morgan requires all students in his twelfth-grade English classes to make a presentation to the class every Friday, explaining and synthesizing their learning of recent lessons. He explained the rationale: "Whether it is acting out part of a play or just giving a PowerPoint presentation about part of a book, I think that type of pressure and openness gets every student to achieve. Everyone's presentation obviously looks very different based on their abilities, but it's all around the same content, and every student is capable of doing something along those lines."

At the NYC iSchool, students routinely produce short video documentaries or other digital products to show their understanding. Jonathan, a ninth-grader, described Kitchen Sink Physics, a "core experience" class for which he made videos about Newton's laws and applied them to his own examples. He said this approach helps him "remember stuff a lot more." After learning about the controversial process of hydraulic fracturing (or fracking) to extract natural gas from reservoir rock formations, iSchool students in Susan Herzog's science class spontaneously organized a vigorous "Think Before You Frack" public information campaign. Their extensive Web site includes a video, a radio play, and an original song that won a city award.[10]

Independent Projects and Extended Learning Opportunities That Build on Special Interests

All six schools require students to carry out independent projects and encourage them to pursue extended learning opportunities that stretch them intellectually—and often socially and emotionally as well. Most schools require a presentation of a capstone project for graduation. Students present before a public audience and are assessed by a panel of teachers and community members, often including experts.

NYC iSchool students begin preparing for their culminating independent project as soon as they choose an academic focus area late in tenth grade. Principal Berger explained that in the junior year, students think about the ways people in that field look at the world and at problems. At the beginning of the year, through a nine-week class called Critical Thinking and History (or whatever the subject area is), they choose the specific topic they want to research. Then they write a summary paper, similar to a literature review, to explain current thinking in the field. This helps them decide what to focus on as a senior.

The senior project is as personalized as it gets, by definition empowering students to choose what interests them most. It also requires students to design their own learning—figuring out what they need to know, setting deadlines, assessing their own progress, determining next steps, and deciding how to apply and share what they have learned.

ELEMENT 3: APPROPRIATE CHALLENGE LEVELS FOR EACH LEARNER

An important part of personalizing curriculum and instruction is providing appropriate levels of challenge for all students. The key is for teachers to know their students well enough to set tasks that are neither too easy nor too hard. For young people, stretching to reach, and then achieve, challenging goals sets in motion a cycle of effort, practice, intrinsic satisfaction, and growing confidence. This often counters feelings of discouragement or humiliation caused by past academic failure.

All six schools in our study infuse individualized levels of challenge into their structure and daily teaching practice. Indeed, challenging and stretching students may be what these schools do best. Achievement gaps cannot be closed by lowering expectations for students but by pushing them to do more, teachers told us. In Brent Goff's language arts class at DECA, students read high-level texts: *Beowulf, Frankenstein, Grendel, Beloved, Native Son,* and the epic poem *Gilgamesh.* "As a teacher here, we never forget where these kids come from," Goff said. "But this doesn't mean that we water down or slow down the curriculum for them, that we do an urban curriculum that isn't as challenging as a suburban curriculum. We don't take our foot off the accelerator."

Teachers in the schools we visited commonly use a variety of strategies to challenge students: scaffolding, differentiating instruction, instilling habits of practice and revision, and providing supports for students with special needs.

Scaffolding

Since the students in most classrooms have very different readiness levels, the student-centered teacher scaffolds instruction and differentiates learning tasks so that each learner is ready for just the right stretch.

Teachers use scaffolding in Alief's AVID classes to help students come up with good questions at several levels of inquiry. "You don't ever want to just start throwing out information," remarked Peggy Breef, who teaches AP English and serves as an instructional coach. She calls their approach "Hook, Line, and Sinker." Breef explained: "I've got to do something to get them into the subject matter. Then I have to do something with them to get that subject matter across, and then I have to let them do something with what they've learned and take it out and beyond."

The principle of scaffolding has shaped the overall design of these schools. For example, DECA launched a middle school when it recognized that too many entering ninth-graders lacked the habits they needed for the challenge and workload they faced; roughly half would leave DECA before the senior year. The vertical learning academies at Noble move students along a path of increasing autonomy and decreasing reliance on the intensive team support they receive as freshmen and sophomores.

Differentiated Instruction

Across the schools, teachers name the same issue as one of their greatest challenges: how to center instruction on individual needs when students arrive with myriad differences in experience and readiness.

The schools embrace differentiation in many ways, summoning their inventive powers and attunement to students. For example, no matter what the content area in Bronx International's multilevel, multilingual classes, every teacher also always teaches English. Yet the language of instruction is determined collaboratively for any day's tasks. Students work in small groups on projects that develop both language and content knowledge. Depending on their needs, students may use both English and their native languages to explore content; those more proficient in English often translate for others. Teachers stay close at hand, helping individual students grasp the material at every turn, said Dolan Morgan: "As a teacher here, the biggest challenge is the variability of what you get as a cohort. Some students already have a whole bunch of strengths from previous schooling, and can acquire language almost just by hanging out. Others have huge deficits in their previous education, either from not being in school or from poor schooling."

Teachers and students alike note how online courses inherently allow students each to take in information at their own pace. Nicky, a tenth-grader at NYC iSchool, said it's a big benefit for students who need points repeated, as well as for those who can move ahead without repetition.

Supporting Students with Special Needs

The six schools set high standards for all students, and heterogeneous grouping is the rule in their classrooms. However, they also spend considerable time and resources supporting students who need something extra, or different, in order to thrive.

Noble High School guidance counselor Shelly Lajoie runs a successful recovery program for failing juniors and seniors who realize they want to graduate with their classmates; she tailors it to fit their individual circumstances. Down the hall, teacher Adina Hunter keeps challenging the high school's "gifted" students. "I'll work with the teacher and with the student to find a curriculum or a project they can do discreetly in class, on top of their regular work," Hunter explained.

Many Bronx International students arrive in the United States and enter the eighth or ninth grade; thus they have only a few years in which to master both a new language and New York State's graduation requirements. To catch them up from the start, the school launched its new Bridges program in 2011 to offer intensive instruction in basic numeracy and basic literacy.

Focus on Practice and Revision Habits So Students Push Themselves

Students work intensely at the six schools we studied, often noting that they spend significantly more time on their work than do peers at other schools. A major reason is the focus on practice and habits of revision, which are critical skills for students to push themselves.

Jordan, a DECA twelfth-grader, gave an example: no students ever pass a gateway the first time they try, and educators always provide feedback to help guide improvements. "You hate them, because it means more work," he said. "But you appreciate them, because the edits make you improve. [They] keep us on our toes, to keep us working. But with the edits comes support. They are always there to help."

By using the term "Not Yet" as an assessment code, Bronx International sends students a clear signal to keep trying again until they get it. Dolan Morgan made the case for that in a 2008 memo to his colleagues: "The traditional grading system promotes the idea that there are failures and there are achievers. It sends the message that opportunities for success happen, and if you miss them, that's it—it's over. The outcomes environment promotes the idea that there are those who have already achieved and those that will. It sends the message that there are multiple opportunities to succeed and that you are encouraged to keep trying."

ELEMENT 4: SUPPORT FOR STUDENTS' SOCIAL AND EMOTIONAL GROWTH AND IDENTITY DEVELOPMENT

An adolescent's central developmental needs involve forming an identity, belonging, being heard, feeling powerful, and understanding the world. These social-emotional needs loom especially large in secondary school, as teachers seek to engage students in academic challenges and foster the work and mind habits they will need throughout their lives.

More traditional models of teaching presume that academic motivation and effort result from the intersection of the teacher's instruction and each student's existing aptitude. A more student-centered teaching approach takes into account the conflicting narratives that adolescent learners often hold about themselves, such as "I am bad at math" or "I can do whatever I put my mind to." Those narratives, fundamentally social, emotional, and cultural in nature, are part of how young people develop an identity based on the dynamic among their beliefs, relationships, and prior experiences.[11] If teachers tune into that ongoing process humming in the background— and intervene strategically at various points—they can help students negotiate their learning targets.[12]

Teachers pointed to an array of practices they believe support students' social and emotional growth and identity development, including knowing students well and educating the "whole child"; requiring student personal reflections; nourishing peer relationships, teamwork, and mentoring; and coaching students on how to present themselves in public.

Knowing Students Well and Educating the Whole Child

Each of the schools in our study would argue that everything about their daily practice is intended to educate the whole child. However, teachers must also know their students well—including both the personal experiences students bring to school and the new narratives they hope to create once there. Most students in the schools studied come from low-income families and many work to support themselves. At Bronx International, 70 percent have been separated from one or both parents during their families' immigration to the United States. In addition, war or other conditions in their countries of origin prevented many of its students from getting adequate schooling previously.

Several DECA seniors offered examples of how their teachers and advisers had put into practice the idea of educating the whole child. According to James, a senior: "When I started at DECA, I was what you'd call immature. The only reason I was here was because my father insisted I come. My adviser picked up on me right away. She and I talked about what were immature actions and what was mature. Then all through the year we did, like, a behavior inventory."

The schools in our study have created formal and informal structures that target a subset of students perceived as vulnerable to failure. For example, Noble students receive special attention during the transition from middle to high school, when many kids face social and emotional difficulties, disengagement, and ultimately academic failure. Teacher Jennifer

England has taken struggling ninth-graders under her wing in a class she created with the neutral title "Study Skills." Her goal was to entice students to come to school each day—a major challenge for many—and to start daily learning with a positive attitude. England told the principal that the class must be held during the first block, and the students must receive full course credit even though they would not be doing typical schoolwork. Instead, they start with a check-in and have breakfast, then might take a walk outside, play basketball, and review for an upcoming exam. "The success has been ridiculous," England said. "It's not magic; it's just giving kids a caring, safe environment . . . and the kids [start] their day in a good space."

Student Reflection

Student reflection is integral to teaching and learning at these schools—and to their demonstrating progress and proficiency. Students must routinely complete reflective writing assignments, keep response journals when reading, record their community service and internship experiences, and discuss their own "takeaways" in reports and presentations.

Three schools require a twenty-five-page autobiography as part of the graduation portfolio. Dante, the twelfth-grader at DECA, compared the task to climbing a rock wall. "Twenty-five pages—that's stiff," he said, noting that the research included interviewing family members about their perceptions of the student and making a list of personal highs and lows. "But I learned so much about myself, things I'd never thought about much before."

At Noble High School, students participate in a public presentation each year. They frame these around essential questions: Who am I? (grade 9); Where am I going? (grade 10); How will I get there? (grade 11); How can I exhibit what I have learned? (grade 12).

Engaging Peers

We have found the norm in most traditional schools is to discourage perceived negative peer influence, reinforced by separating students by age and grade level. The opposite is true at these six schools, which see peer culture as a powerful tool for learning. They understand that peer ties are an essential part of every adolescent's social and emotional development, and they regularly point students to one another as sources of support.

Social interactions among students at the beginning of a school year are especially complex at Bronx International, given the high language barriers to even mundane conversations. Looking back at his sophomore year, one student described a transformation in the way classmates treated and learned from one another. At the beginning of the year, most were strangers: "They be like they looking at each other. And the Africans and the Dominicans, they used to fight because every time the Spanish people used to talk Spanish, the Africans didn't understand them, so they thought that they was talking about them. But now everybody know each other. It's cool. Because we get to know about other people's community, how do they feel, the opportunity that they give them, why they came over here, and to learn about their country."

Starting with advisories, teachers nourish close ties among students across grade levels. A recently instituted program at Noble High School formally pairs struggling sophomores with juniors who are positive role models. Teacher Julie Gagnon explained: "They meet twice a week during sustained silent reading time and touch base, make a connection, get some work done, learn some skills—whatever they need."

When conflicts arise, each school invokes a structure that teaches students to resolve disputes through discussion. Noble uses peer mediation, for example; DECA students take a course in anger management. Bronx International teachers set aside class time for students to share what's causing difficulty among classmates and take responsibility using a "restorative practices" approach that eschews blame in favor of reparations.

Coaching Students on How to Present Themselves Publicly

Presenting oneself publicly with confidence is an important part of the curriculum at each school. Students describe a progression that starts with their becoming more comfortable speaking up in class and grows to include a range of public "performances": cold calls to community members to arrange job shadows or internships; hosting visitors to their schools;

and speaking about their education at public forums and conferences. "I used to be so shy, and now I speak up" was a common refrain.

Teachers coach students well in advance of public scrutiny. For example, in preparing a job shadow, students rehearse a professional handshake and review the importance of making eye contact, speaking clearly, and the role of small talk, said DECA's Marge Mott. DECA freshmen take a "corporate etiquette" class to accustom them to business situations. "We don't expect our students to come with these social skills; it's our job to teach them," Mott said. "When students need to set up phone interviews with strangers in the community, we ask them to first script their introductory remarks and practice them until they have them down."

Perhaps the students' best preparation for developing social confidence comes via the public exhibitions of their work that punctuate their rise from freshmen to graduating seniors. Teachers and advisers work hard to prepare their students for these high-stakes performances.

Student exhibitions at NYC iSchool often take place in the community, when students present to the organizations for whom they act as consultants. For example, one group worked with curators at the 9/11 Memorial Museum in New York, supplying their own perspectives on the attacks as well as those from videoconferences they conducted with youth in Afghanistan, London, Israel, and New Orleans. "It has changed me," Hannah told us, near the end of her sophomore year: "I feel like I'm a lot stronger and I'm not as scared to stand in front of a room and talk to people on a stage or something, or publicly speak. That's a really big strength that I've gotten from being a student here. I'll carry that on with me."

ELEMENT 5: ANYWHERE, ANYTIME AND REAL-WORLD LEARNING

With their developmental drive to "become someone" in the larger world, adolescents often feel constrained when their learning is confined to the classroom. Recognizing this, the schools we studied open their doors wide in all directions. They make schedules flexible, so that students can take advantage of regular learning opportunities outside school, anywhere and anytime. They bring the "real world" into school by welcoming community members as partners in curricula, instruction, and assessment. And they facilitate digital access to the entire globe to stimulate and deepen students' interests, knowledge, and skills.

As teachers and administrators in our research stressed, creating—and managing—opportunities for extended learning outside the school and classroom can be daunting; it requires a huge amount of work. But all agreed the effort has multiple payoffs: increasing student motivation, grounding learning in real-life situations, expanding job awareness, teaching lessons in citizenship, and building personal skills like self-reliance.

Flexible Schedules

NYC iSchool has used technology to render the conventional high school schedule virtually obsolete. Students decide for themselves when to work through the teacher-created online courses that help them prepare for state Regents exams; if they do the work at home, they may take a loaner laptop with them. From any Internet connection, students can access a "virtual desktop" system on which teachers post curricular and instructional materials. Challenge-based modules, seminars, labs, and other classes do meet according to a set schedule, but a lot of the work is exploratory, involving individualized or small-group activities or forays outside the school.

MetWest is also designed around flexible schedules. Students spend two days a week seeking or carrying out community internships. When at school, they meet in grade-level classes, with one teacher-adviser coaching and coordinating their academic development across the curriculum. This permits an extraordinary amount of daily flexibility and differentiation, in both timing and instructional modalities. As a result, much of instruction focuses on building strong, self-reliant habits of work and of mind, whatever the setting.

DECA keeps its doors open for an extended day, providing a nurturing base from which students come and go for anytime, anywhere learning. Marge Mott described a typical day: "Many of our students arrive, by their own choice, an hour before school starts and hit the computers. When classes end, they may return to the computer, go do their community service, join up with a book club, head out for an internship. We don't see this as 'after school.' We see all of this as 'school,' with students making a commitment to learning that stretches throughout the day."

Community Service and Internships

A requirement that all students engage in community service is now common in U.S. high schools. Two of our six study sites have community service requirements: sixty hours at Noble and one hundred hours at DECA. All six schools value community internships as opportunities for learning.

Students at DECA must complete at least two short-term internships before graduation. Bronx International requires a weekly internship for seniors. NYC iSchool requires internship "field experiences" for juniors and seniors and encourages them for ninth- and tenth-graders.

The Learning Through Internship program is central to the MetWest curriculum, in the Big Picture tradition. "For students who are confronted with the reality of poverty, the fact that they're going to need to work is very present in their minds by ninth grade," said Greg Cluster. Working with local businesses for four years gives them a big head start—in confidence and connections. Internships also motivate many to keep coming to school each day, he said: "About 40 percent of our students have parents who didn't graduate high school . . . The question of whether they're going to stay in high school is huge . . . Unless the high school is really connecting with their future and related to the concept of work and a future life path from day one, the odds of their dropping out are extremely high."

Curricular Projects That Engage the World Outside School

Notably among the schools we studied, MetWest and NYC iSchool ground much of their curricula in real challenges from the broader community. Students told us they feel energized by their regular contact with community members and the opportunity to help them solve problems that matter to people. At MetWest, that emphasis emerges naturally from the central role internships play in student learning. For example, several students interning at the American Friends Service Committee collaborated on a media campaign to highlight the situation of undocumented youth after the DREAM act failed to win congressional approval in 2011. Their efforts yielded a press kit and a grant proposal to raise funds for designing and executing a mural outside their San Francisco workplace to raise public awareness about the issue.

In NYC iSchool's short-term, intensive, challenge-based modules, the teacher's role becomes that of facilitator, with an interest in the subject but no expertise. Tapping the expertise of outsiders, principal Alisa Berger said, offers a deeper kind of learning: "When kids are working to build a green roof or creating digital activism campaigns around the humanitarian crisis in Zimbabwe, this is real work . . . Students need access to real people who do this as their jobs."

ELEMENT 6: TECHNOLOGY THAT IS INTEGRAL TO TEACHING AND LEARNING

Technology is changing the way teaching and learning take place in classrooms.[13] When used thoughtfully, new technologies provide ever sharper tools for what student-centered teachers have long practiced the old-fashioned way: adapting instruction to what individual students most need, encouraging students to collaborate in their learning, and providing swift and relevant feedback on their work.

The six schools in the study fall at various points along the spectrum of how much they integrate technology into what they do so well. Three of their distinguishing practices include: online learning adapted to the needs of each student; online tools that promote student collaboration; and heavy reliance on e-mail to reach teachers whenever needed.

Online Learning Adapted to Individual Student Needs

Despite all the paths the digital revolution has opened for personalizing instruction, ensuring the quality and depth of online learning still presents a challenge. Outstanding in this respect was NYC iSchool, which has designed an inventive, efficient hybrid approach to enabling the richest possible learning outcomes for students.

For example, iSchool teachers have far more latitude to design and teach project-based challenge modules, college-style seminars, and targeted science labs because they have created online courses all their students use to prepare for New York State's Regents exams. Those digital learning environments contain Web-based alternatives for mastering content, as well as quizzes containing Regents test questions. Teachers also review the material and rubrics with students in nine-week seminars directly before the test. The advantages are clear: students self-pace their progress through the exam curriculum, acquire a fund of background knowledge, and usually make their way quickly toward the more engaging projects ahead.

Many NYC iSchool students told us that they liked the flexibility of their online courses in both timing and presentation. Jennie, a ninth-grader, said being able to return to the material multiple times provides a big advantage: "I did the best in U.S. history last quarter, and that was because in the videos, there [were] words, and then there [were] pictures. They would explain it; and if you didn't get it, you can watch the whole thing over again."

In another tactic, experienced teachers from the East Bronx Academy of the Future teach AP courses to NYC iSchool students via distance learning. "I didn't have teachers certified to teach these four courses, yet we had students whom they would serve," principal Alisa Berger said. "It's a real commitment on both schools' parts, but our partnership is really important, so we schedule a lot of things around enabling it. And it's very cost-effective."

Online Tools That Promote Student Collaboration

NYC iSchool students have Internet access to all material and communications related to their courses. A virtual classroom software program contains assignments and teacher feedback, reading and multimedia content, class notes, self-correcting quizzes, group discussion boards, and online forums.

Video conferencing via Skype has also proved a powerful collaborative tool at the iSchool, where challenge-based modules routinely ask students to collaborate with outside experts or peers from around the world. In a module called "Sixteen," two classes interviewed teenagers around the world, using anthropological methods to compare adolescence in different cultures. Elijah, an eleventh-grader, told us how the experience changed his thinking: "How they do their marriages [in one African culture] . . . they would continuously jump to see who jumps the highest and that's how they find their spouse. And in some Indian cultures, you just get married to, like, somebody you don't even know. I'm just like, 'Wow!' And I try to understand . . . what would make them do it this way? But that's just how their culture is. That's how they were raised."

DECA's Brent Goff weaves a variety of software into his twelfth-grade language arts classes, providing a platform for collaboration. He described his techniques: "Media and writing can work in tandem. When we read *Frankenstein*, we did a wiki book. In lit[erature] circles, the students would upload their chapter summaries to Google docs, and these became their equivalent of Spark Notes or Wikipedia, except that they had created the content, it was a communal effort. Then when it came to writing about *Frankenstein*, the students could go back and look at the document they had created together and draw upon it."

E-mail

We described earlier how e-mail has become a lifeblood for communication at Noble High School, now that all students and faculty have laptops they carry almost everywhere. "It has transformed how we communicate with each other—between teachers and students, teacher to teacher, parents and teachers, with the community," said Heidi Early-Hersey, director of Noble's Professional Development Center.

The use of e-mail may be less ubiquitous at the other schools, where laptops do not come with membership, yet this vital tool for connecting and sharing information clearly supports many core elements of student-centered learning in many of our six schools. It undergirds strong relationships between students and their teachers, advisers, and community mentors, making it possible to send reminders, ask questions and get answers, seek input, give advice, check in about personal matters, and more. It supports collaboration, comment, and feedback. It encourages the exchange of drafts and revisions, whether by a student seeking input on her college essay or by teachers developing a cross-disciplinary unit. It also enables parents and teachers to communicate outside school hours.

ELEMENT 7: CLEAR, TIMELY ASSESSMENT AND SUPPORT

Training young people in intellectual inquiry in student-centered settings is much like coaching an athletic sport, as Theodore R. Sizer memorably pointed out.[14] Student learning must be not only assessed but also encouraged and guided. This involves several complementary practices, from teacher and novice looking together at exemplary work and analyzing what makes it good, to teachers providing just-in-time feedback to students who are developing new skills and knowledge. It even includes students' providing feedback on the curriculum and instruction. Other common assessment practices include gateways and exhibitions and customized assessments.

We of course recognize that all of these schools exist in the era of high-stakes standardized tests. While we do not diminish the large role such assessments play in what is taught, we focus here on the ways these schools use assessment to uphold their student-centered practices.

Just-in-Time Feedback

The best time to tell learners whether they are on the right or wrong track is when they are most interested in this information, usually right after they complete a task or give their answer to a question. Otherwise, the informational and motivational value of the feedback is diminished—and students may continue to make the same errors going forward. Also, students need frequent feedback, which packs more punch than broad, infrequent feedback.[15] Teaching that embeds just-in-time feedback into the lesson can and does occur in all kinds of high schools, but it is characteristic of student-centered learning environments, which explicitly prize inquiry-based dialogue.

Gateways and Exhibitions

Most of the schools we studied have structures for students to present their work formally in order to demonstrate their readiness to move forward or graduate. These structures vary in pacing (some come quarterly, others at the two-year mark); in the stakes involved (some are more like course assessments, others more like comprehensive exit hurdles); and, notably, in the means and media students employ to present their work. What links the practices is the conviction that the ability to "show what you know" is an important marker of successful—and student-centered—learning. In every instance, students share their work publicly and receive feedback through a detailed rubric that everyone in attendance is encouraged to fill out.

To graduate from Bronx International, as well as meeting course requirements and passing the state Regents exams, students must complete a major culminating task in each core subject area: math; English language arts; social studies; and science. During the senior year, each student assembles these tasks in a portfolio, along with a résumé, a personal essay, and a statement of personal goals for the future, then presents it in an hour-long exhibition before a panel of classmates and teachers, and sometimes community members as well.

DECA students must pass six gateways to graduate. Once their adviser reviews and approves their evidence, they can apply at any time to present a gateway before a panel of teachers, students, and family members. Each gateway has its own requirements, but taken together, students must demonstrate a number of elements: 95 percent attendance over the forty-five days prior to their gateway; 80 percent mastery of a multigenre research topic, as determined by the adviser and presented through media; 75 percent proficiency in academic standards (in relation to the Michigan Educational Assessment Program and ACT College Readiness Standards); increasing self-discernment as evidenced in a personal reflection paper;

active family participation; documentation of community service, internships, and job shadows; and three literary analyses of books. Students must also show their daily planner, completed and signed by the adviser.

Customized Assessments

At Bronx International, Dolan Morgan and his colleagues created customized software where teachers enter the desired outcomes for each course (including academic goals and behavioral habits) and then teachers, students, and families can regularly check individual progress. Failure is not an option; as discussed earlier, outcomes not reached are marked "Not Yet." Assessment that charts growth in this way "fits all kids," Morgan said. "But it's especially empowering for English language learners, who are already struggling with language. You're not acquiring content because of that language, and you shouldn't be punished for it."

Software like this often suits the philosophies of student-centered schools, but several schools are struggling to find a system that combines ease of use and compatibility with the curriculum, programs, and district requirements. NYC iSchool designed the Moodle-based virtual classroom system it used for the first three years, and then transitioned to new software designed by the city's Department of Education. Each such transition, teachers at different schools told us, involves learning on their part and the inevitable frustrations of adapting to a new system.

Student Feedback on Curricula and Instruction

The schools in our study routinely invite student input on shaping instruction and practice. With the easy student-teacher contact that characterizes daily life in these schools, much of this feedback "just happens naturally," as Noble teacher Josh Gould pointed out. "If I'm considering what book I'm going to teach next, I'll give it to a junior during sustained silent reading and say, 'Hey, would you read this and give me some feedback about how you think sophomores will respond to it?'"

At all six schools, we observed teachers checking with students as class ended to see how things had gone: Did the example used help them understand the concept? Did they like the reading? Was the pace too fast or too slow? Not surprisingly in an environment that encourages students to ask questions and seek clarification, teachers told us that some students were quick to let them know when they were not getting it or what they would prefer to be studying.

NYC iSchool's faculty also use digital communications to seek regular student feedback. After each course ends, students offer feedback on its strengths and weaknesses through an online survey. "That information definitely becomes part of our professional conversation as teachers shape their goals for the next session," said Mary Moss, the school's founding co-principal.

ELEMENT 8: FOSTERING AUTONOMY AND LIFELONG LEARNING

A key task in adolescence is to develop the capacity for autonomy, and just about every practice described in this chapter underscores a unique feature of student-centered learning environments: the priority of helping students become independent learners. Teachers at every school in our study strike a fine balance between encouraging students to be self-directed and keeping a close watch on them, stepping in as needed. The schools pair risk-taking with responsibility, and continual planning with continual assessment. They encourage students to pursue their own interests and initiate their own projects. They help students identify the ways in which each one learns and works best. And they provide opportunities for continual practice in the skills and habits necessary to succeed at whatever they take on.

Ultimately, these schools hope to develop young adults who will be self-aware and self-motivated learners for their entire lives. Two of the most important strategies for setting up students for lifelong success are building their capacity to self-regulate and ensuring that they learn how to learn.

Building Capacity to Self-Regulate

Self-regulation includes a variety of essential skills, such as taking initiative, setting goals, planning tasks, managing time, and showing persistence.

We observed students engaged in these habits in every school. DECA students fill out daily planners that not only record their homework but also serve as a tool to check their progress toward gateways and graduation. Bronx International students use laptops to track which outcomes they are working toward each day in each class. MetWest students find and secure their own internships. All of the schools require regular long-term projects that students design, organize, and execute largely on their own.

NYC iSchool designs its online Regents prep curriculum to maximize student independence and self-direction. "A lot of this is about enabling the students, making them feel empowered, that they own their learning and they're in charge of it," explained principal Alisa Berger. "Their teacher doesn't need to master their content; they need to master their content. They want to graduate high school, so to pass the Regents is an authentic motivator."

Angelica, a ninth-grader in NYC iSchool, wrote a reflection on the challenges that autonomous online learning presented. She had figured she would thrive with her newfound freedom, but the experience was not at all what she expected: "In the beginning I was not fond of being both teacher and student simultaneously. It required more effort, patience, self-control, and self-motivation. Not consistently having someone keep tabs on me was surprisingly unnerving . . . I quickly discovered that my 'freedom' was buried beneath layers and layers of responsibility—or in my case, procrastination."

Learning About Learning

If students are to become lifelong learners, it helps if they master metacognitive skills and strategies that can support sturdy learning through adulthood. The core elements help students plan their approach to a learning task, monitor their comprehension, and evaluate their own progress toward completing it. Students learn to reflect on their strengths and weaknesses, set realistic goals for themselves, and sustain their effort over time.

At many of these schools, the lessons come out of formal or informal dialogue, as teachers press students to articulate their growth and development as learners. Often, we saw evidence of such thinking in students' written or oral reflections as they presented work to others at the conclusion of courses or projects.

To deepen students' metacognitive skills, both Noble High School and NYC iSchool created special courses in the science of learning. Nicky, an iSchool tenth-grader, described what he gained from the experience of taking a class called iLearn: "We did personality tests and figured out what kind of student we are and the way we learn best. Like, are you the person who is a good leader and motivator to get everybody else working? Or are you better at just doing what you're told but doing a good job? Are you a visual learner? It's almost impossible for me to learn without seeing it."

TEACHER ROLES IN STUDENT-CENTERED ENVIRONMENTS

The core elements of student-centered teaching overlap and combine in a dynamic relationship, each affecting and contributing to others. Yet analyzing that web reminds us sharply that schools do not rise or fall—and students do not thrive or fail—based on structures and practices alone. Institutions and students alike depend on the ability of staff to take on a range of roles in the course of each day. The schools studied support all teachers in forging a new relationship to teaching—one where they serve in multiple capacities, from curriculum planner, classroom facilitator, and assessor to adviser and community connector. (See "A Quick Note on Professional Development.")

Though challenging, such shape-shifting can lend a distinct appeal to the work of teaching. Noble High School teacher Andrew Korman explained: "We have a culture here that encourages risk-taking—to try something new, to put on a new hat, to reach out to that kid. We also attract teachers who are willing to think outside the box, that are in tune with this culture. And even if you fail in a particular lesson, that's okay. The point is to try to help these kids meet their educational goals."

Students appreciate the multiple parts their teachers play. Looking back after her graduation, Morgan, a former Noble student, named the three

A QUICK NOTE ON PROFESSIONAL DEVELOPMENT

Taking on varied and new roles necessitates support for educators as well as students. The single most important support, teachers told us, is frequent, common planning time so they can collaborate. These teachers constantly compare notes on shared students and plan curricula across content areas.

Combined with other key collegial practices, such as steady mentoring for new teachers and regular observation of one another's classrooms, collaborative planning empowers teachers in the same way they seek to empower students. They improve their practice based on constructive feedback from peers as well as supervisors.

Despite the challenges and frustrations of their profession, these teachers said, they feel part of a learning organization. Reflecting, taking stock, adding and subtracting, reinventing—all lend color, depth, and life to their everyday practice and to the learning of their students.

that mattered most to her: teacher, friend, and mentor: "Most of the time, the teachers here create a very personal relationship with their students. They get involved in what their students care about, they help them and coach them. Finally, there's mentor: beyond that personal relationship with kids, the teachers here also help you discover how to succeed in what interests you."

Curriculum Planner

Developing curricula is a constant aspect of the work at the six high schools. Most student-centered schools replace textbooks with multiple sources for ideas and materials. They choose depth over the breadth of coverage typical of texts. Teachers collaborate with colleagues whenever possible to design and revise lessons. Many go to great lengths to integrate their teaching across disciplines. For example, a Noble High School unit on immigration took the place of regular daily English and history classes for three weeks.

Alief's Peggy Breef, who had been a teacher for twelve years at the time she was interviewed, explained that she used to feel tremendous pressure to expose her students to a large amount of material. Now, she said, her totally different conception of what is important makes the extra planning worth the effort: "This year, I'm struggling to get through two novels and short stories and one play. But it's much more in depth, much more narrow," she said, noting that she spends about 50 percent more time on curriculum planning than in the past. "It forces me to really be thinking, 'What are the essential things that they have to learn?'"

Classroom Facilitator and Coach

In student-centered learning environments, teachers act more as guides than as lecturers. Staff members said this works best when they set up scenarios in which students can explore, ask their own questions, and discover their own answers.

Teachers in the Early College High School Initiative, including those at Alief and DECA, follow the initiative's Common Instructional Framework of six strategies: Collaborative Group Work; Write to Learn; Classroom Talk; Questioning; Scaffolding; and Literacy Groups. Each strategy places the teacher squarely in the role of facilitator, Alief's Peggy Breef noted, and the AVID curriculum further reinforces that: "As a teacher, you don't ever want to just start throwing out information." Instead, she focuses on drawing students in, getting them actively using new material, then pressing them to take it further.

Assessor

The teachers we observed consider assessment an art interwoven with teaching. More than a single test, *formative assessment* is an active process that requires teachers to stay alert to daily evidence of learning and struggle by students, and it is an essential part of student-centered practice. As teachers circulate in class each day, they engage with every student in some way that enables them to measure understanding—and, critically, adjust instruction as needed.

At all six schools, students also take high-stakes standardized state tests, which are *summative*, giving a snapshot of a student's learning at a certain point in time. Those cannot be ignored, for a variety of reasons. Nevertheless, they often lack the emphasis on deeper learning that teachers prefer. As we heard again and again, the assessment data that most help teachers improve their teaching, reflect "what's happening with our students" every day.

Adviser

Though each school structures advising differently, all the teachers in this study see the adviser role as central to their work. At DECA, Jessica Austin meets with her advisory group students individually once a week, in part because many teens get too little support from home. Students remain in one advisory group for grades 7 and 8, then move to another for high school. Austin said she considers the advisory relationship critical to her students' success, both academically and emotionally: "Students build a strong relationship with someone who can support them academically, emotionally, really be there for them, get to know their family, that one-on-one," she explained. "I'm also a motivator and pusher, making sure that students are working on whatever they need."

Connector

The teachers in our study know that interpersonal networks in which adolescents participate make a big difference to their future lives, and they do what they can to help facilitate community connections. For example, at Bronx International, group discussions frequently focus on helping students connect with summer opportunities or postsecondary pathways, said one tenth-grader.

In rural Maine, opportunities can be scarce for teenagers, especially during hard economic times. "I am constantly sending out opportunities via e-mail for summer programs, or scholarship opportunities, or contests that they can enter," said Noble teacher Adina Hunter. "That's a lot of what I do: connect students to opportunities to push themselves above and beyond their classrooms."

BATTLING THE HEADWINDS OF STANDARDIZATION

The six secondary schools falling under our lens have much to show and teach about deep student-centered learning. Each school reflects its origins, including its model and local context of policy, financing, and community interests. And each has evolved and continues to change over time, with staff continually examining, rethinking, and revising, unafraid of getting rid of what does not work and trying new things. Thus, the specific steps these schools take are not neat designs to be replicated. Rather, we regard them as models of how public schools can center teaching and learning on the needs of students, even as each school adapts to its unique environment. These six have grown from both necessity and invention, and so have power to inspire in situations very different from their own.

Despite these inspiring portraits, we fully recognize that student-centered teaching and learning are more the exception than the rule in U.S. schools today. The headwinds are strong in the face of scaling up structures and practices that support a student-centered model. Common Core standards may provide an important lift, assuming those standards are both high and clear enough to translate into widespread practice. Technological advances will unquestionably alter the landscape, though raising issues of both depth and equity. Yet top-down reform, a hyperreliance on testing to measure mastery among both students and teachers, the push for standardization despite the most diverse student body in our nation's history—these and other trends greatly challenge efforts to spread the kind of schooling we have explored.

Nevertheless, the vitality and richness of the student-centered settings and the development of lifelong learners are striking examples of what education could look like. We conclude with one fundamental question for the nation: In the face of today's policy headwinds, how can we give more children—especially those left behind on the basis of poverty, color, language, and other "differences"—the opportunity to learn in schools like these?

CHAPTER 2

Making Assessment Student Centered

Heidi Andrade, Kristen Huff, and Georgia Brooke

ASSESSING STUDENT LEARNING often promotes anxiety among students, teachers, and administrators. In this era of high-stakes testing, school leaders worry about the accountability consequences of showing inadequate progress. Teachers are concerned that tests do not adequately measure what students have learned. And students feel enormous pressure from all sides to succeed according to a single definition of success.

Student-centered assessment, in contrast, can *promote* learning, not just *measure* it. Like any good assessment, it does evaluate progress against developmentally appropriate learning targets and provides feedback about how to deepen learning. But student-centered assessment is distinguished by several additional defining qualities: it is individualized, promotes learning and growth, motivates students, actively engages students in the regulation of their own learning, and is informative and useful to a variety of audiences. Such assessment practices can be incorporated into any educational setting. But they are essential to student-centered approaches, which value differentiation, active engagement, and self-management as critical to the learning process.

We observe that:

- No single type of assessment can inform learning and instruction at the classroom level and simultaneously aid policy decisions. Student-centered assessment should be part of a balanced system of formative, interim, and summative assessments—both formal and informal—that together meet all of a school's and system's assessment needs.
- A variety of classroom-based, student-centered assessments are associated with significant gains in student learning and achievement. These include self- and peer assessments, portfolios, assessments using new technologies, exhibitions, and formative uses of summative tests.
- Schools and districts across the nation report impressive gains in student achievement and deepened professional collaboration when teachers create their own interim assessments aligned to what they are actually teaching.
- Modern assessment technologies hold great promise for student-centered assessment because they can offer immediate feedback to each student and allow teachers to respond to individual learning needs with greater speed, frequency, focus, and flexibility.

A BALANCED ASSESSMENT SYSTEM AND STUDENT-CENTERED ASSESSMENT

No single type of assessment can inform classroom practice as well as school, district, and high-level policy decisions. Therefore, a truly student-centered assessment system requires a balanced system of formative, interim, and summative assessments that, taken together, provide the detailed information educators and other stakeholders need. Such a system may include everything from informal observations of student work to standardized tests.

Types of assessment include:

- **Formative assessment**: The ongoing, minute-by-minute, day-by-day classroom assessment that is administered in the course of a unit of instruction. It is often informal, ranging from classroom observations to check-in conversations with individual students. The intent is to identify individual strengths and weaknesses, assist educators in planning subsequent instruction, and aid students in guiding their own learning, revising their work, and developing self-evaluation skills.[1]
- **Interim assessment**: A more formalized, periodic process of measuring student achievement throughout the school year. The chief goal is to provide information to local educators and policy makers, who can adjust curricula and instruction as needed.
- **Summative assessment**: Also a formal, often standardized, assessment and typically administered at the end of a unit of instruction, semester, or year. The primary purpose is to categorize the performance of a student or education system in order to inform accountability processes and decisions about grades, graduation, or retention.[2]

Ultimately, a system using all three types of assessment, created both inside and outside the classroom, is needed to support student-centered learning. For example, formative student self-assessment is highly individualized and actively engages students in regulating their own learning, but it is not particularly useful to any audience other than the student. In contrast, summative large-scale assessments such as state-mandated, standardized annual assessments provide data to policy makers interested in comparing state-by-state outcomes and implementing accountability systems, but cannot serve their intended purposes if they are individualized. Only a complete system of formative, interim, and summative assessments can be individualized, focused on learning and growth, amenable to actively engaging students in regulating their own learning, motivating, and capable of generating useful information for a variety of audiences.

While most assessment processes have some student-centered features, only a few meet all the characteristics of student-centered assessment:

- **Individualized:** The first and most obvious feature of student-centered assessment is that it is individualized, and focused on each student's strengths, needs, and interests. Individualizing assessment involves differentiating learning targets, assignments, and tasks to each student's current skills group.
- **Focused on learning and growth:** Student-centered assessment does more than measure and report student learning—or the lack thereof—although it does those things as well. It actually promotes learning and growth. Most important, it provides useful feedback about what the student needs to do (e.g., what specific skills and knowledge the student must master) in order to progress toward the learning target. This helps teachers and the students themselves adjust teaching and learning processes to maximize understanding.
- **Actively engaging students in self-regulation:** Students are actively engaged in student-centered assessment in ways that are not possible with traditional assessment practices. Students help manage their own learning and growth—participating in setting goals, monitoring their progress toward those goals, and determining how to address any gaps. Developing these self-regulation skills, as well as core content knowledge and skills, is essential for twenty-first-century college and career success.
- **Motivating:** Perhaps the most surprising aspect of our definition of student-centered assessment is that it is motivating. Many people associate being evaluated with mild to moderate anxiety, not motivation; and research has shown that the use of grades for evaluation can be associated with decreased motivation and lower achievement.[3] Recent studies have shown that formative assessment—particularly detailed, task-specific comments on student work—can activate interest in a task[4] and result in better performance.[5]
- **Informative and useful to a variety of audiences:** Finally, student-centered assessment provides useful information for stakeholders at all levels—including students, teachers, administrators, parents, districts, and states. All of these groups can apply the results to support

learning. For example, public exhibitions of student work engage an audience from the community in discussions of what individual students have learned, and of the education they are getting. An example of an assessment that is informative to a broader group is a state test that guides policy makers at the district or state level in determining where to allocate limited resources or what programs appear to be working best, where, and for whom.

Generally, formative assessment tends to be more student-centered than interim and summative assessment (except for summative, end-of-year exhibitions of student work). Figure 2.1 presents an overview of selected assessment processes, along with our judgments of the "student-centeredness" of each. In this chapter, we focus on the most student-centered types of assessment—those with at least four or five student-centered qualities.

AT THE INDIVIDUAL, CLASSROOM, AND SCHOOL LEVEL: FORMATIVE ASSESSMENT

When it comes to the critical work of improving student outcomes, research has shown that formative, classroom-based assessments are associated with significant gains in learning and achievement.[6] The purpose is to provide timely information to students and teachers about current student progress, gaps in understanding, and targets for deepening learning.[7] Forms of classroom assessment that are particularly student-centered include self-assessment, peer assessment, portfolios, and formative uses of summative tests.

Self-assessment

The purpose of self-assessment is to help students identify areas of strength and weakness in their own work in order to make improvements and promote learning, achievement, and self-regulation.[8] Research suggests that self-regulation and student achievement are closely related: students who set goals, make flexible plans to meet them, and monitor their progress

FIGURE 2-1 Student-centered qualities of select assessment processes

		Individualized	Focused on learning and growth	Student self-regulation	Motivating	Informative to a variety of audiences
Individual, classroom, school	*Formative*					
	Self-assessments	•	•	•	•	
	Peer assessments	•	•	•	•	•
	Portfolios	•	•	•	•	•
	Tests		•	•	•	•
School, district	*Interim*					
	Criterion-referenced tests		•			•
School, district, state, nation	*Summative*					
	Exhibitions	•	•	•	•	•
	Learning progression-based assessments & diagnostics		•			•
	Large-scale tests					•

tend to learn more and do better in school than students who do not.[9] Self-assessment is a key element of self-regulation because it involves awareness of the goals of a task and checking progress toward them.

It is critical to recognize that self-assessment is a formative tool, rather than a summative one. Self-assessment is done on work in progress to inform revision and improvement; it is not a matter of having students determine their own grades. Effective self-assessment involves at least three steps:

1. **Articulate performance targets:** The teacher, the students, or, preferably, both clearly articulate the expectations for the task. Students better understand the nature of the task and how to accomplish it when they are involved in thinking about how quality performance of the task is defined. Co-creating a rubric with students is one effective way for teachers to help make expectations clear. A rubric is usually a one- or two-page document that lists criteria for completion of a specific assignment and describes varying levels of quality, from excellent to poor, for all of the criteria. (See "A Sample Self-Assessment Process.")

2. **Checking progress toward the targets:** Students make a first attempt at their assignment (e.g., essay, lab report, choral recital, or speech). Then they compare their performance-in-progress to expectations, noting areas of strength and weakness and making plans for improvement.

3. **Revision:** Students use feedback from their self-assessments to guide their revision. This step is crucial. Adolescents are unlikely to assess their own work thoughtfully unless they know their efforts can lead to opportunities to make improvements and possibly increase their grades.

Research findings suggest that student self-assessment in writing,[10] mathematics,[11] social studies,[12] science,[13] and external examinations[14] can promote achievement and learner autonomy. Student reactions to self-assessment are generally positive, but they need support and practice to reap the full benefits of the process.[15]

A SAMPLE SELF-ASSESSMENT PROCESS

An example of self-assessment in writing, using a rubric, might look like this:

After writing a first draft of a persuasive essay, students underline key phrases in the rubric with a variety of colored pencils. Next, they use corresponding colors to underline or circle their evidence of having met each criterion in their drafts.

For example, students might underline "clearly states an opinion" in blue on their rubric, then would underline their opinions in blue in their essay drafts. If they cannot find a clearly articulated opinion to underline, they would write themselves a reminder to do so in their revision.

They would continue the process for each criterion in the rubric.

Peer Assessment

The purpose of peer assessment is for learners to provide feedback to one another on the quality of a product or performance.[16] Students can help one another identify strengths, weaknesses, and areas for improvement. Peer assessment happens both inside and outside of school and across different times and contexts, leading to the development of valuable metacognitive, personal, and professional skills.

Effective peer assessment generally involves the following steps:[17]

1. Students and teachers co-create assessment criteria.
2. Peers are placed into pairs or small groups based on similar ability levels.
3. The teacher provides training by modeling how to assess a piece of work using explicit criteria.
4. Students get a checklist with peer assessment guidelines.
5. The activity to be assessed and timeline are specified.

6. The teacher monitors the progress of the peer assessment groups.
7. The quality of the feedback is examined.
8. Reliability is checked by comparing teacher- and peer-generated feedback.
9. The teacher provides feedback to the students about the effectiveness of their assessments.

Research suggests that peer assessment can improve the quality and effectiveness of learning across grade levels, particularly in writing.[18] Furthermore, both the assessed and the assessor benefit from the process.[19] As Topping notes, "[L]istening, explaining, questioning, summarizing, speculating, and hypothesizing are all valuable skills of effective peer assessment."[20] While an initial investment is necessary to establish effective peer feedback groups, it is likely to be worthwhile in terms of student learning.

Portfolios

Academic portfolios are individualized collections of student work that trace progress and highlight strengths. They typically consist of physical artifacts presented in a deliberate order, assembled in a folder or binder or on a computer, incorporating audio, video, graphics, and text. Some portfolios showcase a student's best work; others trace progress from novice efforts to mastery.

For portfolios to be student-centered, students must be actively engaged in their creation. It is especially important for students first to set goals for their own learning and achievement. Later, students select the pieces that will be included in the portfolio and add reflections on what those pieces communicate about their progress toward their goals and their learning over time. For example, a writing process portfolio includes several successive drafts and the students' comments on each. In these ways, portfolios scaffold self-regulated learning and provide nuanced information about a student's knowledge, motivations, and needs.

Portfolios can be useful and informative to students, parents, teachers, and administrators. Research suggests that portfolios are best used formatively, for classroom assessment, rather than summatively as large-scale evaluations, thus limiting their usefulness to audiences outside the school.[21]

Electronic portfolios, or e-portfolios, are becoming increasingly popular. The technology enables linking, multimedia storytelling, archiving, collaborating, and publishing that print portfolios cannot match. Research suggests that the use of electronic portfolios is positively associated with improvements in student performance, goal setting, problem solving, and reflection.[22] (See "Assessment Technologies.")

Samples available on the Web site of New Technology High School in Napa, California, illustrate the wide range of possibilities.[23] A striking example of the potential of e-portfolios to vividly capture student progress is the senior project video of a student named Sean, who spent months mastering Parkour—the sport of moving along a route, typically in a city, trying to get around or through various obstacles in the quickest and most efficient manner possible, often by running, jumping, vaulting, and flipping.[24] His portfolio also contains explicit goals, outcomes, reflections, and a personal statement describing his transformation from a freshman who did not care about learning into a "model student."

Formative Uses of Summative Tests

Traditionally, tests come at the end of a unit of study, and teachers use them summatively to determine grades. But such tests can also be used formatively. Formative uses of summative tests involve two testing events that bookend careful analyses of learning by students and teachers. The results of the first test are used formatively, while the results of the second are used summatively. The explicit goal of the first test is to activate learning about the content of the second. It is not the same process that occurs with a practice test, which is generally more passive. It is not just hearing the correct answers that makes formative uses of testing work; rather, it is the hard thinking that happens in between the tests that matters—students figuring out which skills or concepts they do not yet understand, and then finding ways to learn them.

For example, consider a formative test of students' understanding of the Pythagorean theorem. Before reviewing the correct answers, the teacher asks small groups of students to compare responses and resolve any disagreements using their notes, textbook, and other resources. Only after students have had ample opportunity to discover and correct their mistakes does the teacher go over the correct answers with the class. Students then note the kinds of mistakes they tended to make, what they need to study before the next test, and what concepts they need additional help to understand. A day or two later, the teacher administers the second, summative, test, which has different questions but covers the same content.

Research shows that this process, which is part of *mastery learning*, is related to learning gains, especially for struggling students. It also has positive effects on students' attitudes toward course content.[25] In fact, after reviewing meta-analyses from over forty areas of educational research, Kulik, Kulik, and Bangert-Drowns concluded: "Few educational treatments of any sort were consistently associated with achievement effects as large as those produced by mastery learning."[26]

Of the four classroom assessment processes discussed in this section, formative uses of summative testing are informative and useful to the widest variety of audiences. The usefulness to administrators can be enhanced if the first test is also used as an interim test and analyzed in terms of the instructional and curricular needs of a class or entire grade level.

AT THE SCHOOL AND DISTRICT LEVELS: INTERIM AND SUMMATIVE ASSESSMENT

School- and district-level assessments tend to be more useful to a wider audience than classroom-level assessments, but often at the expense of individualization, student self-regulation, and motivation. However, two types of assessment—criterion-referenced interim assessments developed by teams of teachers for use beyond a single classroom, and exhibitions—can be used in student-centered ways. Criterion-referenced tests

ASSESSMENT TECHNOLOGIES

Modern assessment technologies hold great promise for student-centered approaches to learning. A wide array of computer software provides immediate feedback and enables teachers to respond to individual learning needs with greater speed, frequency, focus, and flexibility. The rapid feedback also has the potential to motivate students by providing specific information about not only their strengths but also how they can improve their work while they are still engaged in the task.

Other key features of student-centered assessment technologies include: systematic monitoring of student progress to inform instructional decisions; the identification of misconceptions that may interfere with student learning; and information about student learning needs during instruction.[27]

Computer-based assessment software integrates the management of learning (e.g., organizing student assignments, assessments, and performance), curricular resources, embedded assessments, and detailed student-level and aggregate reporting of strengths and weaknesses. Examples include DreamBox Learning, Time To Know, Wowzers, Carnegie Learning, and WriteToLearn. Some products, like WriteToLearn, integrate instruction and assessment into one platform. Continued research on the effectiveness of assessment technologies in student-centered learning environments would be valuable, yet there is already some information on their worth.

An Example: WriteToLearn

WriteToLearn is an example of a student-centered assessment technology with research support. It promotes reading comprehension and writing skills by providing students with immediate, individualized feedback.[28] The program, designed for students in grades 4 through 12, has three components: summary writing, where students read and summarize passages from across subject areas; vocabulary exercises in select reading passages; and essay writing, where students write topic-prompted essays. By logging in to WriteToLearn, teachers can set up individualized assignments for each student in their class and then monitor activity and progress. Students can get instant feedback on the quality of their writing according to specific criteria.

One study found a positive relationship between the use of the summary writing feature and student summary scores after just two weeks.[29] It also found that students spent significantly more time generating summaries than students not using the program, suggesting the program may promote motivation and engagement. Another study found that eighth-grade students had significantly higher comprehension scores and writing skills than students who do not use the summary program.[30]

in particular appear to hold promise for focusing on learning and growth and thereby informing adjustments to curriculum and instruction.

Criterion-Referenced Interim Assessments

Schools and districts across the nation are reporting impressive gains in student achievement when teachers create criterion-referenced interim assessments aligned to what they are actually teaching.[31] These assessments are administered regularly and test student achievement of the learning targets set by their teachers in their schools. Teacher teams from within and across schools—in particular, across grades and subject areas—collaborate to design questions that directly measure the curriculum enacted in their classrooms. The teachers use the same assessments on an interim basis throughout the school year (usually about every six weeks). They get together to discuss the results at length and share pedagogical approaches to helping students progress. The key to the success of these efforts is that teachers collaborate to develop the tests and discuss the results, and then adjust their pedagogy accordingly when they return to their classrooms.

The student-centeredness of interim assessments would increase sharply if schools used them the way teachers use formative tests: by involving students in analyzing the results of their performance and making plans to deepen their learning.

Exhibitions

Exhibitions are public demonstrations of mastery that occur at culminating moments, such as at the conclusion of a unit of study or at high school graduation.[32] Their purpose is to support sustained, personalized learning while assuring commitment, engagement, and high-level intellectual achievement aligned with established standards.[33]

Exhibitions are a rare example of a summative assessment process that exemplifies each characteristic of student-centered assessment: they are individualized to student interests; they involve personalized, ongoing feedback from diverse sources before the final performance; they actively engage students in regulating learning by requiring them to set short- and long-term goals and seek feedback; and because the audience for exhibitions typically includes practicing experts, they provide authentic, real-world tasks that can motivate students to do well. By definition, exhibitions provide useful information about student learning and achievement to students, teachers, parents, administrators, and community members.

While the research literature on exhibitions is thin, it suggests that schools placing a central focus on exhibitions have lower dropout rates, higher college-going rates, and improved college performance and persistence.[34]

AT THE STATE AND NATIONAL LEVELS: LARGE–SCALE SUMMATIVE ASSESSMENTS

Large-scale assessments—those that states use for K–12 accountability and those that measure performance based on national norms—tend to be less student-centered than any of the other processes discussed here. However, these tests are ubiquitous in U.S. schools and unlikely to go away anytime soon. Both statewide criterion-referenced and nationally norm-referenced assessments provide useful information to school and district administrators, policy makers, parents, and other stakeholders.

Criterion-referenced interim assessments are regular (e.g., every six to eight weeks) tests of student achievement of the learning targets set by their teachers in their schools, and are used to make timely adjustments to instruction and curriculum. In contrast, *norm-referenced large-scale assessments* are typically used infrequently (e.g., once a year) to compare students' performance on content taught nationwide. *Criterion-referenced large-scale tests* are designed to measure a particular set of state-based learning outcomes, or standards for accountability purposes. Results are reported in terms of the degree to which the student has or has not met the expected performance standard (e.g., Basic, Proficient, or Advanced) and, increasingly, the degree to which the student has improved since the previous year (i.e., growth measures). Norm-referenced tests are not primarily designed to measure curriculum-based knowledge and skills. They are administered nationwide so that student performance can be reported in terms of national norms. For example, the eighty-ninth percentile represents the same performance, regardless of whether the student is from Massachusetts or New Mexico.

Policy makers use the information from large-scale tests to compare performance within states and nationally. Districts and states also analyze the data and often use them to determine where to allocate resources and what kinds of educational programs (e.g., schools with innovative instructional approaches) have the most success with particular groups (e.g., English language learners; students with special needs).

Making Large-Scale Tests More Student Centered

Recent advances in large-scale tests suggest they can be more student centered when crafted with certain priorities in mind. In order to provide useful feedback to students, teachers, and policy makers, large-scale assessments could be improved in three areas. They should: be based on theories of learning; provide instructionally relevant score reports; and address the educational context of a wide array of students.[35]

Evidence-Centered Design. Evidence-centered design is an innovative approach based on learning theory that describes how to measure complex, higher-order thinking, and details the specific assessment features that are required to elicit student understanding. To maximize the educational benefits of assessment, exams should be situated within an aligned and integrated system of curriculum, instruction, and assessment,[36] based on theories of learning. In this system, curricula should sequence learning objectives that reflect our understanding of how students build knowledge and expertise in the domain and instruction should employ strategies that facilitate such knowledge building. Assessment design should be evidence-centered, informed by the same cognitive framework that shapes the curriculum and provides feedback to teachers.

Assessments based on evidence-centered design would be empowering, motivating, and informative for all stakeholders, who would have a shared understanding of the targets of learning, the observable evidence of student work that is required, and the types of tasks that can best support students in providing the required evidence of student learning.

Instructionally Relevant Score Reports. Instructionally relevant score reports are another tool for improving large-scale assessment. Demand has increased for test scores that offer information that is directly relevant to instruction.[37] The problem is that criterion- and norm-referenced large-scale assessments are not designed to provide detailed information about the strengths and weaknesses of individual students. If they were, it might undermine their use for summative assessment.

That said, there are ways to improve the types of information that can be provided. First, large-scale assessments could use an item-mapping or scale-anchoring approach to provide detailed feedback to students without compromising the summative design requirements.[38] A second approach employs a collection of techniques called *diagnostic classification models.* These models provide feedback based on the response patterns of individual students and an analysis of student strengths and weaknesses on specific, fine-grained skills.[39] Although both of these approaches have pros and cons, their ability to provide more instructionally relevant score reports would be greatly improved if they were based on an assessment that was designed with student cognition in mind, such as evidence-centered design.

Learning Progression–Based Assessments and Diagnostics. Learning progressions have great potential to support student-centered assessment practices. Learning progressions articulate in detail how knowledge, skills, and abilities change as one moves from less to more sophisticated understanding in a given content area. Sometimes they are referred to as the building blocks or steps that students need to go through to reach a learning target.[40] For example, if the learning target is for students to understand that it gets colder at night because part of the Earth is facing away from the Sun's heat, they must first understand that the Earth both orbits around the Sun and rotates on its own axis.

Learning progressions can support student-centered classroom assessment by revealing typical mistaken preconceptions that students have and must correct as their understanding of a particular learning objective becomes more sophisticated (figure 2.2). A recent commission on learning

FIGURE 2-2   Excerpt of levels 2 and 3 from a fourth-grade learning progression

Level 2	Level 3
The student recognizes that: • The Sun appears to move across the sky every day. • The observable shape of the Moon changes every twenty-eight days. The student may believe that the Sun moves around the Earth.	The student knows that: • The Earth orbits the Sun. • The Moon orbits the Earth. • The Earth rotates on its axis. However, the student has not put this knowledge together with an understanding of apparent motion to form explanations and may not recognize that the Earth is both rotating and orbiting simultaneously.
Common error: All motion in the sky is due to the Earth spinning on its axis. *Common error:* The Sun travels around the Earth. *Common error:* It gets dark at night because the Sun goes around the Earth once a day. *Common error:* The Earth is the center of the universe.	*Common error:* It gets dark at night because the Earth goes around the Sun once a day.

Source: D. C. Briggs et al., "Diagnostic Assessment with Ordered Multiple Choice Items," *Educational Assessment* 11, no. 1 (2006): 33–63. Copyright © 2012 WestEd.

progressions in science noted that teachers will not be able to track student progress and help them reach the learning goals until they have information about how students' learning in the subjects develops over time."[41]

Unfortunately, research indicates that teachers may not yet have the tools that would enable them to use learning progressions as the basis for their assessments. The research suggests that teachers need explicit detail on "how learning progresses in a domain[,] what the precursor skills and understandings are for a specific instructional goal, what a good performance of the desired goal looks like, and how the skill or understanding increases in sophistication from the current level students have reached."[42]

Fortunately, there is great momentum to use learning progressions as the basis for large-scale assessment.[43] The potential contribution of learning progressions to improved assessment design is significant. Learning progressions can inform the development of achievement-level descriptions, which are the basis of score interpretation and decision making for large-scale, criterion-referenced assessments.

When learning progressions are used as the basis for designing multiple-choice items, the items can then be used diagnostically, such as in the example in figure 2.3. When the information from a learning progression (e.g., figure 2.2), including the steps toward understanding and typical preconceptions or errors, are used as answer choices, student responses to

FIGURE 2-3   Diagnostic multiple-choice test item based on a learning progression

---

It is most likely colder at night because:

A. The earth is at the furthest point in its orbit around the sun. *[Level 3 response]*

B. The sun has traveled to the other side of the earth. *[Level 2 response]*

C. The sun is below the earth and the moon does not emit as much heat as the sun. *[Level 1 response]*

D. The place where it is night on Earth is rotated away from the Sun. *[Level 4 response]*

E. The Sun and Moon switch places to create night. *[Level 2 response]*

Source: D. C. Briggs et al., "Diagnostic Assessment with Ordered Multiple Choice Items," *Educational Assessment* 11, no. 1 (2006): 33–63. Copyright © 2012 WestEd.

the item yield information about the students' understanding that far surpasses what can be learned from simply classifying the student response as right or wrong.[44]

Although these types of items help assessments meet the student-centered criteria for focusing on learning and growth and for being informative to a variety of audiences, there are challenges to using them on large-scale assessments that are designed for summative purposes. Researchers are investigating ways to incorporate learning-progression-based diagnostic items into large-scale summative assessments.[45]

The Role of Context

One challenge for large-scale assessment that needs further attention is the role of the student's learning context. Allowing students to learn and build deep conceptual knowledge in "real-life" environments is a key to developing the twenty-first-century skills required for college and career success. However, assessing the knowledge and skills that are important regardless of context is challenging. For example, suppose two high school biology teachers are conducting a unit on the various ways in which DNA is transferred to the next generation. One teacher is in Chicago, so she uses quagga mussels as the context for her students' project. They collect samples from Lake Michigan, conduct experiments, and record their observations. The other teacher is in Glenwood Springs, Colorado, so he uses the narrow-leaved paintbrush, a native plant that grows along the Colorado River, as the context for the unit. How can both sets of students be assessed on the foundational knowledge and skills without putting either set at an advantage or disadvantage?

The developers of large-scale assessments routinely face this challenge. The role of context is not yet resolved, but progress can be made with more advances in assessment technology (e.g., simulation-based computerized assessments) and more sophisticated psychometric and assessment design innovations (e.g., the use of task models that can produce "families" of items that measure the same target but have different contexts).[46] Solving the problem of context in large-scale assessment would be a first step toward helping large-scale assessments be more individualized, which is the first defining characteristic of student-centered assessment systems and the one most challenging for large-scale assessment to attain.

ASSESSING TO LEARN, LEARNING TO ASSESS

We believe that a balanced system of formative, interim, and summative assessments can support student-centered assessment and learning. Yet even an exquisitely balanced assessment system would present challenges. For one, the sheer quantity of assessment data threatens to be overwhelming. Emerging technologies hold great promise to facilitate more student-centered assessments; but the available digital tools have yet to catch up to innovative practitioners or the demands of national accountability systems. Even as new assessment processes and technology are created, educators must work to ensure they are useful to and used by the appropriate audiences—students, teachers, schools, districts, and policy makers alike.

Students must learn how to take advantage of feedback to improve their work, deepen their understanding, and regulate their own learning. Teachers must learn how to individualize instruction and assessments and to make adjustments to instruction based on assessment results. Schools and districts must learn how to combine formative, interim, and summative results and interpret them in meaningful ways. And policy makers must learn to create and use balanced assessment systems that inform but do not overburden or overwhelm those they are designed to assist.

It is also critical to continually assess the assessments to make sure that advances in design—and their implementation—are as student centered as possible.

PART II

Next Steps

*How can teachers use student-centered approaches
to create positive learning environments in which
increasingly diverse learners thrive and develop?
Specifically, how do advances in digital media allow us
to move away from the myth of the average learner?
How can educators use cultural and social identities
to enhance literacy and mathematics instruction for
black, African American, and Latino/a students?*

In recent years, the mythical image of the average learner
has given way to the reality that curriculum and pedagogy
must be as articulated and differentiated as the learners
themselves if we are to maximize each learner's potential.
Part 2 offers aspirational portraits of what student-centered
curricula and practices could look like if we were attending to the needs, contexts, and identities of the most
underserved populations in our schools today.

CHAPTER 3

Using Digital Media to Design Student-Centered Curricula

David H. Rose and Jenna W. Gravel

MOST CLASSROOMS ARE *curriculum centered*; that is, they are designed around curricula whose core elements—textbooks and other print materials—are standardized or, as the saying goes, "one size fits all." But students are anything but uniform. As a result, teachers face inherent hurdles in meeting the needs of all their students, and students struggle to learn from curricula that are often inaccessible to varying degrees.

Technological advances make possible new curricular designs that offer exciting ways to create classrooms that are student centered.[1] To help the wide variety of today's students master the skills needed to succeed in college and careers, curricula must be as differentiated as the learners themselves. In the digital age, that level of differentiation is both feasible and optimal, as captured through the field of universal design for learning (UDL), which supplies guideposts for designing curricula that are individualized enough to meet the needs of diverse learners. The three main principles of UDL—provide students with multiple means of representation, multiple means of action and expression, and multiple means of engagement—align closely with student-centered practices.

In this chapter, we argue that:

- There is no mythical "average" learner. Advances in neuroscience reveal that the brain is highly differentiated and specialized, with a vast array of strengths and weaknesses, not only between different people but also within individuals.
- Multimedia technologies provide an encouraging foundation for student-centered learning, offering educators the ability to customize how and what we teach each student.
- UDL's research-based framework combines neuroscience and technology to optimize learning for every student.
- Using the UDL framework, student-centered classrooms can harness the flexibility of new media to provide a diverse range of students with the multiple means of representation, expression, and engagement each needs to become a thoughtful, strategic, and motivated learner.

NEUROSCIENTIFIC FOUNDATIONS OF VARIABILITY AND CUSTOMIZATION

An explosion of research in neuroscience, arising from new digital imaging and analytic tools, profoundly alters our ability to understand learning and individual differences.[2] Images of the brain in action reveal that its functions are both specialized and highly differentiated. For example, at least twenty different regions of the brain specialize in vision. Even more striking, people process information about faces in certain brain regions and objects like utensils or cars or flowers in other regions.

Such findings are crucial for education because different people exhibit astounding variation in strengths and challenges. From reading to mathematics to musical ability, most brain specializations lie along a continuum: from "gifted" to those who are "disabled." Moreover, most individuals have a wide array of strengths and weaknesses within themselves. Gifted writers may struggle in math; dyslexic students may excel at science; people with autism may have perfect pitch in singing.

Indeed, all individuals are complex composites of variation in a great many different capabilities. This is true not only within a single perceptual modality like vision or hearing but also at higher levels of brain function, such as cognition, language, and memory. Variation is not only universal; it is ubiquitous.

It is important to consider the sources of individual variation. Confronted with the sharp differentiation of brain images, many educators and researchers have assumed that the roots of individual differences are largely genetic. In reality, the human brain, at any stage in its development, reflects a complex history of the interplay between genetics and environment. What we see in a brain's individual pattern is as much a result of that person's interactions with people, places, things, and ideas as of genetics.

As one example, consider perfect pitch. We know that genetics plays a role: individuals with Williams syndrome or with autism have a much higher than average incidence of perfect pitch. But it is also true that culture plays a role—the incidence of perfect pitch is much higher in some cultures than in others—specifically in cultures where pitch is an important factor in communication and social development. Nowhere are the effects of cultural differences more sharply drawn than in the role of culture and society in differentiating not only how mathematics is realized but also how it is learned, as detailed in chapter 5. In this new landscape of richly differentiated functionality in the brain, general global measures like IQ seem anachronistic and uninformative.

What are the implications for a student-centered curriculum? On the face of it, it seems clear that a curriculum cannot really be considered "student centered" if it is appropriate for one individual but not another.

For students in the margins, this point is especially evident. A poster or map that highlights Republican states in red and Democratic states in blue would represent political information well for most students but would hardly be considered student centered for those who are blind or even just color blind. Nor would a math lesson that requires excellent reading skills seem student centered for a student who is dyslexic. At the other end of the spectrum, a ninth-grade history text written with a sixth-grade vocabulary and syntax (as many are) is hardly student centered for ninth-graders reading at level, let alone the student who needs to be challenged with the vocabulary and syntax of a twelfth-grader.

How many sources of variation must a lesson designer consider to create material that meets the criteria for "student-centered" learning? Students with sensory and physical disabilities—even students with dyslexia—are striking cases, but not entirely representative. In what ways must it be possible to "customize" a curriculum so that it is student centered enough to reach the diversity of learners in a single classroom?

Another, equally important question: for the full population of students, does the availability of options—customization—actually improve performance? A considerable body of research shows it does, with various types of customization.[3] However, plenty of studies show no effects.[4]

Clearly, customization itself is not the answer. For customization to be effective in any educational setting two things need to be considered. Designing a lesson that can be student centered first depends on recognizing the important variations from student to student that might make it less accessible or less informative for some. Second, it depends on recognizing the important variations in the design and implementation of tasks or lessons. Of particular concern are aspects of the task that are not *construct relevant*—that is, where aspects of the lesson design may interfere with what is being taught. In the civics map example, color is actually construct irrelevant because the lesson is about politics, not color discrimination. The use of a color in the map requires each student to have the same abilities in color discrimination—that is, the color is helpful (i.e., student-centered) for most but poses an unacceptable barrier for a few.

Yet effective customization also requires paying attention to aspects of tasks that *are* construct relevant. For example, a civics teacher who wants to develop students' persuasive writing skills might assign an essay that asks them to describe their perspectives on the benefits of living in either a "Red" or a "Blue" state. In this case, developing persuasive writing skills is the construct-relevant goal, so customizing the assignment by allowing students to make a poster or create a skit on the topic would interfere with a student's opportunity to learn. Instead, it would be optimal to offer other kinds of customizable supports but only for those aspects of the task that are not essential to the goals of learning. For example, the teacher might offer students the option of utilizing a graphic organizer, speech-to-text technology, or word-prediction software. With these scaffolds in place, the teacher could customize the assignment for different students, providing options that would focus both student and teacher on the goal: developing the higher-level strategies of persuasive writing.

In summary, advances in the neurosciences have resulted in a radical alteration of the idea of what it means to be student centered. Any student-centered classroom must meet the challenge of diversity, providing a curriculum that is as articulated and differentiated as the learners themselves. Given the hundreds of ways students differ from one another, what guidance is there for teachers and curriculum designers on what is essential to include and what can be ignored? What options must be provided so that a curriculum can support student-centered learning—for all students, not just a few? We propose that the field of universal design for learning provides a framework and guidelines for making decisions about instructional designs that meet the challenge of diversity.

UNIVERSAL DESIGN FOR LEARNING

The theory of UDL derives in part from the concept of *universal design*, a practice that began in architecture, where the goal is to engineer products, buildings, or environments for the widest possible range of users, regardless of age or abilities. All U.S. architects are now legally required to design buildings in ways that reduce or eliminate architectural barriers for diverse groups of people. This practice is recognized as more cost-effective and more equitable than retrofitting buildings or providing customized accommodations to individuals who cannot navigate poorly designed structures. While originally conceived to meet the needs of individuals with disabilities, universal designs have proven to be widely beneficial. A common example is the wheelchair ramp, which is also ideal for people pushing strollers or using handcarts.

Universal design for learning is part of this overall movement. Its purpose is not just to provide access to information but also to ensure that the means for learning—the pedagogical goals, methods, materials, and assessments of instruction—are accessible to all students.

At its simplest, UDL is based on three principles, each corresponding with one of the three broad divisions of "the learning brain" and three critical features of any teaching and learning environment:

- **Multiple means of representation:** Corresponds with the pattern recognition and perceptual capabilities of the posterior regions of the cortex.
- **Multiple means of action and expression:** Corresponds with the motor and executive capabilities of the anterior regions of the cortex.
- **Multiple means of engagement:** Corresponds with the affective or emotional capabilities of the most central regions of the nervous system.

From the three principles, nine guidelines form the foundation of UDL (see figure 3.1). These guidelines are based on research and practice from multiple domains within the learning sciences—education, developmental psychology, cognitive science, and cognitive neuroscience. Their main purpose is to guide educators and curriculum developers in using research-based means of addressing the wide range of individual differences in any classroom. Each guideline recommends options, as no single tool, method, or path will be optimal for each student.

The top of each column in figure 3.1 emphasizes a basic principle of UDL. At the bottom of each column is a basic goal: students who are, each in their own way, resourceful and knowledgeable; strategic and

FIGURE 3–1   Universal design for learning guidelines

Principle I. Multiple means of representation	Principle II. Multiple means of action and expression	Principle III. Multiple means of engagement
Guideline 1: Provide options for perception	**Guideline 4: Provide options for physical action**	**Guideline 7: Provide options for recruiting interest**
Checkpoints:	Checkpoints:	Checkpoints:
1.1 Offer ways of customizing the display of information	4.1 Vary the methods for response and navigation	7.1 Optimize individual choice and autonomy
1.2 Offer alternatives for auditory information	4.2 Optimize access to tools and assistive technologies	7.2 Optimize relevance, value, and authenticity
1.3 Offer alternatives for visual information		7.3 Minimize threats and distractions
Guideline 2: Provide options for language, mathematical expressions, and symbols	**Guideline 5: Provide options for expression and communication**	**Guideline 8: Provide options for sustaining effort and persistence**
Checkpoints:	Checkpoints:	Checkpoints:
2.1 Clarify vocabulary and symbols	5.1 Use multiple media for communication	8.1 Heighten salience of goals and objectives
2.2 Clarify syntax and structure	5.2 Use multiple tools for construction and composition	8.2 Vary demands and resources to optimize challenge
2.3 Support decoding text, mathematical notation, and symbols	5.3 Build fluencies with graduated levels of support for practice and performance	8.3 Foster collaboration and community
2.4 Promote understanding across languages		8.4 Increase mastery-oriented feedback
2.5 Illustrate through multiple media		
Guideline 3: Provide options for comprehension	**Guideline 6: Provide options for executive functions**	**Guideline 9: Provide options for self-regulation**
Checkpoints:	Checkpoints:	Checkpoints:
3.1 Activate or supply background knowledge	6.1 Guide appropriate goal-setting	9.1 Promote expectations and beliefs that optimize motivation
3.2 Highlight patterns, critical features, big ideas, and relationships	6.2 Support planning and strategy development	9.2 Facilitate personal coping skills and strategies
3.3 Guide information processing, visualization, and manipulation	6.3 Facilitate managing information and resources	9.3 Develop self-assessment and reflection
3.4 Maximize transfer and generalization	6.4 Enhance capacity for monitoring progress	
Goal: Resourceful, knowledgeable learners	*Goal:* Strategic, goal-directed learners	*Goal:* Purposeful, motivated learners

Source: CAST, Universal Design for Learning Guidelines Version 2.0 (Wakefield, MA: Author, 2011).

goal-directed; and purposeful and motivated. Each column articulates guidelines for achieving each goal, as well as customizable "checkpoints" elaborating on the guidelines.

An interactive, Web-based version of the guidelines is available; in this version, clicking on any checkpoint brings up a box with critical additional information.[5] Each contains three points essential for educators: an elaboration of the meaning and importance of the checkpoint; links to practical examples of the recommended options; and links to research evidence for the efficacy of such options.

In figure 3.2, one of the checkpoints—providing options that guide appropriate goal setting—is highlighted as an example of how the guidelines are supported. In the Web-based version, clicking on any checkpoint brings up a box like that illustrated in figure 3.2, also containing the three points noted above.[6]

Similarly, clicking on the "view latest evidence and scholarly research" link brings up a bibliography of relevant research findings and scholarly opinions or summaries. (See figure 3.3 for a partial sample.)[7]

All of this is a little hard to demonstrate in print, yet the challenge illustrates the difference between new and old media. Just as it is difficult to present the UDL guidelines in print, constructing or implementing a curriculum that is student centered is too hard a task to undertake with tools dating from the sixteenth century. (See "Print's Disabilities.") Using UDL's three principles, teachers in student-centered classrooms can harness the flexibility of new media to provide a diverse range of students with the multiple means of representation, expression, and engagement each needs to become a thoughtful, strategic, and motivated learner.

STUDENT-CENTERED MEANS OF REPRESENTATION

Students differ widely in how they best perceive information, comprehend it, and turn it into usable knowledge. Any one medium of representation—a text, a video, an image, an audio recording, a simulation—will

FIGURE 3-2   Universal design for learning guidelines: Detail

Guideline 6: Provide options for executive functions
Checkpoints:
6.1 Guide appropriate goal-setting
6.2 Support planning and strategy development
6.3 Facilitate managing information and resources
6.4 Enhance capacity for monitoring progress

Goal: Strategic, goal-directed learners

• **Checkpoint 6.1: Guide appropriate goal-setting**
It cannot be assumed that learners will set appropriate goals to guide their work, but the answer should not be to provide goals for students. Such a short-term remedy does little to develop new skills or strategies in any learner. It is therefore important that learners develop the skill of effective goal setting. The UDL framework embeds graduated scaffolds for learning to set personal goals that are both challenging and realistic.

Tell Me More!
• Provide prompts and scaffolds to estimate effort, resources, and difficulty
• Provide models or examples of the process and product of goal-setting
• Provide guides and checklists for scaffolding goal-setting
• Post goals, objectives, and schedules in an obvious place
■ Checkpoint 6.1: View examples and resources

Get Evidence!
■ Checkpoint 6.1: View the latest evidence & scholarly research

(top of post)

Source: CAST, Universal Design for Learning Guidelines Version 2.0 (Wakefield, MA: Author, 2011).

ultimately privilege some students over others. To create a curriculum that can support student-centered learning, it is critical to provide a variety of options for presenting information.

Unlike print, new media have a wide range of capabilities for presentation, from text to spoken language, to full-motion video, to 3-D graphics, to virtual reality, as well as various combinations of these formats. A format such as digital text can be manipulated in terms of size, color,

FIGURE 3-3   Partial sample page of relevant research

Checkpoint 6.1: Guide appropriate goal-setting
Summary

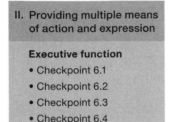

Learning can be inaccessible when it requires effective and realistic goal-setting and where there are no options for individuals who differ in such executive functions. Long term and even short terms tasks can raise barriers to learning without the proper embedded support for such goal-setting. The experimental and quantitative evidence listed here indicates the advantages of supports—such as highly explicit goal-setting instruction, varied models, and embedded prompts and scaffolds to estimate effort and task difficulty—for this facet of executive functions. The scholarly reviews and opinion pieces provide additional arguments for why it is important to supports students' in setting their goals. Although some of these articles are dated, they nonetheless continue to provide guidance on supporting effective goal-setting.

■ Do you have additional evidence to support this Checkpoint? Tell us!

Experimental and Quantitative Evidence:

Butler, D. L. (1997). The roles of goal setting and self-monitoring in students' self-regulated engagement in tasks. Paper Presented at the Annual Meeting of the American Educational Research Association (Chicago, IL, March 24-28, 1997).

Earley, P. C. (1985). Influence of information choice and task complexity upon goal acceptance, performance and personal goals. *Journal of Applied Psychology*, 70(3), 481-491.

Fleming, V. M. (2002). Improving students' exam performance by introducing study strategies and goal setting. *Teaching of Psychology*, 29(2), 115-119.

Fuchs, L., Butterworth, J., & Fuchs, D. (1989). Effects of ongoing curriculum-based measurement on student awareness of goals and progress. *Education and Treatment of Children*, 12(1), 63-72.

Fuchs, L. S., Fuchs, D., Karns, K., Hamlett, C. L., Katzaroff, M., & Dutka, S. (1997). Effects of task-focused goals on low-achieving students with and without learning disabilities. *American Educational Research Journal*, 34(3), 513-543.

Source: CAST, Universal Design for Learning Guidelines Version 2.0 (Wakefield, MA: Author, 2011).

or form of emphasis to make it easier for students to see or to comprehend main points. Text can also be transformed into entirely different modalities, such as voice, American Sign Language, Braille, or other languages. Moreover, new media can easily convey motion, interaction, and sequence—through video, sound, or simulations—and provide options

PRINT'S DISABILITIES

Thanks to Johannes Gutenberg, print has served as an inexpensive, portable way to convey the narratives and knowledge of our culture for five hundred years. In contemporary classrooms, it remains the primary technology for communication and instruction. However, as a platform for student-centered learning, print is far from ideal. It is a fixed, inert, standardized, one-size-fits-all medium—perfect for any classroom in which students are essentially alike.

The challenge (and opportunity) of diversity is increasing in the modern era because our culture has demanded education that is equitable and inclusive—reformed to include not only wealthy white males but women, minorities, people who do not own land, individuals with disabilities, and English language learners. Print is a poor fit for such diversity, but with no obvious alternatives, students and teachers have adapted to its limits. Classrooms are textbook centered rather than student centered because students have seemed more adaptable, flexible, and malleable than their textbooks.

Yet not all students are malleable enough. For some, the strictures of print impose rigid barriers. For example, rendering verbal information into print makes it inaccessible to students who are blind. In fact, the limits of print are so onerous for a variety of people that the need for alternatives became obvious as soon as appropriate technologies were available. By 1931, when audio recordings and Braille editions were possible, Congress mandated that alternatives to print be provided to individuals who are blind, have poor vision, are physically disabled, or have organically based reading disabilities.

In the 2004 Individuals with Disabilities Education Act, Congress used the then-new term *print disabilities* to convey the challenges these individuals face. This term is now prominent in federal and state legislation requiring every school and classroom in America to provide alternatives to anyone with a print disability. This represents a watershed, a harbinger of the future that will have profound effects on the ways we understand what it means to have student-centered learning.

The revolutionary aspect of the term *print disabilities* subtly but remarkably shifts the focus of learning. While most labels reflect only the role of the individual—identifying disability in personal handicaps or weaknesses—this new term emphasizes the role of the learning environment, specifically the environment of print. The handicap is recognized as not residing wholly in the child but rather in the interaction between the child and the medium.

New media differ fundamentally from old ones: computers, televisions, cell phones, video, iPods, and other technological devices store information as numbers (digitized) rather than physically embedding (printing) information in a particular medium. From the numbers, new representations can be recreated as needed, separate from their original display. As a result, information is continually transformed from one format to another—from an image to digits in order to store it; or from digits to a printed (or, say, projected) image in order to view it. In these transformations, new media take on a very different character, with much greater malleability and other significant advantages over analog or print media. Recognizing these abilities is critical to understanding their potential for student-centered learning.

Whereas the soul of old media is its permanence, the soul of new digital media is the flexibility with which it can be modified, customized, transformed, represented in many formats, manipulated. Moreover, that flexibility can be gained without sacrificing permanence.

that demonstrate relationships in time and space, dynamic cause and effect, and processes and procedures in real or slow motion, among other possibilities.

Not only do digital technologies provide better options for customizing presentations to meet the challenge of individual differences, but they also vastly increase the range of concepts that can be conveyed for any student. For example, instead of explaining the concept of fractions orally or modeling problems on the board, teachers can turn to online tools that enable students to interact with the content.[8]

STUDENT-CENTERED MEANS OF ACTION AND EXPRESSION

A curriculum is not student centered when all students must express or demonstrate what they have learned in exactly the same way. Students are as varied in their abilities for expression and action as they are in their abilities for accessing information.

As noted above, student variation can be seen at three levels: at the level of physical or motor action (e.g., students with cerebral palsy differ significantly in the ways they can express themselves from many other students); at the level of specific skills or fluency in a particular medium (e.g., students with dyslexia differ significantly in the ease with which they can express themselves in written text); and at the level of executive function (e.g., students with ADHD differ significantly in the ways in which they can plan, organize, sustain effort, and complete any significant composition or expression). As a result of these individual differences, some students may be able to express themselves well in writing but not orally, or in a diagram but not in an essay, for example. No one means of expression will be optimal for all students; providing options for expression is essential.

One set of options, the most general, is to allow or encourage students to express themselves in a variety of media. A digital environment opens up many possibilities. Consider a class learning about mitosis (a type of cell division). In addition to encouraging students to write an essay or make a poster describing the process, teachers can suggest that groups of students work together to create an animation using free online software such as SAM Animation, which enables users to produce stop-action animated video.[9] Alternatively, teachers could ask students to start with a drawing of the process, then upload that drawing into VoiceThread, a free tool for sharing and commenting on images or video files, and narrate the different stages depicted in the image.[10] Finally, the class could co-create an online book about mitosis using CAST UDL Book Builder, a free tool for creating and sharing digital books with embedded learning supports.[11]

An astounding array of digital technologies can provide options for student expression, and we must find ways to effectively weave these new tools into the classroom.

Nevertheless, simply providing options of media formats is not the most important or pedagogically effective way to make expression more student centered. What is really important is to provide within any medium the graduated supports and scaffolds of a cognitive apprenticeship. That is, rather than just provide the scaffolds and supports an early learner needs, a student-centered approach would calibrate and adjust those scaffolds and supports to the changes in skill and development—and eventually students' ability to direct their own learning—that come with practice. New technologies can provide vastly more differentiated support and scaffolding than was available in the classrooms of print. Consider a few examples.

Modeling

One of the most effective techniques for teaching a new skill or strategy is to model it. While human teachers are the best source of modeling (as long as they are themselves skillful in the domain), new media make it possible to embed virtual modeling in almost any learning environment. And while print can provide models of outcomes—a model of an essay, for example—new technologies can provide virtual or simulated models of the process for reaching those outcomes.

The explosion of how-to videos on YouTube is one indication of the power of new media to model and the popularity of doing so. Thousands of people have posted videos in which they demonstrate how to do everything from sharpening knives to juggling them. The advantages of this kind of modeling are immediately obvious when compared with the tortured and confusing explanations that come in the printed directions for assembling a new bike or countless other products. Viewing a video of a high-quality, step-by-step demonstration—one that could be watched as many times as needed—would invariably be more helpful to many people.

In schools, almost any digital medium can embed tutorial videos or animations, providing effective modeling for skills that seem virtually impossible to model effectively in print: public speaking; scientific inquiry; painting; composition; social interaction.

Furthermore, digital media offer new opportunities for modeling complex concepts through simulations and animations that visually display abstract ideas, highlight critical features, and connect to students' everyday lives. For example, SimCalc Mathworlds®, an interactive computer software program, develops students' understanding of the mathematical concepts of proportions, rates, and linear functions by embedding a range of models, simulations, and animations to promote student learning. The software aims to support students in "linking visual forms (graphs and simulated motions) to linguistic forms (algebraic symbols and narrative stories of motion)."[12] SimCalc Mathworlds has a statistically significant effect on students' ability to understand the concepts of rate and proportionality.[13] One student comments on its benefit: "You can really see what you're doing instead of just like on a sheet of paper . . . you can actually see it moving and it's like you can experience it so it's easier to understand."[14]

Graduated Scaffolding

Providing opportunities for practice is a critical aspect of growth and development in the nervous system.[15] A key aspect of teaching any form of skillful expression is guided practice with scaffolding that increases students' responsibility for their own learning, and today's new technologies have the flexibility to incorporate these important instructional supports. Well-designed digital media offer a broad palette of learning supports and challenges to find what Lev Vygotsky calls the *zone of proximal development*—that place where optimal learning occurs for individual students.[16] With carefully designed digital technologies, students can practice new skills or new knowledge with just the right amount of challenge and support, which can be adjusted to reflect the student's evolving needs—a key aspect of student-centered learning.

There is a growing body of research and development in using technology to provide the supports and scaffolds that promote effective practice. To give an example from our own work, C. Patrick Proctor and his colleagues conducted a study of a UDL online vocabulary and reading comprehension intervention designed for both English- and Spanish-speaking students.[17] The tool included a range of embedded supports: Spanish translation; a multimedia glossary; Spanish and Spanish-English bilingual "coaches" to prompt for understanding; illustrations depicting the content of the text; and an electronic work log that gathered students' responses to comprehension prompts. The embedded supports significantly improved vocabulary knowledge.

Other research reveals the positive effects of graduated scaffolding across a wide spectrum of learners. Consider, for example, research on Literacy by Design, a technology-based approach to literacy instruction that combines UDL principles with research-based reading instruction for young students who have significant cognitive disabilities.[18] LBD embeds a range of scaffolds into the design of the online environment, such as text-to-speech; a multimedia glossary; videos and photo essays to supply background knowledge; prompts to apply reading comprehension strategies (e.g., predict, question, retell, connect); prompts to echo read, partner read, and read independently; and pedagogical agents who offer prompts, think-alouds, and models. Research indicates that using LBD led to significant gains on a test of reading comprehension (the Passage Comprehension subtest of the Woodcock-Johnson III Test of Achievement, among others) and that the digital scaffolding has a strong effect on students' word attack skills, listening comprehension, and understanding of alphabet and book knowledge.[19]

Progress Monitoring

Very few skills can be developed without timely, relevant feedback. Increasingly, new media learning environments can provide ongoing assessment data by carefully monitoring student progress and providing relevant, challenging feedback to both students and teachers. New digital tools can support teachers in collecting valuable data for measuring student growth as well as making necessary adjustments to instruction. These technologies do not replace teachers in monitoring the progress of students; rather, they provide valuable, timely, and student-centered sources of information. With that information available, teachers can teach more effectively, making strategic, knowledgeable, and motivating decisions for all of their students.[20]

Moreover, these digital technologies can be updated and improved on the basis of learner feedback—something essential to effective student-centered practices but generally missing until recently. Historically, few educational technologies have been as responsive to the user as even rudimentary video games, which monitor progress and adjust the level of challenge and support accordingly.[21]

Technologies are now available to remedy that situation. For example, in 2002, Carnegie Mellon University launched the Open Learning Initiative to develop online postsecondary courses that "enact the kind of dynamic, flexible, and responsive instruction that fosters learning."[22] OLI courses both complement face-to-face instruction and serve as stand-alone courses that do not require official instructors.[23] To support student learning, the courses embed a range of features, including simulations, options in navigation through content, and frequent opportunities to practice new knowledge. Furthermore, the OLI courses support students to monitor their own progress and provide them with immediate, targeted feedback. "Mini-tutors" offer students hints and advice as they practice new skills and are designed to focus on common mistakes and common misconceptions.[24] When an OLI statistics course was used by itself, student learning gains "were at least as good as in a traditional, instructor-led course;" and when used in conjunction with face-to-face instruction, students in the treatment group "learned a full semester's worth of material in half as much time and performed as well or better than students learning from traditional instruction over a full semester."[25]

The above are examples of scaffolding. It is not that print technologies cannot provide scaffolding; it is that the lack of versatility and inertness of print limit the most critical aspect of scaffolding: the ability to adjust to the changing relationship between the learner and the goal of instruction. In contrast, well-designed (especially universally designed) learning environments, like well-designed video games and simulations, often provide many types of scaffold, many levels of scaffolding, and many levels of challenge so that students are always in their zone of proximal development.

OPTIONS FOR ENGAGEMENT

A curriculum is not student centered when it uses only one means to engage and motivate all learners. As several chapters in this volume indicate, a strong research base indicates that at the core of teaching is providing the motivational foundation for learning and preparing students for a lifetime of further, intrinsically motivated learning. One of print's biggest limitations in helping teachers achieve that goal is in adjusting for the level of frustration, boredom, challenge, or threat that tasks in this medium present to each individual learner. The same reading assignment may bore one student, terrify or threaten another, and bewilder a third. None of these situations is constructively engaging.

The UDL guidelines call for multiple means of engagement because students differ markedly in the ways in which they can be engaged or motivated to learn. Spontaneity and novelty engage some students; those same things disengage, even frighten, others. Authentic tasks are one source of engagement, but "authenticity" is highly culturally and developmentally sensitive—what is authentic to one student seems foreign to others. In reality, no one means of engagement is optimal for all students; providing multiple options for engagement is essential.[26]

New digital technologies widen the range of options for student-centered engagement. The UDL framework comprises three aspects of engagement: recruiting interest; sustaining effort and persistence; and building self-regulation.[27]

Recruiting Interest

In order to learn, students must attend to the information at hand. Teachers devote considerable effort to recruiting interest, or securing learner attention and engagement. It is no news to them that "learners differ significantly in what attracts their attention and engages their interest," in the words of a guideline under UDL's principle III.[28] New media can provide a rich, interactive panoply of resources to recruit interest. For example, students seeking to learn about orangutans can take a virtual field trip and see these animals via live webcams at the San Diego Zoo.[29] They can also communicate with bloggers and videographers studying these animals in China or Africa. These resources are engaging because they are connected to experts in the field doing real-time research and are normative, not because they are novel.

Given their facility and comfort with technology, it is no wonder that today's students find print to be anachronistic. Marc Prensky uses the term *digital natives* to describe these students, who "have spent their entire lives surrounded by and using computers, video games, digital music players, video cams, cell phones, and all the other toys and tools of the digital age."[30] Print is certainly not the dominant medium of their culture, nor the one into which they will matriculate.

Sustaining Effort and Persistence

The learning of skills and strategies requires not just a student's initial interest but sustained attention and effort. Sustaining effort and persistence differs from student to student depending on their initial motivation, their skill at self-regulation, and their distractibility. New media provide extended and authentic opportunities to build communities of practice among students, which can help sustain effort and persistence. Digital tools expand the lines of communication and collaboration for students across districts, states, and counties. For example, ePals, a free online community, enables students around the world to connect and share experiences. Glogster is a free tool that enables students to create "interactive posters" to communicate ideas. And Blogger, another free resource, enables students to create their own blogs.[31]

Hoot.Me exemplifies the idea of using digital technologies to foster collaboration and communication.[32] This new company seeks to provide students with a way to turn their Facebook pages into what it calls "study mode"—connecting peers and their teachers through chat options, video/ voice conferencing, screen sharing, and other features. Such tools make it easier for students to collaborate and learn from one another.

Building Self-Regulation

The third guideline for UDL's principle of engagement is to build each student's capacity for self-regulation, or the intrinsic ability of a person to regulate his or her own emotions and motivations. One of the self-regulation skills that students need to develop is the ability to recognize and react to appropriate feedback.

Students are quite diverse in how they initially react to feedback, and the capacity of digital technologies to adjust both the level and kind of feedback can help in providing multiple means of engagement. Most important, the UDL guidelines recommend options that develop students' self-assessment and reflection skills as a way to promote self-regulation. It is essential for students to build an awareness of their individual strengths and weaknesses so that, when offered an array of options and flexibility in the student-centered classroom, they can select the tools and strategies that provide the right amount of challenge and support. With young children, teachers may need to support students in selecting the options that work best for them. As students grow older, it is important that they develop skills that enable them independently to seek out the customizable features that optimize their learning.

In sum, the student-centered classroom can harness the flexibility of new media to provide a diverse range of students with multiple means of representation, expression, and engagement. It can also harness the flexibility of new media for the teacher, providing a rich set of tools and resources to elevate and differentiate teaching. In that rich environment, the teacher can be both a content provider and the classroom's most experienced and savvy teacher/learner, a model of the kind of expert learner students can emulate.

A FEW CAVEATS

While digital technologies have numerous advantages over print, they have limits as well, including

Poorly conceived tools: The usefulness of digital tools depends on their design, which must provide both broad access and learning supports. Poorly conceived digital learning tools give the illusion of progress when in fact they simply replicate print versions. This is the case when scanning a printed document into a digital version.

The digital divide: Many families still lack access to essential technology. According to a Pew Research Center report, 87 percent of U.S. households making more than $75,000 a year have Internet access at home, compared with only 40 percent of households making less than $30,000 a year.[33] A survey of a diverse group of economically disadvantaged youth in California found that 91 percent of the students believe that the Internet is either "highly important" or "important" to their schoolwork.[34] Yet only 31 percent of students have high-quality Internet access at home, 35 percent have low-quality access, and 34 percent have no access. This limited access causes a significant amount of stress among students.

Cost: New media can be expensive, especially when the technological infrastructure of whole schools or districts must be modernized. The short-term cost can be daunting, despite the long-term costs of not implementing change—creating a generation of high school graduates unprepared for college and careers.

Professional development: Simply acquiring technology does not make learning student-centered. Technology must be woven into instruction to support student learning. We must prepare teachers to do this—and provide ongoing training as digital technologies change rapidly.

Standards and curricula: Even the best new technologies are not good for some elements of instruction. For example, although digital technologies are effective in supporting students in reaching standards through features such as modeling and progress monitoring, they are not effective in setting those standards. Distilling critical aspects of content domains and crafting thoughtful curricula that challenge all learners is the work of experts in content and pedagogy.

Human relationships and social learning: Finally, technologies are not good at the "emotional work" of the classroom, which is ultimately about building and enhancing relationships. Computers and online tools and programs are not equipped to do this profoundly human work. That responsibility lies in the hands, hearts, and minds of classroom teachers. What universally designed materials can do is provide the supportive tools that enhance a teacher's ability to excel.

A NEW ECOLOGY FOR LEARNING

The education landscape is slowly embracing the framework of UDL as a basis for student-centered learning. Its proponents are laying the necessary groundwork in the realms of public policy, state and district initiatives, market models, and classroom practices. The number of classrooms where these practices happen is growing rapidly. And there are many signs of relevant advances in the kinds of tools and methods that teachers use every day. (See "The Movement Toward UDL.")

It is important to emphasize, because it is often a concern for traditional educators, that these new environments for learning are not dominated by computers or technology, nor are students isolated by their computer screens. Rather, the classrooms are active, vibrant, inquiring, and social. Students have more ways to communicate and build knowledge together. And with more ways to communicate, more students succeed.

We believe, and recent policy directives suggest, that the way education is practiced can change dramatically in coming years. One key change could be a shift away from rigid curricula—where learners have to adapt to various barriers and inefficiencies—and toward flexible, customizable curricula that are designed for diversity. Digital technologies and principles like those in the UDL framework can play an essential role in these

THE MOVEMENT TOWARD UDL

National

- The 2004 reauthorization of the Individuals with Disabilities Education Act established National Instructional Materials Accessibility Standard (NIMAS), stipulating that students with print disabilities have a civil right to an alternative version of textbooks and related instructional materials. NIMAS represents a marked change in how educators think about disability and remediation by placing the blame on the inflexibility of print rather than on students.[35]

- The establishment of the National UDL Task Force in 2008 has continued to make UDL a powerful player in the education policy landscape, attaining definition in federal statute.

- The Higher Education Opportunity Act of 2008, enacted with strong bipartisan support, signifies a federal recognition of the power of UDL to enhance instruction and increase learning opportunities for all students.[36]

- The U.S. Department of Education's National Educational Technology Plan, released in 2010, provides numerous strong recommendations for UDL. The plan consistently cites UDL to promote the use of technology to expand learning opportunities for all students.

- Trends in federal funding—for example, the National Science Foundation's adoption of a UDL-based initiative to develop science curricula—show promise for the implementation of a more student-centered, digital curriculum.

State and District Initiatives

- Maryland's Universal Design for Learning Act (HB 59/SB 467) adopts UDL to guide curriculum design for all students. Enacted in 2010, it is the first state-level UDL legislation.

- Strides in implementing UDL can be seen in the California State University via Ensuring Access Through Collaboration and Technology (EnACT), which focuses on providing faculty with comprehensive training on UDL and an online library of accessible materials and resources.[37]

- Since 2003, Bartholomew Consolidated School Corporation, an Indiana district serving eleven thousand students, has been scaling up a UDL pilot. UDL principles now are applied in all nineteen of the district's schools.[38]

Market Models

- NIMAS has sparked some textbook publishers to get ahead of the curve. For example, Pearson introduced fully accessible e-versions of its traditional printed textbooks in 2009.[39]
- Platform makers such as Inkling are exploring customized supported learning environments and developing interactive, multimedia versions of textbooks for the iPad that offer such features as links to primary sources and videos, assessment questions with instant feedback, and the ability to share notes and questions with peers and the teacher.[40]

changes. Like many cultural advances, these would begin by addressing the needs of those who are most obviously marginalized and disadvantaged by existing practices, but they would ultimately benefit everyone. The aspirations of school reformers going back to *Brown v. Board of Education* to make a high-quality education available to all are, perhaps for the first time, actually possible.[41]

The shift to universally designed curricula foreshadows a future where change is continuous rather than intermittent. Traditional curricula are limited in their ability not only to adapt to the differences between students but also to adapt to changes in students or the environment (e.g., new discoveries in a field). By contrast, one reason that new media can be powerful and motivating is because, like video games, they can monitor individual progress at a very granular level and adjust the level of challenge and support accordingly.

Another important way in which the future holds promise is that it is possible to design media, especially social media, that grow smarter with use. Users can develop and continually enhance these media by adding content, evaluations, pedagogy, models, and data. What will make a modern learning environment student centered is not just that it will be responsive to learners but that they will co-construct it.

Ultimately, what will separate new curricula from old is a new environment for learning, one that puts students at the center of the learning environment. And all students will not only learn, each in their own way; they also will teach. Every curriculum will not only teach, it will learn. New media make possible this optimal ecology for learning, one in which the paths to learning are rich and diverse enough for all our students.

CHAPTER 4

Identity and Literacy Instruction for African American Males

Alfred W. Tatum

MILLIONS OF AMERICAN YOUNG PEOPLE struggle with reading and writing, despite substantial efforts by school, districts, states, and the nation to increase literacy. Although their difficulties are not unique, a high percentage of African American male adolescents fail to demonstrate proficiency on national reading tests. Statistics illustrating the point abound, but one finding from my research stands out: in preparing this chapter, I could not identify a single U.S. urban school district where at least 40 percent of African American males in the eighth or twelfth grades scored Proficient in reading on the National Assessment of Educational Progress.

Recent attempts to improve these students' literacy through assessment and accountability measures, while warranted, underestimate the depths of their needs. What is required is a cross-disciplinary approach that addresses both internal and external factors particular to African American male adolescents, especially those living in high-poverty urban areas. This approach absorbs lessons from the literacy practices of African American males of the past who embraced literacy as a source of personal dignity as well as social, political, and economic power.

Student-centered approaches to learning have great potential to advance the literacy of African American male adolescents as well as others across the race and class spectrum. In this chapter I discuss how:

- Student-centered practices embrace the individual's experiences, interests, and needs as the starting point of education. These practices can build resiliency and other critical resources that African American male adolescents must have in order to succeed in school and in life.
- Student-centered approaches to learning take into account instructional, sociocultural, and personal factors likely to determine success or failure, and they have the potential to boost internal and external protective resources.
- The role that reading and writing has played for these youth historically serves as a productive starting point for student-centered approaches, including conceptualizing teaching practices, selecting texts, and structuring instructional contexts.
- Four sets of "vital signs" of literacy development—reading, readers, reading and writing instruction, and educators' approaches—offer an alternative framework of effective literacy curricula and instruction for African American males. This framework starts with developing students' identities rather than the goal of raising test scores.

Going further, there is a reciprocal relationship between the concepts of student-centered learning and the goal of advancing the literacy development of African American male adolescents. Not only are the concepts of student-centered learning important for advancing the literacy development of African American male students, but the concepts of advancing their literacy development have important implications for student-centered practices for all students. The literacy development of African American male adolescents is impacted by educational policy, reading research, urban school reform and all it entails, and a wide array of personal, social, economic, and political forces.

RACE, GENDER, AND STUDENT-CENTERED LEARNING

This chapter seeks to help educators think pragmatically and strategically about pathways to reverse long-standing trends of reading underperformance among African American male students, and also to provide insight into factors that lead many of them to excel in reading. While other contributors to this book focus on cognitive, psychological, and biological alignments with student-centered learning, this chapter adds a sociohistorical perspective, one that complements the other alignments but is often ignored in large-scale efforts to reform literacy education. This perspective is useful because of the persistence of many problems that African American males experience, including low expectations, bias, and discrimination. Student-centered approaches to learning can help these youth access their voice (which today's school often silences) to overcome low expectations and achieve at high levels.

There is promise in recent national priorities to improve the U.S. education system by adopting standards and assessments that prepare all students to succeed in college and compete in the global economy, and to ensure a great teacher for every classroom and a great leader for every school. Yet these goals are too generic for advancing the literacy development of African American male adolescents. In fact, urban schools and districts can be in full compliance with state and federal mandates yet see only small upticks in reading achievement.

However, virtually no empirical evidence identifies practices and programs that significantly improve the reading achievement of many of these students who enter urban high schools as struggling readers. What guidance there is has been extrapolated from reading research on elementary-aged children, where the literature is more robust.

Often, the reading instruction offered to African American male adolescents is based on assessment scores framed in the context of data-driven instruction. And often, poor reading scores land these youth in remedial reading classes, where they may receive less-demanding or poorly conceptualized reading instruction, including underexposure to quality texts.[1] Such academic marginalization often cements low levels of literacy and reifies social inequality.[2]

This assessment of ability and subsequent placement is too often made without regard for a variety of considerations that may have affected the students' past achievement, such as poor instruction, inadequate assessment practices, and insufficient attention to their individual experiences, needs, and interests. Reading difficulties combine with out-of-school forces to place a disproportionate number of African American males, particularly those from low-income urban neighborhoods, at risk for academic failure and maladaptive behaviors.[3] Literacy instruction must be broader than just developing the skill to perform well on reading assessments. Because reading comprehension is the foundation for learning just about anything after fourth grade—and for functioning in society— educators need to pay more attention to how literacy instruction can safeguard the academic and personal well-being of these youth.

By considering the broader contexts in which their literacy development is situated, student-centered approaches to learning can provide the robust, effective literacy practices needed for addressing the needs of African-American males. Student-centered practices define the same high rigorous standards for all students, but they customize learning to each individual student. Thus, by considering the broader contexts in which their literacy development is situated, these approaches can provide the robust, effective literacy practices needed for addressing the needs of African American male youth.

Compare the current framing of instruction and curricula with a proposed model that, quite literally, puts students at the center. Figure 4.1 depicts the current high-stakes assessment and accountability climate: to avoid sanctions, schools focus on standardized test scores and making Adequate Yearly Progress, positioned at the center of the diagram. Standards focus on traditional "honored" curricula (i.e., canonical texts and

FIGURE 4-1   Current framing of instruction and curricula

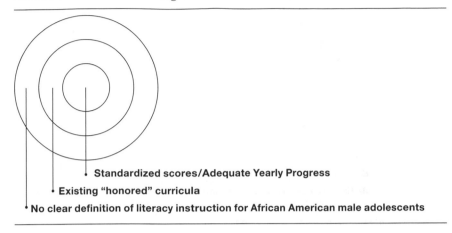

Standardized scores/Adequate Yearly Progress
Existing "honored" curricula
No clear definition of literacy instruction for African American male adolescents

content-area textbooks). The needs of particular students seem an after-thought; particularly relevant for this chapter, there is no clear definition of literacy instruction for African American male adolescents.

Figure 4.2, by contrast, makes students' identities the clear priority for schools. They are the anchoring point for learning. Curricula provide multiple entry points—including personal, economic, social, cultural, and political—into texts in order to reach a variety of students. Surrounding these inner circles, the quality of both instruction and the texts themselves is high. This diagram is better aligned with historical pathways to literacy development for African American males, suggesting the need for a model for (re)orienting learning pathways for these youth.

Factors Affecting the Reading Achievement of African American Males

Over the past decade, a large body of research has looked at both in-school and out-of-school factors that contribute to the general academic performance of African American males. Drawing on this research, I distill three types of factors that may affect their reading achievement: instructional, sociocultural, and personal.

FIGURE 4-2   (Re)envisioning framing of instruction and curricula

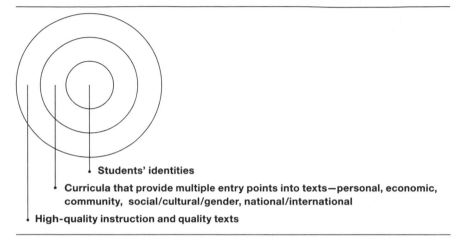

Students' identities

Curricula that provide multiple entry points into texts—personal, economic, community, social/cultural/gender, national/international

High-quality instruction and quality texts

Instructional research: Instructional research has identified essential elements of teaching reading comprehension, such as differentiating instruction, building subject-matter knowledge, expanding vocabulary, integrating reading and writing, encouraging classroom discussion, and exposing students to a large volume and range of motivating texts. Research on motivation is particularly important for student-centered practices, including research showing that texts that capitalize on students' interests contribute to motivation.[4]

Sociocultural research: Research into sociocultural factors provides evidence that many variables—such as culture, social class, home experiences with literacy and language, family background, and environmental factors—work together to interrupt reading achievement. For example, far too many African American male adolescents come from home environments that contribute to a language differential that places them on an unequal academic playing field when they enter school. Studies confirm that students in urban schools often have unique needs.[5]

Research into personal factors: Research into personal factors shows that certain individual experiences and behaviors contribute to reading achievement. These include effort, time, persistence, and participation, as well as positive attitudes toward school, connection with long-term goals, and the belief that education may help overcome adversity and contribute to a better life. Moreover, embracing an ethnic group identity and paying attention to their masculine identities may enhance school engagement for African American male students, which in turn increases achievement. This contradicts the notion of "oppositional identity" that minorities may form in response to the majority culture, and it rejects the idea that such students do not want to be viewed as smart lest they be perceived as "acting white." A final significant factor is the expectation that students will continue their education beyond high school.[6]

These factors do not act independently; rather, it is their overlap—the multifactor impact—that determines pathways of success or failure. Addressing all of them is essential to addressing the needs of individual African American males and keeping them engaged in literacy development.

Nurturing Protective Internal and External Resources

Student-centered approaches to learning have great potential to advance the literacy of African American male adolescents by helping them build resiliency and other critical protective resources needed to address the above factors. Researchers have identified both internal and external sources of these protective resources. Internal factors include strong academic skills and a strong self-concept. Specific external factors that promote resilience include community supports, positive expectations, opportunities for meaningful participation, and the involvement of a consistently caring adult—all priorities of student-centered approaches.

Adolescents are more likely to be resilient if they feel secure in the presence of adults who clearly communicate high expectations with realistic goals and who support students' meaningful participation by engaging them with authentic tasks and real-world dialogue.[7] For individual students, certain protective resources will be in greater demand depending on both the student's characteristics and contextual factors, such as the accumulation of failure. Teachers should acknowledge these characteristics and factors and combine them with other resources to help improve reading achievement and shape positive literacy and personal trajectories.

Quality teaching and texts are also essential. To provide these, educators need a clear concept of the role of literacy instruction, a sincere interest in contributing to the personal development of African American males, and knowledge of a wide range of texts across disciplines that can help prepare these youth for engaged citizenship at the local, national, and international levels.

Not surprisingly, student-centered approaches to learning, which make career and college readiness the goal, relate closely to effective literacy practices for African American male adolescents. It is important to recognize that in a student-centered approach, several external resources affect students' internal resources. Both internal and external resources can be influenced by a student's home life and cultural, environmental, and economic contexts, which ultimately can affect school- and society-based outcomes.

A HISTORICAL PERSPECTIVE

Understanding the roles that reading and writing historically played for African American male adolescents serves as a productive starting point for conceptualizing student-centered practices that may better meet their learning needs, including developing quality teaching, selecting texts, and structuring instructional contexts. Most of the strategies currently proposed for increasing the reading achievement of these students are ahistorical; that is, they do not consider the pathways of literacy taken by African American males historically.

A sociohistorical perspective provides insight into the wide range of reasons that African American males of the past practiced literacy. They viewed reading, writing, and speaking eloquently as protective pillars. Literacy instruction was deeply principled and purposed to help them gain and maintain authority over themselves.[8] In the nineteenth-century educational movements of the urban North, for example, African Americans pursued literacy in order to improve their social and economic status, strive for racial uplift and full membership in American society, tear down the walls of discrimination, advance human liberty, and advance the economic, social, and political aims of the community, among other reasons.[9] Other historical practices include a focus on developing self-identity, personal engagement, and transformation.[10] For example, African American males, including some teenagers, formed literary societies in Northern cities in the early 1800s, and they did so not only to improve their reading and writing skills but also to cultivate a scholarly way of life.[11]

The specific documents African American males were reading and writing—and the local, national, and international contexts that shaped these choices—were the most important signatures of their literacy development. For more than two centuries, these men turned to written texts to make sense of their present conditions in the United States and to shape possibilities for their futures. Historical accounts are laden with references to "enabling texts"—those that move beyond a sole cognitive focus (e.g., skill and strategy development) to include a social, cultural, political, spiritual, or economic focus.[12]

Today's emphasis on standards, rigor, and assessments lacks the connection to the historical model of African Americans' literacy development with its link to students' identities and embracing of reading as a cultural practice. Most federal, state, district, and school efforts to improve reading emphasize skills and strategies in isolation, rather than helping these young men strengthen their identities and embrace reading as a cultural practice in meaningful contexts. Although many teachers are effective in teaching reading to African American male adolescents in urban high schools, literacy reform efforts for a large percentage of this population are ahistorical and apolitical, often ignoring or suppressing the students' need for intellectual development.

Using a sociohistorical perspective also sheds light on the low expectations some educators have for their African American male students. As a former eighth-grade teacher, reading specialist, and now literacy program developer, I am often asked about effective curricula and instructional practices for African American males. Although I assume the teachers and administrators who approach me have good intentions, I have heard such questions as: "Does it matter what African American males are reading as long as they are reading?" and "Should I correct the spelling or language of African American males when they are writing or speaking?"

Historically, the goals of reading were much more than reading for reading's sake; such questions imply that this might not be the case today. Allowing students to speak or spell poorly would have been viewed as reprehensible—a caving in to a racist perception of the uneducable, inferior African American male. And although resources were limited, teachers were determined to find the best texts to engage their students, not those that were most readable.

Historical Accounts of African American Writing

Historical accounts also illuminate the types, characteristics, and roles of writing embraced by African American males as they sought to protect their dignity in a racist society. Analyses of their work suggest that African American writers focused strongly on the social, political, and economic concerns of their communities.[13] Themes of literacy and liberation were consistent across their writings, which often depicted teaching and learning literacy as communal acts that valued tight connections across the stories of black people.[14] In addition, the politics of race, class, and sex were common, and often entwined, concerns.[15]

African American males wrote to provide perspectives on the current events and historical orientations that informed their lives. They penned both narrative and expository texts to fight for fair treatment and equal pay, create an accurate historical record to counter their depiction as inferior in society's dominant narratives, and discuss the liberating potential of education. They wrote poems, speeches, essays, pamphlets, short stories, and novels to reimagine their experiences in the United States.[16] Four salient characteristics—defining self, becoming resilient, engaging others, and building capacity—appear repeatedly in much of this work, both in creative fiction and expository writings.[17]

African American male adolescents have been severed from the literacy tradition of these writers. It is essential to reconnect today's youth with the historical roots of African American writing and reading.

A FRAMEWORK FOR DEVELOPING STUDENT IDENTITIES

One way to reconnect African American male adolescents with their historical traditions of reading and writing, and thus to improve their achievement and meet their out-of-school needs, is to focus on multiple facets of literacy development, rather than building only foundation skills. I propose a broad framework that shifts the focal point to developing student identities. This framework, which emerges from several bodies of literature, is based on my work on four sets of "vital signs" of literacy development: reading, readers, reading and writing instruction, and educators' approaches (discussed in detail below).[18] This framework is student centered by definition, philosophy, and practice. Ultimately, it is designed to help practitioners provide literacy instruction to increase the number of African American male high school graduates who are prepared for postsecondary academic studies.

The vital-signs framework uses a central metaphor: literacy instruction as a human body. As such, it is a more "anatomically correct" model than those currently in use—and more student centered as well (see figure 4.3). Theoretical strands—the "head"—focus on defining the role of literacy instruction for African American male adolescents in their immediate contexts, creating curricula that empower them, and using culturally responsive approaches. These theories guide the instructional methods—the "body" of the model. Like a body without a head, even the best instructional methods will fall flat unless they make use of texts that interest, engage, and motivate students.[19] Professional development—the "legs"—prepares teachers to engage all students.

FIGURE 4-3   A comprehensive framework for literacy teaching

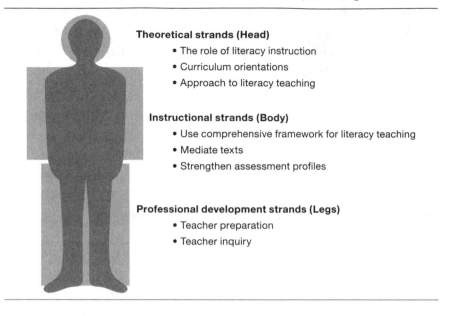

Theoretical strands (Head)
- The role of literacy instruction
- Curriculum orientations
- Approach to literacy teaching

Instructional strands (Body)
- Use comprehensive framework for literacy teaching
- Mediate texts
- Strengthen assessment profiles

Professional development strands (Legs)
- Teacher preparation
- Teacher inquiry

Central to this framework are quality instruction and rich texts with multiple entry points—personal, economic, and community; social, cultural, and gender; local, national, and international. (See "Quality Texts Are Critical.") This has implications for all three strands.

The theoretical strands should be considered when planning how best to provide literacy instruction and professional development. They address how one conceptualizes the role of literacy instruction and approaches teaching, and must include an idea of improving the life circumstances of African American male adolescents. And it includes a dual focus on both college and career readiness, with a long-term aim of increasing earnings as well as helping these learners become good men and restoring their confidence in reading and writing as tools of human development.

The instructional strands focus on knowledge of effective reading and writing research practices, strategies for mediating texts, and developing a useful comprehensive assessment profile.

QUALITY TEXTS ARE CRITICAL

Secondary school teachers confront myriad challenges in their work with struggling adolescent readers.[20] Overcoming resistance to reading among African American male students is particularly challenging. Many are simply bored with the books teachers provide and will not go past the first few pages. Some refuse to read at all.

Too often overlooked is the importance of engaging African American male adolescents with quality texts. Rather, well-meaning educators frequently base their selection of books or excerpts solely on reading level, but the subjects of these selections can be childish and irrelevant to young men facing harsh realities of urban poverty. Choosing texts that students find meaningful is essential, as is inviting students' input and participation in this process. Both are key to a student-centered learning environment.

Historical accounts of the lives of African American men are laden with references to "enabling texts" that include a social, cultural, political, spiritual, or economic focus.[21] Unfortunately, many African American male adolescents who struggle with reading cannot identify any texts they find significant. Instead, they are more likely to find "disabling" texts—texts that neglect their local contexts, ignore their adolescent desire for self-definition, and reinforce their self-perception as struggling readers.

I have identified a number of enabling texts by examining biographical and autobiographical documents written by esteemed African American male writers and thinkers from the past century—as well as the writings of contemporary African American male adolescents. Four characteristics of texts appear to be meaningful to these learners: they contribute to a healthy psyche; they focus on the collective struggle of African Americans; they provide a road map for being, doing, and acting; and they heighten awareness of the real world.[22]

During a ten-month case study I conducted of one young man, we talked extensively about his experiences in school and his thoughts about texts he chose from a list I provided. His reaction to one such book, *Yo, Little Brother: Basic Rules of Survival for Young African American Males* by Anthony C. Davis and Jeffrey W. Jackson, is telling:

I wasn't going to read it at first, but I sat down, and said, "Let me read this book." So as I flip over the pages and I start out reading, I'm like, I like this book for a reason, so I'm going to try to read, and then I seen this say "Street Smarts" right at the top. I know I know a lot about the street, so I just read to see what they were talking about. Then some of the things they was saying was true . . . As I was going along I wanted to stop, but I couldn't. I was like, I started it, and I ain't going to sleep 'til about six in the morning. That's how into it I was, and I didn't know I could get into a book like that. To tell you the truth, I forgot I was reading . . . This is a good book, it help you out a lot.

Introducing enabling and engaging texts is obviously just part of an effective student-centered strategy for addressing the literacy and personal development needs of African American adolescent males. However, without them, any strategy will fail. Ultimately the goal is reading high-quality texts across the disciplines, including the traditional canon. Among the selection of all best possible texts that should be made available to African American youth, there is also a place for literature that speaks directly to local contexts and their adolescent desire for self-definition and reinforces their self-perception as successful readers.

Selected Reading Recommendations for Middle School Level

With Every Drop of Blood: A Novel of the Civil War, by James Collier and Christopher Collier (1992). A fourteen-year-old white boy from Virginia, attempting to bring food to besieged Richmond, is captured by African American Union soldiers, one of whom is a former slave his own age. The boys ultimately become friends.

The Beast, by Walter Dean Myers (2003). A young man leaves his neighborhood in Harlem to attend a college prep school and confronts his anxieties about his future when he returns for winter break to discover that his girlfriend has become addicted to drugs.

47, by Walter Mosley (2005). The narrator remembers himself as a young slave named "47," living in Georgia in 1832. A mystical runaway slave called Tall John inspires him to fulfill his destiny and lead his people to freedom.

Selected Reading Recommendations for High School Level

There Are No Children Here: The Story of Two Boys Growing Up in the Other America, by Alex Kotlowitz (1991). A *Wall Street Journal* reporter tells the true story of two brothers, ages eleven and nine, who live in a violence-ridden Chicago housing project.

Rite of Passage, by Richard Wright (1994). Set in Harlem in the late 1940s, this posthumously published book tells the story of a bright fifteen-year-old boy who suddenly learns that he is a foster child and is being transferred to a new foster home. He runs away and struggles to survive in a harsh world.

Yo, Little Brother: Basic Rules of Survival for Young African American Males, by Anthony C. Davis and Jeffrey W. Jackson (1998). In direct, down-to-earth language, this book offers advice for African American youth from their older counterparts.

Reallionaire: Nine Steps to Becoming Rich from the Inside Out, by Farrah Gray (2005). A self-made millionaire and philanthropist at age twenty, the author tells his personal story of growing up on the South Side of Chicago and rising to success.

Professional development strands focus on initial teacher preparation and ongoing professional development to provide additional support. Even knowledgeable teachers may require this to lead African American male adolescents to high achievement. Many teachers who have a solid grasp of the basics of reading instruction still struggle with teaching literacy to such students, especially in high-poverty schools. An example is an e-mail I received from a veteran educator: she was concerned because, despite her fundamental knowledge of teaching literacy, she was not competent enough in other areas that could help her reach her African American male students.

Vital Signs of Effective Literacy Instruction

Continuing the anatomical metaphor, there are vital signs of effective literacy instruction for all students (see table 4.1). These are essential elements for improving reading achievement. The vital signs are aspects of instruction that should be cultivated in classrooms and tailored to the characteristics of educators and students. As the veteran teacher's e-mail indicates, she has the tools to teach her African American male students to read *but not to be readers*. A comprehensive literacy instruction framework calls for addressing all four sets of vital signs. When any one vital sign shows trouble, the whole body could fail.

The four sets of vital signs, all of which affect reading outcomes, are:

- **Vital signs of reading:** The vital signs of reading are the *what*—the basic minimum tools that all students must master in order to read and write independently. They include decoding, self-questioning, monitoring comprehension, and summarizing.

TABLE 4-1   Vital signs of literacy instruction

	Reading	Readers	Reading and writing instruction	Educators' approaches
Objectives	Providing the working tools (What?)	Improving the human condition (Why?)	Rescuing the significance of teaching (How?)	Interacting with students, not scorecards of achievement (Who?)
Vital signs	• Knowledge • Fluency • Writing • Decoding • Self-questioning • Monitoring comprehension • Summarizing	• Home life • Culture • Environment • Language • Economics	• Appropriate text • Quality instructional support • Context • Assessment • Technology	• Competence • Commitment • Caring • Accountability • Courage
Gaps addressed	Reading achievement gap	Relationship gap	Rigor gap	Responsiveness gap

- **Vital signs of readers:** The vital signs of readers are the students and their everyday lives. This vital sign answers *why* educators must pay attention to students' experiences both in school and outside of it in order to build supportive relationships. These vital signs are also useful for considering ways to improve the human condition as it acknowledges the historical links that enable students to connect to an identity as a reader.
- **Vital signs of reading and writing instruction:** These vital signs consider *how* appropriate texts, quality supports, assessments, and the potential uses of technology maximize opportunities for rigorous learning experiences. They are useful for conceptualizing literacy teaching as developing individuals who can fulfill their potential as people. (Some would say these vital signs are intimately related to reclaiming the significance of literacy instruction in an era focused on assessment and accountability.)
- **Vital signs of educators' approaches:** The fourth vital signs comprise the *who*—or the qualities of the educator who pays attention to the other three signs. Teachers need a strong foundational background geared to the vital signs of reading, readers, and literacy instruction. Educators must embody a sense of shared responsibility and advocacy for their students, shaping educational environments characterized by competence, commitment, caring, and accountability. Adolescents benefit when they know they belong in the learning community and feel they are in the presence of an adult advocate who has the courage to not give up on them.

Stifling literacy mandates and the imposition of one-size-fits-all reading and writing standards over multiple years have narrowed the focus of literacy instruction to the vital signs of reading, with little regard for the others, and in particular the essential roles of texts in reading instruction. Providing quality, student-responsive instruction and quality texts to support students' reading, writing, and human development is central to an effective model of literacy instruction for African American male adolescents.

This model is critical for addressing gaps that align with the four vital signs of literacy instruction: the reading achievement gap that exists between high- and low-performing readers; the relationship gap between teachers and students of different ethnic groups; the rigor gap between those students who receive rigorous instruction and those who do not; and the responsiveness gap that often leads to home and school each holding the other culpable for African American males students' failures to develop literacy.

A NEW PATHWAY TO LITERACY

The sociohistorical approach taken here suggests that student-centered learning is conceptually sound for advancing the literacy development of African American male adolescents. For this group, student-centered learning has to be essentially race- and gender-based. It also has to be placed in the broader local, national, and international contexts for African American males.

Historically, mastering a set of common skills and learning to read and write with propriety were main staples of the literacy development of African American males and the aims of effective teachers who held high expectations and impressed their students with the need for achievement. That tradition also shares a purpose with student-centered approaches to learning, which characteristically have aimed at larger goals than basic skills attainment—personal development, racial uplift, economic power, political enfranchisement. Any examination of the position of African American males in the academic and social hierarchy in the United States shows that these needs persist today.

Each of these needs aligns neatly with the concepts of student-centered learning. However, it is premature to suggest a causal relationship between student-centered learning and improved reading and writing outcomes. At this point, student-centered learning is a suggested pathway for advancing the literacy development of African American male adolescents.

The concepts of advancing the literacy development of African American male adolescents certainly hold important insights for student-centered practices for all students. While the comprehensive framework and vital signs are grounded theoretically in the literacy needs of African American young men, they do not exclude other populations and may even be useful in promoting the literacy development of all students.

However, adopting these approaches will not occur without resistance from those who believe that all students are the same or that there is no need to honor students' differences. Thus, it is crucial for the new strategies to be well thought out to avoid becoming just another failed experiment. The current political climate affecting schools, policies, and curricula can lead to a symbolic, piecemeal approach to student-centered strategies rather than a substantive change in the ways literacy instruction—particularly for young males—is conceptualized and enacted in racially segregated classrooms and racially diverse classrooms.

CHAPTER 5

Making Mathematics Matter for Latin@ and Black Students

Rochelle Gutiérrez and Sonya E. Irving

TOO MANY AMERICANS struggle with mathematics, and far too many in this group are Latin@ and black adolescents, particularly from low-income backgrounds.[1] This chapter focuses on how to better engage these populations in mathematics and improve their achievement by offering a comprehensive vision of what student-centered learning in mathematics could be and how it could support Latin@ and black students in particular.

Recent research focusing on mathematics as a social activity rather than as a matter of cognition alone suggests that school instruction in how to "think mathematically" is not a sufficient solution. Using new perspectives on learning outside of school, mathematics teachers need to initiate students into mathematical communities and practices, helping adolescents see themselves as "doers" of mathematics.

Key findings from this research include:

- The forms of mathematics that U.S. schools value are not the only mathematics that people use. Different cultures practice different kinds of mathematics, learn them in different ways, and use them for different reasons. Studying math around the world—and valuing the range of students' cultural backgrounds in math—can help more students connect to math instruction.
- How students feel about themselves while doing mathematics is critical to how much they engage with it. Out-of-school experiences in mathematics can help them develop confidence, a larger repertoire of math strategies, and a math identity built upon their culture or community—all of which contribute to school learning.
- Small-group math learning, which is more common in afterschool programs than in regular classrooms, provides more opportunities for students to explain their thinking, get feedback quickly, and refine their thinking using a variety of perspectives.
- Teaching mathematics through social justice issues can motivate adolescents—especially those who have lost interest in traditional mathematics—to learn the math skills necessary to solve complex problems.

THE PROBLEM WITH MATH

Ask a few random people what they think of mathematics and you are likely to get some spirited replies. Some may say they have always loved doing math, but more will shudder in horror or sheepishly admit it is one of their biggest weaknesses. The very word *mathematics* often conjures up memories of sitting in class trying to memorize formulas and understand disconnected topics that do not seem to apply to the real world. After all, when does anyone ever use a quadratic equation outside of school? As a society, we perpetuate a myth that there are two kinds of people—those who are good at mathematics and those who are not—and that this is just the natural order of things. But is it?

Researchers who study the brain and the way people process numbers and concepts have shown that in fact we are all hardwired to learn mathematics.[2] Even babies as young as six months old can distinguish between small and large quantities.[3] This is true of every culture, race, and gender. It is not until we enter school that we start to see a fall-off in the number of people who do mathematics well or enjoy doing it. By the fourth grade, we see a real decline in the number of students who understand basic concepts, and this is particularly true for Latin@ and black students. So, if there is nothing wrong with our brains, no genetic predisposition for difficulty understanding math, what is causing this great deficit in mathematical competency? Part of the reason may have to do with how we define mathematics and where we look for it.

This chapter focuses on Latin@ and black students in the United States because of the persistent trend in these populations (especially among low-income students) for low performance on standardized tests and their lack of representation in advanced mathematics courses and mathematics-based careers.[4]

More than their white peers, Latin@ and black students are strongly affected by the rigor of the mathematics curriculum, the quality of their teachers, and the beliefs teachers hold of them. For example, a review of studies asking teachers to assess the current or future ability of this group shows a statistically significant bias toward negative stereotypes and low expectations.[5] Many teachers mistakenly believe the black-white achievement gap is at least partially genetic and so may be inadvertently sustaining it through a self-fulfilling prophecy. In a survey of 379 secondary mathematics teachers, respondents attributed the achievement gap most to factors that were student dependent: student motivation, work ethic, and family support.[6] Moreover, respondents located in schools with a high Latin@ population were more likely to highlight language issues as a problem.

Some researchers have suggested that because Latin@ and black students worry about fulfilling negative stereotypes, they face additional pressure and vulnerability that can lower their performance on standardized tests.[7] In one review of the literature on teacher beliefs and expectations with respect to black students learning mathematics, teachers' expectations, perceptions, and behaviors were found to sustain and perhaps even expand the black-white achievement gap.[8] In fact, some researchers have documented the additional work that must be done by Latin@ and black students to maintain a positive self-identity and negotiate mathematics classrooms when images from the media and society paint them as intelligently inferior.[9] And studies of adults show that negative stereotypes and poor achievement in mathematics classrooms continue to impact individuals throughout their lives as they struggle to overcome both real and perceived barriers to learning and using mathematics.[10] (This "stereotype threat" research is explored further in chapter 7.)

Moreover, Latin@ and black students are more likely than their white peers to be placed into lower tracks, have mathematics teachers who are not credentialed in mathematics, or attend schools that offer fewer advanced mathematics courses (e.g., AP calculus).[11] Given that so many of the challenges that these adolescents face in school relate to how they are racialized (seen as inferior to whites and Asians), we take a combined approach to understanding and improving their learning in mathematics. Even so, we highlight when and where the literature has something to say about a particular group.

Historically, our understanding of Latin@ and black student achievement in mathematics has tended to focus on comparisons to middle-class white students; today we call this the *achievement gap*. In these comparisons, Latin@ and black students often come up short, reinforcing stereotyping by teachers and others in society about the mathematical capacities of students of color. However, because these studies rely primarily on one-time responses from teachers and students, they capture neither the history nor the context of learning that have produced such outcomes.[12] In addition, most people are unaware that the distributions of achievement for Latin@s, blacks, whites, and Asians largely overlap; in general, there is more variation in achievement within a group than between groups. Perhaps most important, the knowledge captured by standardized tests does not reflect the state of the art about what kinds of mathematical understanding, practice, and disposition are important in order for students to pursue a mathematics-based career, work in an increasingly technological society, or become participating citizens in a democracy.

BUILDING MATHEMATICAL IDENTITIES

If scores on standardized achievement tests capture only a fraction of the issues we think are important in mathematical learning, where else should we turn our attention? The recent release of the Common Core State Standards suggests that mathematics should comprise more than just mastering eight key mathematical properties (moving from "novice" to "apprentice" to "expert"). Students are also expected to develop a "character" that relates to mathematics.[13] This notion of building a mathematical identity is something the research community in mathematics education takes very seriously. In fact, teachers are being asked to "start each unit with the variety of thinking and knowledge that students bring to it."[14] And they are exhorted to "empower all students to build a relationship with mathematics that is positive and is grounded in their own cultural roots and history."[15]

Perspectives on mathematics as a social activity and how people learn outside of school offer a unique starting point for rethinking the problem of ensuring mathematical achievement for all students, and for Latin@ and black students in particular. This focus on student-centered learning can inform different ways of teaching and organizing schooling so that more Latin@ and black students are engaged and learn.

Over the past two decades, research in mathematics education has moved from an emphasis on cognitive psychology (mathematics as something that happens in the minds of individuals) to mathematics in social interactions.[16] For example, we now see knowledge as intricately tied to a person's context, including why and with whom he or she is doing mathematics. Many skilled teachers understand that more than just getting their students to think mathematically, their role is to initiate students into mathematical communities and practices." As Sal Restivo writes:

"The historical, social, and cultural contexts cannot be separated from the substance of mathematical objects, concepts, and ideas."[17]

This social perspective is so prevalent that when talking about what students know, many mathematics education researchers do not just consider whether students have mastered a set of predetermined procedures or facts; they also place great emphasis on identity—whether students think of themselves as people who do mathematics and how they position themselves with respect to each other in the mathematics classroom.[18] Given the research on teachers' beliefs and use of stereotypes, issues of building strong and positive identities for Latin@ and black students are especially important to consider in teaching and learning mathematics.

Drawing on the common themes that emerge across different fields of research, we recommend four key elements for expanding student-centered approaches to math education and improving math achievement, especially among marginalized groups:

- Build on the personal and cultural experiences of learners to make math meaningful.
- Nurture confidence and a mathematical identity in learners.
- Use authentic problems and peer learners to increase mathematical rigor.
- Leverage community members to personalize curricula and challenge notions of "novice" and "expert."

Build on the Personal and Cultural Experiences of Learners to Make Math Meaningful

Traditionally, mathematics education has not taken into account the personal and cultural experiences of learners; nor has it offered meaningful connections to the real world. By contrast, student-centered practices might encourage mathematics students to draw on familiar games, hobbies, community customs, or effective approaches to learning and using mathematics from other countries.

The research raises important questions for student-centered approaches to learning mathematics in U.S. schools. For example, would students find mathematics more interesting if they learned the history of math and the different ways that cultures across the world still use math today? Would students who are immigrants learn more if schools encouraged them to use forms of mathematics they practiced in their home countries?

For the most part, schools do not teach the global history of mathematics. More often, students learn that mathematical theorems and discoveries are credited to individuals of European descent, such as Newton, Euclid, and many others. Few realize that the Pythagorean theorem was known by the Babylonians and Chinese more than a millennium before Pythagoras lived, or that the numeral system we use today is Hindu-Arabic. Omitting this dynamic history from the classroom can give students the impression that excellence in mathematics is the exclusive domain of Europeans.

Two sources of educational activities and lesson plans are particularly useful in introducing how people use mathematics around the world—the Exploratorium museum in San Francisco and Culturally Situated Design Tools. (See "Global Mathematics in the Classroom.")

Even with such tools, educators will need to learn more of the global history of mathematics and to learn about which current-day cultural experiences are most meaningful to their students. Typically, it is community members who know students deeply, rather than teachers, who have facilitated processes like these. Community walks, projects that allow students to apply mathematics to problems in their lives, and more personal conversations with students all would help teachers improve student-centered learning for Latin@ and black adolescents.

Nurture Confidence and a Mathematical Identity in Learners

Secondary mathematics classrooms tend to focus on mastering predetermined content, with little attention to students' social or emotional development. Yet Latin@ and black adolescents, like all young people, reap the benefits of programs that attend to both their academic and their

GLOBAL MATHEMATICS IN THE CLASSROOM

Educational activities that integrate mathematical practices from around the world into U.S. classrooms are rare. The authors found two exceptions:

The Exploratorium

One set of ethnomathematics activities available for teachers was generated and piloted by the Exploratorium museum in San Francisco (http://www.exploratorium.edu/who/educators/).[19] Its fourteen inquiry-based activities begin with historical background and make suggestions for teachers to launch and assess each one. Suggested topics include ancient Egyptian numeration, the quipus numerical system of the Inca, a game of solitaire from Madagascar, Mayan numeration and calendars, African sona (sand) drawings, and basket-weaving patterns of many cultures.

Culturally Situated Design Tools

Focusing on the fact that many cultural designs are based on mathematical principles, Ron Eglash has developed software called Culturally Situated Design Tools (http://csdt.rpi.edu) to target Latin@, black, and Native American students.[20] The tools enable students to learn standards-based mathematics and reproduce art by leveraging underlying mathematical principles in various art forms: Latino-Caribbean percussion and hip-hop rhythms (ratios); graffiti (Cartesian and polar coordinates); cornrow hairstyling (transformational geometry, fractals); break dancing (rotational and sine function); and pre-Columbian architecture (symmetry, pre-algebra). Students learn about the cultural backgrounds of the art and get tutorials on how the software works, then invent their own designs. Teachers get lesson plans, evaluation materials, suggestions for how to use the design tools, and connections to the standards of the National Council of Teachers of Mathematics.

social/emotional needs. Learners show greater confidence and are better able to find an answer—and they can reflect on how reasonable that answer may be—when they have opportunities to (1) be active in a learning space; (2) use the languages they speak at home; (3) use mathematics to analyze injustices in society; and (4) build on familiar contexts and personal and cultural experiences. However, learners need help translating their everyday knowledge into more abstract forms of mathematical modeling and representation. Manipulatives (objects designed so that a learner can perceive some mathematical concept by manipulating them) are useful tools to help make this translation, as are community members, especially people from a familiar context.

Incorporating the history of mathematics and the views of community members can go a long way toward helping students see that mathematics is not a singular entity, that many cultures have created (and are still creating) it, and that we can combine our personal identities with mathematical ones. Creating opportunities for students to have a stronger voice in the kinds of mathematics being studied and the forms of interaction in a learning environment can also help Latin@ and black learners see themselves as "math people." And when they do, they are more likely to persist in solving difficult problems or addressing novel situations.

Research suggests that how students feel about themselves while doing mathematics is critical to whether or not they engage fully in the activities. Important steps to motivate students who might not otherwise be engaged in mathematics classrooms include developing their confidence, using a larger repertoire of mathematical strategies, and fostering a mathematical identity that builds on their culture or community.

It seems reasonable that if adolescents are encouraged to model phenomena with which they are familiar and expected to look for generalizations in the data they are generating, they may be more likely to learn the abstract, formal mathematics that is required in school. Civil rights leader Robert P. Moses has been applying these ideas successfully for years in his student-centered model The Algebra Project, now used in more than two hundred middle schools across the country. As a black male who taught mathematics to his daughter and her four younger siblings, he has seen the need to make a college preparatory mathematics sequence accessible to all students, particularly those from marginalized populations.

Moses starts with fundamental mathematical questions: What is algebra? Why should students learn it? What kinds of process give all students access to it? One of his key contributions has been recognizing that in getting students to transition from understanding arithmetic to understanding algebra, they must develop a whole new way of thinking—and it is easier to do this when grounded in real-world situations that they share. Young people must be able not only to count (number); they must also consider direction (positive versus negative numbers). Algebra Project participants first do this by taking a subway trip and then mapping out their route, answering questions about how many stops and which way they went. Essential to the program's philosophy is starting with where the students are in their mathematical understanding and using experiences common to all. Then students reflect on those experiences, draw conceptual connections to them, and finally apply the ideas to their conceptual work. Evaluations of The Algebra Project indicate some success with this approach.[21] In Arkansas, seven out of the eleven cohorts of students that were followed longitudinally showed at least a 10-point increase in mean-scaled scores on the SAT-9 a year after being in the program. Moreover, students scored at or above the proficiency level at all of the Arkansas sites, as compared with controls who declined or stayed at their proficiency levels.

Studies of Latin@ parents learning mathematics suggest that building on students' previous cultural experiences—what some researchers have termed *funds of knowledge*—can help address issues of equity in schools. One model is for teachers to go into the community and observe and interview families about the kinds of activities (e.g., chores) students do at home. Teachers then can build on these forms of expertise in the classroom. However, a funds of knowledge approach to teaching is not simple.[22] It can lead to stereotyping about particular cultural groups (e.g., presuming what kinds of experiences Latin@ adolescents bring to school) or require copious amounts of time getting to know students and their communities.

Nevertheless, teachers can do a lot to make the school walls more permeable. They could take kids into the community to study how people use mathematics in their everyday lives or invite community members into the school to talk about the kinds of things they do and how that relates to mathematics. Students might then gain a better sense of themselves as doing mathematics and become more interested in knowing how their practices relate to the formal, abstract mathematics taught in school. Moreover, if students were encouraged to draw on their out-of-school experiences to offer multiple representations for the mathematics classroom, they might be more willing to see connections between their out-of-school mathematical practices and their in-school mathematical practices. Such approaches might also serve to position as mathematical experts students who were not previously seen as competent, based on school performance.

Use Authentic Problems and Peer Learners to Increase Mathematical Rigor

For decades, mathematics problems have tended to be of this kind: "Here is an example where I have worked out a solution, now you do thirty of them." In fact, these are not problems but mere exercises. The teacher and the students both know there is only one right answer, and probably only one sanctioned way of representing the solution. In fact, the current push for failing schools to better prepare students for standardized exams almost ensures that Latin@ and black youth will continue to get this form of instruction. Problems in the real world, by contrast, involve many overlapping variables and the solutions can be far from clear-cut.

By beginning with problems grounded in the interests of Latin@ and black students, we make it more likely that they will be engaged in higher-order thinking. Such problems invite learners to build on previously acquired knowledge to help in deciding how best to develop a solution. Broad social issues, such as social injustices that affect these adolescents, might be the most motivating.

The potential for higher-order learning increases further when individuals work with peers. Dozens of studies of afterschool learning point to the importance of various forms of collaborative learning.[23] Collaboration often requires greater levels of energy and attention to detail, and small-group problem-solving sessions also can require more of learners. Particularly when collaboration is structured around an authentic, open-ended problem, Latin@ and black adolescents can benefit from working in small groups. They can hear a variety of perspectives and strategies, refine their thinking, and justify their ideas to others—just as in real-life collaborations. In doing so, they are more likely to persist in a trajectory from novice to apprentice to expert.

Leverage Community Members to Personalize Learning

Most schools operate under the idea that one mathematics teacher can effectively support twenty-five to thirty students with whole-class instruction. This organizational structure presumes the teacher needs few opportunities to understand deeply what individual students know or can do—both before they walk into the classroom and after they walk out of it. However, even when teachers choose to have young people work in small groups, their students generally benefit more when they have time to check in with one another about the status of their work, their growth, and their misconceptions.

Bringing in community members, particularly older people who may be unfamiliar with today's mathematics curricula, strategies, and technology, can be more helpful than it might at first appear. Adolescents can "teach" adults about things with which they are familiar, even as they learn from individuals who have a lifetime of knowledge of how mathematics relates to the real world. This blurring of our ideas of novice and expert can help students develop meaningful personal relationships and offer opportunities to "try on" mathematics identities.

We offer these four elements in order to inform and inspire mathematics practitioners to craft innovative pedagogies to better support Latin@ and black youth in student-centered ways. Focusing on mathematics that students learn outside of school (where it happens more naturally) and on mathematics applied to personal, cultural, or community issues that students bring to school may better highlight the competencies, interests, and needs of these students as learners. Starting with mathematics as a social activity (as opposed to a set of skills that schools need to impart to students) may better foster individual student identities as capable "doers" of mathematics. And using authentic, real-world problems both can make mathematics more meaningful to students and increase curricular rigor.

A DEEPER LOOK AT RESEARCH

A variety of research fields that have developed within mathematics education speak to the question of how people learn mathematics outside of the institution of schooling. For this chapter, we examined a wide range of research in order to broaden popular conceptualizations of mathematics achievement of Latin@ and black students, including ethnomathematics, adults learning to use mathematics as part of their everyday practices, afterschool mathematics programs, and social justice mathematics. Although similar, each of these approaches operates with assumptions and goals that have left them largely disconnected. By both looking deeply within and across these bodies of research, teachers can help their students, especially Latin@ and black students, to become more engaged with and successful in mathematics.

Ethnomathematics

There is not a single mathematics found everywhere. Anthropologists who study mathematics have documented that not only do all people around the world do mathematics, but a variety of sophisticated forms are practiced in different cultures. Many believe that humans on different parts of the globe developed mathematics in order to describe their environment and help them solve everyday problems.

Having developed within countries that were once colonized and that today oppose importing Western curricula, one of the primary goals within ethnomathematics is to highlight the contributions of different, mainly non-Western cultures to the field of mathematics. At one level, this work includes documenting the mathematics that have developed in ancient cultures such as ancient India, China, Egypt, Babylonia, and other parts of the Arab world.[24] However, this work also shows that today's indigenous peoples with diverse perspectives on the world develop diverse mathematical practices.[25] (See "Mathematics Around the World.")

A common approach is for an anthropologist with extensive knowledge of mathematics to spend large amounts of time within a given population, learning how to do the mathematical work that local people do. For example, researchers studying number and pattern in South African cultures highlighted the roles women play in reproducing geometrical patterns and tessellations through the weaving of baskets and cloth.[26] Much of the readily available ethnomathematics research highlights the games that are played in many African cultures, such as mancala, and how those games draw on mathematical principles familiar to Western mathematics.[27]

Ethnomathematicians also document that what the West often takes to be the exclusive knowledge of professionally trained mathematicians exists throughout the world. Among other examples, researchers have shown that in the Marshall Archipelago, where sailing is integral to life and wave piloting is essential, the use of stick charts (maps) relies on unique geometric and algebraic renderings of the oceans. Few of the peoples documented in these studies have had formal schooling. Rather, they have developed these ways of using mathematics through learning from others in their community.

Contemporary studies in ethnomathematics seek to highlight the asymmetrical power relations that arise when different mathematical practices are developed and maintained in one place. For example, a recent study focused on a group of landless peasants in Brazil fighting to maintain the effective system they developed for measuring land plots before the school testing industry and government officials began requiring an official European system.[28] Peasant testimonies indicate that the new method of doing mathematics in school denies them knowledge they have developed outside of school and are accustomed to using. On the

MATHEMATICS AROUND THE WORLD

In looking across cultures, researchers have classified the general forms of mathematics that are practiced by all humans around the globe. The most cited classification system, developed by Alan Bishop, argues for six basic categories:[29]

- *Counting:* "The use of a systematic way to compare and order discrete phenomena. It may involve tallying, or using objects or string to record, or special number words or names."

- *Locating:* "Exploring one's spatial environment and conceptualizing and symbolizing that environment with models, diagrams, drawings, words, or other means."

- *Measuring:* "Quantifying qualities for the purpose of comparison and ordering, using objects or tokens as measuring devices with associated units or 'measure-words.'"

- *Designing:* "Creating a shape or design for an object or for any part of one's spatial environment. It may involve making the object, as a 'mental template,' or symbolizing it in some conventionalized way."

- *Playing:* "Devising, and engaging in, games and pastimes, with more or less formalized rules that all players abide by."

- *Explaining:* "Finding ways to account for the existence of phenomena, be they religious, animistic, or scientific."

other hand, testimonies also reflect the belief that the peasants' school-based mathematics education has not given them enough formalism and abstraction to help them negotiate a language that has traditionally kept them as outsiders.

Recent studies focusing on the perspectives of learners seem to point to the importance of learners having reference items for doing mathematics. A study of women fourteen years and older in the city suburbs of Brazil indicates that being able to work with familiar materials (e.g., beans, rice, sugar) makes doing school mathematics problems easier.[30]

What we learn from ethnomathematics studies is that the forms of mathematics we privilege in school (e.g., Euclidian geometry; Cartesian coordinates; the base-10 counting system) are not the only mathematics that people use. Moreover, the mathematical practices that have developed among different cultures serve a purpose. That is, people do mathematics not just to display knowledge to others (get good grades) as happens in school, but also to accomplish practical tasks in everyday life. We see that people learn mathematics not necessarily from someone called a teacher, but also from people in their environment who have initiated them into a culture-specific way of doing mathematics. Furthermore, individuals do mathematics in the particular ways they have learned because they make sense. Finally, when students are connected to the things they are studying—for example, through topics based on cultural experiences and ideas they already have—they may be more motivated to learn.[31]

Math in Everyday Contexts

The typical argument made by schools and teachers for why individuals need to learn mathematics is that the knowledge they gain is general enough to transfer to their everyday lives. Yet studies of people using mathematics in their everyday lives seem to challenge these claims. For the most part, individuals do not apply rules or ideas they have learned in the mathematics classroom to real-life problems. Rather, they draw heavily on a familiar context in which they participate.[32] Poor children selling candy and melons on the streets of Brazil, for example, can calculate complex sums in the context of their work but not in similar paper-and-pencil, "school-like" problems.[33] The same has been found for adult carpet layers, grocery shoppers, interior designers, retailers, and restaurant managers.[34] For many of these individuals, the "naked" (stripped of context) problems that researchers presented to them as equivalents to what they were doing in everyday practice were seen as not equivalent at all, and attempts to solve them led to nonsensical solutions.[35] Looking across a variety of

FIGURE 5-1   Learning mathematics: In school versus out of school

In school	Out of school
• Individual thinking	• Shared thinking
• Pure thought	• Using tools
• Manipulating symbols	• Contextualized reasoning
• Generalized learning	• Situation-specific competencies

studies, some researchers have sought to categorize more broadly how in-school mathematics learning differs from mathematics learning outside of school and have identified four significant differences, summarized in figure 5.1.[36]

The distinctions are important: they point to why school mathematics does not always make sense to students and may make them feel incompetent. Consider the example in figure 5.2 of a mathematical exercise on combining like terms that students might see in an algebra course. It is not difficult to see how a student can make errors (e.g., combining unlike terms when working with variables) if manipulating algebraic symbols never involves thinking about what those symbols refer to (how each variable represents a different entity that prevents it from combining with another).

Although significant reform efforts in mathematics education have been under way since these studies were reviewed in 1987, the four differences persist. Even highly technical professionals like radiologists reading x-rays or nurses calculating drug dosages use processes different from those

FIGURE 5-2   Combining like terms: In school versus everyday life

In school	Out of school
$2x + 3y = 5xy$ Could seem to make sense	2 apples + 3 bananas = 5 apple-bananas No such thing as "apple-bananas"
Errors persist	**Reality tells us this is incorrect**

taught in medical schools, through textbooks, or on medical rounds.[37] Their mathematical reasoning tends to be grounded in the situations in which they are working and in relation to others with whom they work. Studies of mathematical learning in out-of-school contexts also highlight the importance of apprenticeship.[38] Teaching in out-of-school contexts is not explicit; it is observed. Here, signs of learning are in the form not of individual acquisition of knowledge but of greater participation (performance) in the practice.

A small number of studies have looked at adolescents practicing mathematics outside of school.[39] Observations of black middle and high school basketball players indicate that they are competent at calculating averages and percentages for the free-throw shots of a given player when the context of the problem is a basketball game rather than a school mathematics worksheet. Furthermore, like the findings in ethnomathematics, the kinds of strategies used in the basketball context differ. For the school mathematics problem, players tend to incorrectly remember or misapply algorithms; their strategies for finding an answer are reduced to mere manipulation of the symbols.

Like those who have studied ethnomathematics and shown that differences in mathematical practices create power dynamics, some researchers who study multiethnic classrooms have found that schools often ignore or even reject the knowledge that students possess from their experiences outside of school.[40] (Most of the studies on learning and using mathematics in everyday contexts focus on adults, not the adolescents with whom we are concerned. Even so, findings from these studies raise important issues for teaching and learning mathematics with Latin@ and black students.)

All of these studies have been qualitative and with fairly small numbers of students. However, the ethnographic approaches (data gathered from students, teachers, and community members as well as school observations and structured tasks) and the repeated patterns across sites provide a convincing picture that when it comes to the mathematics classroom, students are implicitly taught to ignore their out-of-school experiences.

Afterschool Mathematics Programs

Studies on mathematics learning in afterschool settings suggest that some of the constraints normally imposed by teachers and curricula disappear after the school bell rings. Regardless of where the activities occur, afterschool mathematics programs can provide opportunities for greater personalization, collaboration, student talk, manipulatives, multiple representations, connections to the community, positive student identity, and, to a certain extent, more rigorous learning. Similar trends have been found in afterschool science programs led by indigenous peoples in their communities.[41]

A broad range of afterschool programs targets low-income youth, but the available studies consistently highlight the generally positive nature of such programs on mathematics achievement.[42] One meta-analysis of thirty-five afterschool programs and summer schools found small but statistically significant gains in mathematics for low-achieving students.[43] The size of these gains (effect sizes of about 0.13) are meaningful when compared to those of low-achieving students who did not participate in afterschool programs, but they are insufficient to close achievement gaps between low-achieving youth and their more advantaged counterparts. However, secondary students seem to benefit more from afterschool mathematics programs than do elementary students.[44]

One possible mechanism for the increase in student achievement that is generally tied to afterschool mathematics programs is a sense of personalization. For example, programs that attend to both students' social and academic needs show greater effects than programs focused only on academics.[45] Surprisingly, even programs focused on youth development (rather than academics) improve student achievement and engagement.[46]

The impact of personalization extends beyond the social nature of learning (motivating students to attend) to include the number of people who can focus on each student's needs. Learning in small groups, which is more common in afterschool mathematics programs than in typical mathematics classrooms and summer schools, has a stronger impact than does whole-group instruction or one-on-one tutoring. This suggests that students may benefit from peer interaction as they collaborate to solve nonroutine problems—and that they benefit from more opportunities for rigorous mathematics thinking.

For example, a three-year study of twenty-four Latin@ and black middle school students in an afterschool program showed increases in the variety and sophistication of reasoning with respect to proofs.[47] The activities contrasted with those of the math classrooms in which the students typically participated. For example, they engaged in open-ended, group problem solving; tackling problems with more than one answer; collaboration, sharing, and supporting one another's solutions; the use of manipulatives; and asking students to prove things that could not be proven. The afterschool setting also offered students a more relaxed environment for testing their ideas and making them public. Success was measured not by grades or teacher approval, but by peers' opinions of the reasonableness of an individual's argument.

Research on afterschool mathematics programs also suggests that when students work in small groups, they receive feedback more quickly than they would from a teacher in a large class and they are more likely to be engaged in higher-level problem solving and making connections to the real world.[48] Students in small groups have more opportunities to explain their thinking, clarify their ideas, and justify their strategies to one another. They can hear, challenge, and build on a variety of other perspectives as they refine their own thinking.

Afterschool programs also seem to offer opportunities for students to develop a kind of identity around mathematics. In the study of students developing reasoning, one outcome was that students in the afterschool mathematics program later reported feeling more confident about asking questions, completing homework, and challenging the mathematical justifications of others.[49] This sense of confidence can go a long way toward helping individuals see themselves as mathematical people and persist in solving difficult mathematics problems.

One multisite afterschool research project focusing on the relationship between culture, language, and mathematics is particularly pertinent for our concerns for Latin@ youth. Situated in the Center for the Mathematics Education of Latinos/as, a Center for Learning and Teaching funded by the National Science Foundation, the project conducted a number of research studies at afterschool programs in the Southwest and the Midwest that sought to connect teachers, Latin@ students, and community members in doing mathematics.

The studies looked at a fascinating range of programs: middle school students and their parents voluntarily doing mathematics together in a *tertulia*, or mathematics circle similar to a book discussion group; elementary students observing and interviewing community members about the ways they used math at work in a bakery, auto shop, or candy store; and other students participating for several years in a bilingual afterschool math club.

The findings highlight that engagement, confidence, and ability to apply a range of strategies increase with adaptation to the unique needs of students, opportunities to tap into funds of knowledge from one's own culture, connections to the everyday lives and communities of participants, and taking problems from real-life settings and collaboratively trying to solve them. Engagement increased the most for students who otherwise were quiet or disruptive in mathematics classrooms that required English communication.

Still another site in this larger study suggests a positive connection between participation in an afterschool mathematics program and students' increased participation in their regular mathematics classrooms.[50] Low-income Latin@ students in third through fifth grade who participated over a three-year period in a bilingual mathematics club had opportunities to choose and create mathematical tasks, become the authorities on problem situations, and solve problems in ways that made sense to them, using their preferred methods. Initially, students in the afterschool program were unwilling to communicate their thinking verbally or through models and drawings, but over time they learned to take more risks than in their mathematics classrooms. They also learned to ask more questions, give longer responses, use more tools to represent their thinking, and work better with others. Students also developed more positive identities around mathematics.[51]

Although much of the research on learning mathematics in afterschool settings points to the benefit of breaking with school traditions and supporting students in more personalized ways, some limitations in the research are worth noting. For example, few evaluation studies report the number of students dropping out of the program. Thus, the effects could be inflated, with the most academically motivated students staying in the program.[52] In addition, although reports generally highlight the more personal nature of adult involvement, some research suggests that, because of low pay and high turnover, adults in these settings may be less likely to possess deep content knowledge or familiarity with today's mathematics curricula, especially reform-oriented formats.[53] If that is the case, recruiting better-qualified staff should increase mathematical gains associated with these programs. Several successful programs targeting Latin@ youth have been run by mathematics professors, graduate assistants, undergraduate assistants, or a combination of the three.

The research also seems to suggest important effects in terms of motivating students who might not otherwise engage in mathematics classrooms. Developing students' confidence, enlarging their repertoire of mathematical strategies, and creating a mathematical identity that builds on learners' culture or community may be as important as increasing scores on standardized tests.

Social Justice Mathematics

It is always easier to engage students in subjects they care about. Teaching mathematics to engage Latin@ and black adolescents using social justice issues, which starts with contexts familiar to students and appeals to their sense of fairness, can motivate them to learn the mathematical skills necessary to solve complex problems. This appears to be an especially effective approach to reengaging students who may have lost interest in mathematics. It not only connects with their personal and cultural experiences; it also shows the practical applications of mathematics outside the classroom. Students use mathematics as an analytic tool for developing an understanding and awareness of injustices in society, their place within history, and their ability to make changes in society.[54]

The goal is for students to develop mathematical arguments that, when accompanied by representations of data, they can use as they seek to convince others to take certain action to solve a deeply felt problem. For example, students might examine the areas and percentages of different countries on a world map to see how some countries are represented as larger or smaller than their actual land mass warrants.[55] Or they might survey the community on experiences with the police to calculate the likelihood that, in given neighborhoods, a police officer will pull over a brown or black, versus a white, driver.[56] Using the math to make their point, the students might present the information to their local police department and ask that officers rethink how they profile drivers.

In one study, a class of sixth-graders composed predominately of working-class blacks, Dominicans, and Puertorriqueñ@s compared their overcrowded school with the magnet school serving wealthier students one floor below. They calculated the number of students per square foot in both schools and presented it to the school board to ask for help in rectifying the inequity. Angel, a sixth-grader in the social justice unit, explained this was a much better way to do math than "learning it straight." Because students were solving a real problem, one that mattered to them personally, "we would actually, like, really get into it, and that made it easier . . . Like the facts [about the school], they made you want to find out the answer. Like we wanted to know," Angel said.[57]

Although this form of learning may sound more like what you might see in a social studies classroom, mathematics teachers have tried and succeeded with a surprising number of topics. Examples include: calculus,[58] proportional reasoning,[59] geometry,[60] measurement,[61] estimation,[62] percentages,[63] operations with fractions,[64] and statistics.[65] But in most of these studies, teachers are reporting on their own practices. More rigorous research is needed to show just how effective this approach is in helping students connect to mathematics, develop confidence and a larger repertoire of mathematics strategies, build a robust mathematical identity, and learn the mathematical skills necessary to solve complex problems.

Research has promoted the theory of connecting social justice issues with mathematics for some time.[66] Yet it is difficult to determine the number of teachers who are implementing social justice mathematics in their classrooms. Mathematics education has only recently begun to embrace issues of identity and power.[67] In addition, such instruction presents challenges for teachers to carry out.[68] That said, the radicalmath.org website, created in 2007 by a Brooklyn public school teacher, is dedicated to educating the public, offering resources for teaching mathematics for social justice and promoting an annual conference on the topic, entitled "Creating Balance in an Unjust World."[69]

Another benefit of a social justice approach is the development of a stronger sense of community in the classroom, which makes students more comfortable engaging in difficult conversations about previously taboo topics.[70] In addition, students become more likely to believe they can make a difference in their own lives as well as in the lives of others.[71] For example, students developed more sophisticated understandings of broader social issues (e.g., using data to learn that banks were not necessarily racist, even if they tended not to loan money to blacks). From the point of view of one of the students of Eric Gutstein (a professor and researcher in mathematics education): "It got everyone thinking for themselves. It made some people come up with powerful things to say about the math involving those problems. All my views have changed. The world before wasn't very interesting to me because I wasn't aware of all the issues that were happening. Now, math made everyone interested in the real world because it's something that catches everyone's attention."[72]

Even so, this type of teaching is complex. Some of the challenges include: getting to know the students well enough to develop social justice projects that are meaningful to individuals; balancing the demands for rigorous mathematics with sufficient detail to a social justice issue; avoiding overly influencing students with the teacher's point of view; finding time in the curriculum to fit in social justice projects; and helping students develop a sense of agency rather than despair about injustice.[73] Even mathematics teachers who work in schools with a social justice theme report these challenges.

When presented with social justice issues, it is difficult for individuals to be indifferent; most people want to take a stand on a controversial topic. The approach appears to be especially effective at engaging students who have lost interest in mathematics, a large percentage of whom are Latin@ or black. By connecting mathematics to the world outside of school, teaching mathematics for social justice also has a way of illustrating for students that mathematics will be part of their lives after schooling. The consequences for getting a "wrong answer" or having unconvincing data for an argument mean more than a poor grade.

Although more rigorous research on social justice mathematics is needed to capture the kinds of learning opportunities this approach provides, several benefits remain clear. The main contribution of teaching mathematics for social justice is that it can supplement typical mathematics curricula with topics that may be more interesting for students, increasing their engagement in mathematics. Moreover, because this approach often embeds work in the students' local contexts, it can present problems without simple solutions and motivate students to want to understand challenging concepts.

A BROADER VIEW

We have offered some of the ways that teachers might adopt strategies found in out-of-school settings for mathematics instruction. However, the point of placing students at the center of learning is not to take all of the components of learning that have occurred outside of school hours and squeeze them into the classroom. Schools, as institutions, are constrained by, among other things, their organizational structures, goals, and teacher credentialing processes. One of the greatest tensions for secondary mathematics teachers is attending to issues of depth versus breadth: Do I move on with tomorrow's topic if not everyone understands today's, or do I sacrifice time on the next topic in order to develop greater understanding of this one?

Teachers and schools organize their work (and subsequent student learning) around how much of a prescribed curriculum can be covered in the amount of time available during the school day. In the case of today's schooling, whole-class delivery, standardized assessments, and multiple sections of the same course offer few options for mathematics teachers other than to either move on with the whole class or keep the whole class focused on the topic for a longer period.

In contrast, the interdisciplinary nature of life, the desires of individuals and communities, and the assessment of (and consequences for) successful problem solving all drive a very different process in learning outside of school or in situations that interface with social and community issues. To create more opportunities for student-centered learning, we must think differently about the enterprise of education—where and when it happens, and who benefits from its forms.

The research reviewed in this chapter is a starting point for building student-centered approaches to improving mathematics learning for Latin@ and black youth. However, the lack of literature and of longitudinal data on large groups of these populations is a disadvantage. We recommend scaling up the most successful projects and following them for longer periods so that more Latin@ and black adolescents can benefit. In addition, to better understand which formats best serve which purposes, we stress the need to develop more rigorous assessments, pilot them with students of varying ages, and cover a broader range of mathematical topics. As with any educational movement, teachers need support to understand, implement, and assess the ability of these projects to serve their students. Educational researchers and schools of education can offer assistance in this area.

We might also take some guidance from other countries that have embedded the notion of education as a social responsibility, where the walls separating communities, businesses, schools, adults, children, learners, and educators do not exist or are much more permeable than in the United States. Spain is a country that offers a way of thinking about learning centered on students. Using a model called *comunidades de aprendizaje* (learning communities), hundreds of Barcelona schools leverage community resources, technology, schools, and modes of regular and intergenerational dialogue to translate abandoned and low-income neighborhoods into vibrant places with increased mathematics achievements for youth, greater ownership and strong community, and lifelong learning opportunities for adults.[74] If we are to take seriously the idea of placing Latin@ and black students at the center of learning, we recommend engaging the broader public in the endeavor, especially community-based organizations that have vested interests in supporting youth.

PART III

The Future of Student-Centered Learning

*What do advances in the emerging mind, brain,
and education field tell us about how people learn? What
roles do agency, motivation, and engagement play in
learning? Given the diversity of students in a classroom
and the unique ways each one learns, how can educators
understand the variety of motivations and provide a
range of growth opportunities that motivate and
engage students, both collectively and individually?*

Part 3 steps back from the classroom to discuss the science
and theory undergirding the student-centered approaches,
assessments, and arguments. The author of these chapters
merge what educational researchers and theorists have
known for years with cutting-edge research in the science

of learning and the brain, and in the interdependence of motivation, engagement, and learning. These chapters provide a strong support for the kinds of practices, classrooms, schools, and systems envisioned by *Anytime, Anywhere* and the Students at the Center project.

CHAPTER 6

Applying the Science of How We Learn

Christina Hinton, Kurt W. Fischer,
and Catherine Glennon

RESEARCH IN BIOLOGY and cognitive science is more relevant for education than ever before. Powerful brain-imaging tools enable neuroscientists to study the learning brain in action for the first time. New genetics technologies enable researchers to explore complex gene-environment interactions. Innovative cognitive science methods for analyzing learning enable researchers to track alternative learning pathways. Such advancements have led to a global emergence of the field of mind, brain, and education, synthesizing research in biology, cognitive science, and education to create a learning science that can inform education policy and practice.

This chapter considers the field of mind, brain, and education and its implications for student-centered learning. Many student-centered approaches to learning are well grounded in—or are intuitively in keeping with—research on how young people learn. While this chapter focuses specifically on the transdisciplinary findings in mind, brain, and education research, it also complements the chapter on motivation, engagement, and student voice.

Recent research findings about the brain have important implications for student-centered approaches to learning. Some of the most significant are:

- The brain is continually changing as learning experiences shape its architecture. Students' abilities are not fixed, but rather always developing.
- The brain is learning virtually all the time, in both formal and informal contexts.
- The brain changes that underlie learning occur when experiences are active, not passive.
- Each student has a complex profile of strengths and limitations and learns best through experiences tailored to his or her needs and interests.
- Underserved students, including low-income youth and English language learners, sometimes thrive with different instructional techniques than their middle-class and more privileged peers.
- Learning and emotion work together in the brain.

HOW THE BRAIN LEARNS

Perhaps the most important insight for education from the field of neuroscience is that the brain is highly adaptive, or *plastic*.[1] The brains of students continuously adapt to their experiences and their environments, including school, home, workplaces, community centers, and so forth. As students learn in these places—mastering reading, playing online chess, or practicing word processing—these experiences gradually sculpt the architecture of the brain.

The brain is made up of networks of billions of interconnecting nerve cells, called *neurons*. Learning experiences are translated into electrical and chemical signals that cascade among many neurons in many areas of the brain. In fact, reading just the words in this sentence activates millions of neurons.

Each neuron has many inputs from other neurons. When students learn, certain connections are activated, while others are not. Over time, the most active connections are strengthened, while those that are less active are weakened or eliminated.[2] These experience-dependent changes in the efficacy of neuronal connections are thought to be the biological substrate of memory. Gradually, the electrical and chemical signals traveling through the brain modify connections between neurons in certain areas of the brain, and those areas are reorganized. Over time, these changes can aggregate to significant reorganization in certain brain structures involved in certain types of learning.[3]

One of the most extensive areas of research on the brain's plasticity is in the domain of music. Seminal work by Thomas Elbert, Christo Pantev, and their colleagues demonstrated that learning to play the violin leads to changes in the organization of certain areas of the cortex, which are involved in many types of learning.[4] Elbert et al. showed that the area of the brain representing the fingers of the left hand is larger in violinists than in nonmusicians.[5] Moreover, this area is also larger for violinists' left hands than for their right hands. This suggests that this area is enlarged as a result of practicing the violin, rather than, for example, a genetic predisposition that could lead individuals to become violinists. As a student practices the violin, neuronal connections underlying finger dexterity in the left hand are activated, which strengthens them.

Learning to play the violin also influences the *auditory cortex*, which is involved in processing sound. Pantev et al. found that the area of the auditory cortex representing musical tones is larger in violinists than in nonmusicians.[6] Moreover, later research showed that short-term musical training led to stronger neuronal connections in this area.[7] This supports the notion that as students practice the violin, neuronal connections in the auditory cortex get stronger, which eventually leads to large-scale reorganization. Research has demonstrated this type of plasticity in the brain as a result of other types of learning as well,[8] including motor learning, language learning,[9] and learning Braille.[10]

Neuroscience research demonstrates that individual abilities are not fixed, but rather continuously developing throughout life. The brain is learning virtually all of the time, in both formal and informal contexts.[11] In essence, the more a student learns in a particular area, the more intelligent the brain becomes in that area. This plasticity enables students to overcome many learning challenges. For example, many dyslexic students develop alternative neural circuitry to support reading when given appropriate educational support.[12] The educational environment plays a crucial role in shaping the brain's abilities and determining students' academic achievement.

Brain research in several specific areas has important implications for student-centered approaches to learning. The following sections discuss neuroscience research on active learning, individual differences, language learning, literacy, and mathematics.

Active Learning

Neuroscience research suggests that active engagement is necessary for learning. In a seminal experiment, Gregg H. Recanzone and his colleagues found that when monkeys actively attended to finger stimulation because it was relevant to their goals, they learned the association between the stimulation and their goals.[13] Moreover, the brain area representing the stimulated finger became enlarged. However, when monkeys received the same finger stimulation passively, it did not lead to changes in the brain. Researchers found the same pattern in plasticity when the stimulation was auditory.[14] When monkeys were actively engaged in learning auditory information because it earned them rewards, it led to the expansion of the brain areas involved in processing that information. However, when the same auditory stimulation occurred and monkeys passively heard it, it did not lead to changes in brain. Recent imaging work suggests that brain plasticity is conditional on active engagement in humans as well.[15]

Together, this research suggests that active engagement is a prerequisite for the changes in brain circuitry that are thought to underlie learning. In educational terms, this suggests that active engagement with educational material, within or outside of school, will support learning. Conversely, passively sitting in a classroom while a teacher lectures will not necessarily lead to learning.

Individual Differences

Why do some students whiz through chemistry while others struggle? Why do certain students show uncommon resilience in the face of adversity? These variations are grounded in part in individual differences in the brain.

Students' genetic predispositions interact with learning experiences to give rise to a wide range of individual differences.[16] All people are born with certain genetic tendencies, and as they interact in different ways with the world around them, their experiences reinforce or counteract their genetic inclinations. For example, a student may have a genetic predisposition for shyness[17] yet grow into a gregarious person because of supportive social experiences at home, in school, or in the community.

Since genetics and experience interact to shape the brain, each brain is unique. Mind, brain, and education research does not support the simplistic notion that a given student is either intelligent or not. Rather, it recognizes that each student has a complex profile of strengths and limitations. A student may struggle in one area, such as mathematics, and yet thrive in another, such as interpersonal intelligence. Moreover, within each domain, students can have both talents and limitations. For example, students who have perfect pitch typically struggle with singing a melody in a different key.

Research on reading instruction illuminates the shortcomings of educational approaches that neglect individual differences. While most students learn to read by linking sounds with letters to form words, some students never master the higher-level skill of reading to learn.[18] That is, they are unable to extract meaning effectively from text they read. This educational failure means that these students never become fully literate. Much of the problem stems from the fact that students follow different learning pathways when learning to read and build comprehension, but the curriculum is structured as if all students follow the same pathway.[19]

Rather, to be in keeping with research, curriculum should take into account the different ways students learn, and the different languages, cultures, values, goals, and interests they bring to school.[20]

Student achievement arises from the interaction of a student's profile with instructional techniques; and adjusting instruction to meet each student's particular needs can often move students from failure to proficiency. For example, the performance of students who have a gene that is linked to anxiety can vary significantly according to instructional technique.[21] When students with this anxiety-linked gene engage in a computer literacy instruction program without feedback, they perform lower than students without this gene. However, when the program is adjusted to include positive feedback that motivates and informs students as they work, those with the anxiety-linked gene have higher outcomes than those without it.

Much more research is needed on how to accommodate a wide variety of individual differences. Education literature is overwhelmingly based on studies of middle-class individuals of European American ancestry.[22] Given that instructional methods can be differentially effective for different subgroups, it is problematic that evidence-based practice is, by and large, based on evidence from one particular subgroup. In fact, recent research suggests that studies of middle-class people of European American ancestry are unlikely to generalize to other populations.[23] For example, the degree to which Intelligence Quotient (IQ) is influenced by genetics and the environment seems to vary dramatically depending on students' socioeconomic status (SES).[24]

Language Learning

The brain is genetically primed to acquire language. Noam Chomsky proposed more than fifty years ago that the brain is predisposed to process certain stimuli according to universal language rules.[25] Recent research confirms that there are brain structures that are genetically specialized for language.[26] A part of the brain called *Broca's area* is involved in a broad range of linguistic functions, including language production.[27] Another part of the brain, called *Wernicke's area*, plays a key role in semantics.[28]

Although certain brain structures are biologically primed for language development, experience acts as a catalyst to initiate the process of language acquisition. Research shows that there are sensitive periods in brain development during which certain areas of the brain are most receptive to particular aspects of language learning.[29] For example, acquiring the accent of a language is learned most effectively between birth and about twelve years of age.[30] There is also a sensitive period for learning the grammar of a language.[31] If the brain is exposed to a non-native language between one and three years of age, grammar is processed by the left hemisphere, as it is in native speakers. However, brain-imaging studies reveal that when initial exposure occurs at the ages of eleven, twelve, or thirteen years, there is an alternative processing strategy involving both hemispheres. The brain circuits genetically primed to learn grammar are most plastic early in life. Therefore, when foreign language exposure occurs later in life, the brain must rely partially on other circuits that are not genetically specified for learning grammar. This may account for the deficits in grammatical processing often found in students who were first exposed to non-native language instruction late in their schooling.[32]

However, it is certainly possible to learn language throughout life.[33] If adolescents and adults are immersed in a non-native language, they can learn it very well, although particular aspects, such as accent, may never develop as completely as they could have if the language had been learned earlier. Additionally, there are individual differences; some adults can master almost all aspects of a new language.

Literacy in the Brain

While the brain is genetically primed to learn language, literacy arises through cumulative experience-dependent changes in brain architecture.[34]

Cultural evolution, which takes place in the span of generations, has vastly outpaced biological evolution, which occurred over billions of years and has endowed the brain with certain genetic predispositions.[35] As a result, cultural inventions such as literacy and formal mathematics are not built into the genetic blueprint of the brain. However, because of the brain's incredible plasticity, it can adapt to create complex networks that support this cultural knowledge.[36]

Literacy is a prime example of this phenomenon. The brain structures genetically predisposed to support language, including Broca's area and Wernike's area, are at the core of reading networks. As a student learns to read, these areas connect with additional areas that were not genetically destined for literacy but rather recycled to fit this function.[37] While there are biological constraints on which areas can be recycled for this purpose, the degree to which certain areas are involved and the recruitment of supplemental areas can vary based on experience.

The dual-route theory provides an overview of what happens in the brain when a native English reader reads a word.[38] As the reader looks at a word on a page, the primary visual cortex processes the stimulus first. The dual-route theory posits that processing then follows one of two complementary pathways for native English readers. One has an intermediate step of converting letters into sounds, which involves Broca's area. The other consists of a direct transfer from word to meaning, and seems to involve the visual word form area.[39]

Since there are genetically specified language areas in the brain and biological constraints on which brain areas will fit a literacy function well, many of the areas involved in reading are shared across languages.[40] However, learning to read in different languages does produce some differences in the brain network that supports reading. For example, English has an inconsistent match between letters and sounds—consider the pronunciation of the letter g in the words *girl* and *tough*. The English language is riddled with these types of inconsistency. Therefore, it is efficient for the brain to read English using a combination of phonetic decoding and whole-word recognition.

Italian, by contrast, has a highly consistent match between letters and sounds. As a result, it is efficient for the brain to rely primarily on phonetic decoding when reading in Italian. Indeed, learning to read in Italian creates a brain network that depends less heavily on the visual word form area, which is central to whole-word recognition.[41] Native Italian readers use this brain network even when reading in English, indicating that the skill of reading has been built somewhat differently as a result of experience learning to read in Italian.

Research on reading in the brain illustrates that there are individual differences in reading networks based on experience learning to read in a particular language. One implication of this work is that English language learners may be processing written information in somewhat different ways than native English speakers. Thus, standard reading instruction techniques may not be the right fit for their needs. More broadly, this research illustrates how experience shapes the brain, giving rise to individual differences.

Proficiency in the language of instruction strongly predicts academic achievement among immigrants.[42] As discussed above, neuroscience research indicates that there are sensitive periods for certain aspects of language learning early in life.[43] Students who receive non-native language instruction in preschool or primary school have a biological advantage for mastering certain aspects of that language. Therefore, teaching English language learners the language of instruction as early as possible gives them a biological advantage for learning that language, which ultimately supports their academic achievement.

Mathematics in the Brain

Like literacy, mathematics understanding is created in the brain through a synergy of biology and experience.[44] Just as there are brain structures that have been designed through evolution for language, there are analogous structures for quantitative sense. As students learn mathematics, these structures connect with other brain areas that were not genetically destined for numbers but are plastic enough to be shaped for this function through experience. Therefore, mathematics draws on a complex network of genetically determined brain structures and experience-dependent brain areas.

Recent research has characterized students' genetically endowed basic quantitative sense as including a concept of one, two, and three.[45] Infants can precisely discriminate these quantities from one another and from larger quantities. Moreover, the concept of these numbers seems to be abstract; for example, infants are able to connect the quality of "two-ness" across two sounds and two objects.[46] This initial quantitative sense includes the ability to approximately discriminate among larger numbers as well.

There is also evidence that this quantitative sense includes intuitions about simple mathematical operations. Karen Wynn found that when one object is placed behind a screen followed by a second object, infants expect to see two objects when the screen is removed, suggesting that they know that 1 plus 1 equals 2.[47]

An area of the brain called the *parietal cortex* is likely the site of this genetically endowed quantitative sense and seems to play a central role in developing many mathematical skills.[48] Damage to it has devastating effects on mathematical abilities. For example, patients with parietal damage sometimes cannot answer a question as simple as which number falls between 3 and 5. However, they often have no difficulty solving analogous serial tasks across other domains, such as identifying which month falls between June and August. Moreover, they can also sometimes solve concrete mathematics problems that they cannot solve abstractly. For example, they sometimes know that there are two hours between 9 a.m. and 11 a.m. but still cannot subtract 9 from 11 in symbolic notation.

Such results illustrate two principles about mathematics in the brain. First, mathematics is at least partially dissociable from other cognitive domains.[49] This means that talents or deficits in mathematics do not generally predict talents or deficits in other domains. That is, if a student excels in mathematics, you cannot use this to predict how well he or she will perform in, for example, language or history. Second, abilities within the domain of mathematics can be dissociable from one another. That is, a talent or weakness in a certain mathematical skill is not necessarily predictive of ability in another mathematical skill. This casts doubt on the validity of tracking students based on performance of basic mathematics skills, which may not necessarily relate to their abilities in advanced mathematics skills. In fact, research suggests that higher-level operations rely on partially distinct neural circuitry; the brain areas underlying algebra are largely independent of those used in mental calculation.[50]

As students learn mathematics, the parietal cortex links with other brain areas to give rise to a rich array of mathematical skills.[51] As in the case of literacy, which areas are connected depends partially on experience. Different instructional methods can result in a different underlying neural circuit. For example, Margarete Hittmair-Delazer and colleagues found that learning by drill was encoded in a different neural substrate than learning by strategy.[52] This means that two students may both answer that 15 plus 15 equals 30, but if one student learned this fact through memorization while the other learned to calculate this answer using double-digit addition, the students are using distinct neural circuitries. Teaching by strategy seems to lead to a more robust neural encoding of mathematical information than teaching by drill, resulting in greater accuracy and transferability. More neuroscience research is needed to explore how different instructional methods influence mathematics in the brain.

EMOTION AND LEARNING

Over two thousand years ago, Plato argued that, "All learning has an emotional base." Modern neuroscientists also argue that emotion is fundamental to learning. In the words of Mary Helen Immordino-Yang and Antonio R. Damasio, "We feel, therefore we learn."[53] When a student has a learning experience, emotion and cognition operate seamlessly in the brain.

Emotion acts as a rudder to guide learning, tagging experiences as either positive and worth approaching or as aversive and worth avoiding. The emotions students feel during an experience become salient labels that steer future learning and decision-making. Emotions direct students' learning processes, helping them gravitate toward positive situations and away from negative ones.

Brain-imaging studies are beginning to elucidate the neural substrate of this system. When students encounter a situation, the brain quickly and automatically appraises it.[54] The *prefrontal cortex* is the site of this appraisal, marking whether the situation brings positive or negative feelings.[55] When events are positive, the left prefrontal cortex shows more activity, with higher-frequency brain waves. When events are negative, activation in the prefrontal cortex occurs dominantly in the right.

The prefrontal cortex is also the seat of executive functioning, which involves goal setting, appropriately selecting learning strategies, monitoring progress, and assessing outcomes.[56] Therefore, emotion and executive function are physically integrated in the brain. The prefrontal cortex is still maturing in adolescence, so executive functioning skills are still developing.[57] Education can support the development of these skills by giving students opportunities to practice setting goals, tracking progress toward them, adjusting strategies along the way, and assessing outcomes.

Since cognition and emotion are interrelated in the brain, individuals can regulate their emotions cognitively.[58] For example, individuals can regulate the emotional impact of negative experiences to an extent.[59] This mollifying effect is manifested in both the subjective experience of the emotion and decreased activation of the *amygdala*, a brain structure centrally involved in emotion. However, since the prefrontal cortex is still maturing in childhood and adolescence, students in primary and secondary school are still developing their emotional regulation skills.[60] In fact, one study showed that students between eight and twelve years old were virtually unable to reduce negative emotions, and students between thirteen and seventeen years old demonstrated only half the regulatory control of adults.[61]

Education can support the development of emotional regulation skills, which strongly predict academic achievement.[62] Emotional regulation skills may be particularly important for students from underprivileged backgrounds. Recent research suggests that one of the main differences between disadvantaged students who succeed in school and those who do not is their ability to regulate emotions.[63]

Neuroscience research on the fundamental role of emotion in learning settles long-standing ideological debates about whether educators should be responsible for emotional development.[64] If educators are involved in intellectual development, they are inherently involved in emotional development as well.

Motivation

Motivation in the brain is driven by emotion: individuals are motivated to engage in emotionally positive situations and avoid situations that are emotionally negative.[65] Motivation recruits brain areas involved in emotion, including the prefrontal cortex and amygdala.[66] Much more brain research is needed to explore the mechanisms underlying the complex and varied motivations of students in educational contexts.[67]

However, there is extensive education psychology research on student motivation. Pioneering work by Carol Dweck is beginning to connect neuroscience with this established body of education psychology research on motivation.[68] For example, she has shown that students tend to hold one of two distinct attitudes toward intelligence.[69] In one approach, students treat intelligence as if it were fixed: it is an *entity*. This belief holds that a student is either smart or not. In the other attitude, students believe that intelligence is achieved: it is *incremental*. According to this belief, a student can become more intelligent by working hard to learn. Students with an incremental theory of intelligence are more likely to persist in the face of challenge use mistakes as opportunities to develop understanding, and ultimately succeed academically.

Dweck connects these attitudes with brain research.[70] One brain region (frontal) responds strongly to negative feedback about performance, while another region (temporal) activates with efforts to correct mistakes in performance. Students with an entity attitude show a stronger frontal response to negative feedback when they make a mistake than do students with an incremental attitude. They react strongly to errors but do not take advantage of the opportunity to learn more effectively. Students with an incremental attitude react less strongly to errors and work more effectively to learn from their mistakes. Understanding these types of individual differences in motivation can help educators adapt pedagogy to each student's emotional needs.

Stress

Stress is an emotion that is highly relevant to education. Low to moderate levels of stress can be positive or tolerable and may even contribute to motivation. However, high levels of frequent or prolonged stress can be toxic to the brain.[71] *Positive stress* involves short-lived stress responses, including brief increases in heart rate or mild changes in stress hormones. Examples of positive stress include giving a class presentation, feeling challenged by a mathematics problem, and trying out for a sports team. This kind of stress is a normal part of life, and learning to adjust to it is an essential feature of healthy development. *Tolerable stress* refers to stress responses that could affect brain architecture but occur for brief periods or in the presence of support so that the brain can recover. Tolerable stress can range from taking a high-stakes exam to experiencing the death of a loved one with nurturing guidance from a parent, teacher, or school psychologist. *Toxic stress* refers to strong, frequent, or prolonged activation of the body stress management system in the absence of support. Toxic stressors include chronic poverty, abuse, bullying, and trauma without support.[72]

Toxic stress leads to quantifiable changes in areas of the brain that are centrally involved in learning and can result in learning problems.[73] Furthermore, toxic stress can change the stress system so that it responds at lower thresholds.[74] This means that a situation that would not threaten most students may trigger a stress response and interrupt learning in students who have experienced toxic stress. This can manifest in a problematic aggressive attitude that damages students' relationships with teachers and peers.

Fortunately, supportive school environments can buffer students' brains from the impacts of unhealthy levels of stress.[75] Gabrielle Rappolt-Schlichtmann and colleagues studied the level of the stress hormone cortisol in students of low and middle socioeconomic status (SES).[76] Results reveal that low-SES students typically come to school with higher levels of cortisol than their middle-SES counterparts. However, when students from disadvantaged backgrounds are in high-quality schools, their cortisol levels decline throughout the day. The better the school, the more the cortisol levels decline. Therefore, a quality learning environment can help students reach healthy cortisol levels, leading to better emotional regulation and more favorable learning outcomes.[77]

Research suggests that students from disadvantaged backgrounds are more likely to experience toxic stress.[78] Student-centered learning that extends into afterschool and summer programs can provide the kind of child-friendly learning spaces that shelter students from toxic stress.

Relationships

The human brain is primed for emotional bonding, which supports learning.[79] The brain is tuned to experience empathy, which intimately connects individuals to one another's experiences. When a teacher sees a student cry, some of the same neurons in the teacher's brain fire as when the teacher cries him- or herself. Similarly, when a student sees a coach swing a baseball bat, some of the same neurons in the student's brain fire as when the student swings the bat him- or herself.

The brain is biologically primed to attune to and bond with others, which sustains interactions with students and teachers that support learning. Adults and more-expert peers provide scaffolding that enables students to grapple with advanced knowledge, which leads to richer and more rapid learning than would be possible through individual exploration.[80]

IMPLICATIONS FOR STUDENT-CENTERED APPROACHES TO LEARNING

The mind, brain, and education research discussed here provides an evidence base for many aspects of student-centered approaches to learning discussed in this book. This research suggests that student-centered practices are consistent with how many different types of students learn and what motivates them to learn. Below we review how research supports particular aspects of student-centered practices.

- **Individualized instruction**: Student-centered approaches to learning differentiate instruction to accommodate individual differences and thus meet the needs of a wide variety of students. Research on individual differences, language learning, literacy, and mathematics suggests that students learn most effectively through experiences that are tailored to their needs and interests.

- **Formative assessment:** Formative assessment is an integral part of student-centered approaches to learning. It involves ongoing formal and informal assessment throughout the learning process. Educators use formative assessment for the purpose of gathering the information they need to adjust instruction in real time to help each student continually progress. Formative assessment recognizes that students' abilities are always developing as new learning shapes the architecture of the brain.

- **Out-of-school experiences:** Student-centered practices take advantage of learning experiences outside of school, such as afterschool enrichment, internships, mentorships, or community programs. This approach is consistent with research on brain plasticity that indicates the brain is learning virtually all the time, in both formal and informal contexts. A student-centered program would formally recognize and credit informal education experiences with nontraditional educators, as well as more traditional school experiences.

- **Active learning:** With student-centered learning approaches, students are empowered to engage in active learning that is relevant to their lives and goals, rather than be expected to sit passively in a classroom listening to a teacher present decontextualized information. This practice is consistent with neuroscience research that shows the changes in the brain that underlie learning occur when experiences are active, not passive.

- **Progressing at own pace:** Student-centered practices allow students to follow different pathways to core skills and standards—and to progress at their own pace through learning experiences that meet their particular needs and interests. This is crucial not only for different types of students, but also for students who excel in some areas but have difficulty in others. Without such flexibility, difficulties in a certain domain may unnecessarily interfere with learning in another domain. This approach is supported by neuroscience research that suggests each student has a unique profile of strengths and limitations, and ability in one domain does not predict ability in another.

- **Serving underserved youth:** Student-centered approaches provide low-income youth, English language learners, and other underserved students with different instructional techniques than their middle-class and more privileged peers. This is informed by research findings that different techniques can be more effective for these groups.

- **Attending to emotion:** Students are more likely to thrive academically if educators provide a positive learning environment, encourage a sense of community, teach emotional regulation strategies, and shelter students from toxic stress—all priorities of student-centered approaches to learning. Neuroscience research indicates that emotion and learning are biologically interdependent, making it essential for educators to attend to both.

- **Teaching executive functioning:** Student-centered practices give students opportunities to be self-directed and responsible for their own learning, which requires executive functioning skills such as goal setting, planning, and monitoring progress. Research shows that these crucial skills are still developing in teenagers, as the prefrontal cortex is still maturing in adolescence. Educators can support this development by explicitly teaching metacognitive skills of "learning how to learn," including how to set appropriate goals, track progress toward them, appropriately adjust learning strategies, and accurately assess outcomes. When students first begin learning these skills, educators can provide a good amount of targeted support or scaffolding.

CHALLENGES AND FUTURE DIRECTIONS

To benefit fully from research in mind, brain and education, the education system has to build a stronger infrastructure to support interactions between researchers and practitioners. Without this infrastructure, educators' practices can be outdated or driven by ideology rather than evidence, and researchers' studies can be virtually irrelevant to practice. A related challenge is that implementing student-centered learning requires extensive professional development for educators, who need to be skilled in understanding research, using multiple forms of pedagogy, effectively differentiating instruction, carrying out formative assessments, and connecting with community members. A key solution to these issues is to build a network of research schools, which are living schools that partner with universities to carry out practical research, train educators, and disseminate useable knowledge.[81] This network of research schools can provide a fundamental infrastructure to connect research and practice in education.

A second major challenge of student-centered learning approaches arises from evidence that suggests that students follow different learning pathways: a system that treats students differently risks creating further inequity. If the system is not regulated properly, it could lead to unintentional tracking or widening of the achievement gap. In particular, much more mind, brain, and education research is needed on education of underserved youth.

Research in mind, brain, and education suggests that student-centered learning approaches could lead to a more effective and equitable education system, but the challenges just noted, as well as others, must be dealt with before such practices can be effectively and holistically implemented. In reference to progress in education, Howard Gardner notes, "This task may take one hundred years or more; but as a French military leader once famously remarked when facing an especially daunting task, 'In that case, we had better begin today.'"[82]

CHAPTER 7

Prioritizing Motivation and Engagement

Eric Toshalis and Michael J. Nakkula

IF YOU SPEND TIME in middle and high school classrooms, you are likely to realize that teachers work exceedingly hard to motivate and engage their students, to convince them that the day's lessons are worthy of their attention and effort. Using strategies ranging from inspiration to coercion, teachers are forever attempting to persuade students to participate meaningfully in class activities and to propel them to achieve. When these techniques succeed, classrooms come alive with exploration, discovery, and learning. When they fall short, students tune out, disengage, and learn little.

Figuring out what motivates individual students and engages them in school is as important as it is challenging. Indeed, this observation underscores why student-centered approaches to learning can be so powerful. Practitioners, scholars, and policymakers all agree that the chances of students' academic success are enhanced greatly when they are motivated enough to achieve and adequately engaged in classroom learning.

However, today's teachers confront large classes, fast-paced academic calendars, and standardized assessments all of which create pressures to lump all students together and "teach to the middle" as if all students' motivations and desires were the same.[1] The contemporary national dialogue about how to reform our schools is often guided by assumptions that are out of sync with what we know about how students learn and why they choose to do so. Concerned about how to balance standardized mandates with the unique needs of each student, teachers rightfully wonder how to: understand the wide variety of their students' motivations; address their different ways of engaging; respond when students are not motivated or engaged; and provide growth opportunities for everyone in the classroom. To help educators focus their efforts on how to engage and motivate each and every student in large, diverse classrooms, we provide here a tour through cutting-edge and enduring research on achievement motivation and school engagement. We highlight both the general concepts and specific strategies that promote academic achievement and discuss the implications for student-centered practices. In the end, readers will recognize that schools have many powerful, student-centered tools at their disposal to inspire all kinds of students, increase their learning, and raise their achievement.

Some of the major findings include:

- Research shows that both intelligence and motivation are malleable and highly context dependent. Helping students understand that they can acquire new skills and improve existing skills through effort, regardless of past achievement, increases their motivation to try.
- Tracking students based on perceived intelligence or motivation can be harmful. Separating "less intelligent" or "unmotivated" youth from their higher-achieving peers will likely exacerbate existing motivational dispositions and intellectual capacities.
- Many students have difficulty engaging in school, even when they feel motivated. For these students, it may be necessary to teach

self-regulation skills to help them stay on task, set goals, monitor their learning, ignore distractions, and change strategies as needed.

- General praise can in fact be demotivating. Instead, teachers should link approval to specific skills or achievements and use it to foster students' self-determination and persistence.

- Providing students with opportunities for choice, control, and collaboration are potent strategies for increasing academic achievement. Young people are likely to be more motivated and engaged in an activity when they feel they have a voice in how it is conducted and a choice in how it concludes.

A DYNAMIC RELATIONSHIP

Motivation, engagement, and student voice are fundamentally interrelated—as depicted in figure 7.1—and all can contribute in some way to an individual's ability and desire to learn. Each construct represents various experiences of human emotion or thought, behavior or action, and expression and influence. Each contributes to and can be an outcome of the others. However, engagement plays a distinctive role in that it is the only absolute prerequisite for learning, as the figure illustrates. A student simply cannot learn without being engaged.

Consider an example of how the concepts connect and reconnect: one can be motivated to learn through feelings of inspiration or fear. That motivation can result in or be a product of opportunities to engage deeply in school, which in turn can create or be a result of students voicing their opinions on key aspects of their educational interests. As a result of this engagement, students move from being motivated to actively learning. When such chains of events evolve over moments or months, students come to think differently about their educational possibilities, both positively and negatively. Students change their behavior depending on whether these thoughts are reinforced or contradicted, and their engagement in school may increase or decrease as a result.

FIGURE 7-1   The dynamic relationships of motivation, engagement, and student voice

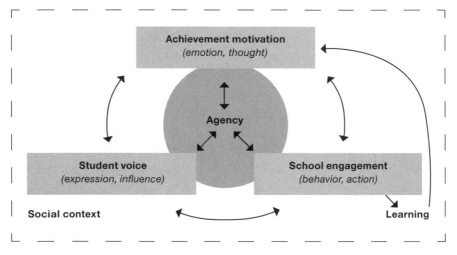

To put this very complex matter in the simplest terms, students have to want it (motivation) in order to stick with it (engagement). They have to stick with it (engagement) in order to learn it. And whether they want it or stick with it is greatly influenced by their level of control over the learning activity and their ability to express their desires about how and what they learn (student voice).

Human Agency

When we look inside middle and high school classrooms, we find adolescents striving and struggling to make an authentic life for themselves, a life that makes sense to them, in their world. Research on motivation, engagement, and student voice frequently addresses this struggle because the individual adolescent's desire for authenticity directly involves goals, hopes, desires, identities, behaviors, and expressions that are as important to academic success as they are to psychosocial well-being. Consequently, our perspective on the literature addressing these three phenomena that share a common basis central to student-centered approaches to learning: the experience of human agency.

As figure 7.1 illustrates, two other factors play key roles in each student's level of motivation and engagement: individual agency and social context. In using the term *agency,* we are attempting to capture the individual's capacity to act in a way that produces desired change. Note the importance of desire in this definition. We are motivated by desire; we engage out of a desire to do so; and, if fortunate enough, we can voice our desired wishes and intentions. Desire is a powerful human instinct, and it is very much at the center of the literature we address here. If education is, at least in part, intended to help students effectively act on their strongest interests and deepest desires, then we need a clearer understanding of how to cultivate their sense of agency.

Social Context

Also affecting the ways that motivation, engagement, and student voice interact is the student's social environment: family, peers, culture, community, resources, and supports. This context can greatly influence the level of motivation students possess, the extent of engagement they commit to academic activity, and the degree to which they feel they have a voice in any of it. As discussed in chapter 5, a student's environment interacts with her ability to learn in a multitude of ways that are observable even at a neurological level. Given its pervasiveness, a student's social context envelopes his or her whole motivation-engagement-agency-learning processes, as depicted in figure 7.1. Conceived in this way, the individual's capacity to act in a way that produces desired change is not just about a person's ability; it is also about the extent to which an environment will *allow* that person to move in her/his desired direction. Social context and agency are therefore always mutually interdependent.

ACHIEVEMENT MOTIVATION

Motivation is generally understood as the driving force behind all of a person's actions. A student's achievement motivation is the emotional will, interest, or desire to pursue school-based educational experiences. Decades of research show that achievement and motivation are inextricably linked. However, no single motivational pathway guarantees academic achievement. Each student is a unique blend of individual interests, backgrounds, stories, and needs. Each is motivated in different ways at different times. Rewards and punishments may temporarily convince some youth to increase their effort (more on the downsides to this approach later), while greater autonomy or more peer interaction may be more effective motivators for others. To meet the challenge of reaching every student in today's diverse classrooms, customized teaching approaches that differentiate instruction tend to work better than one-size-fits-all techniques.

Achievement motivation has been one of the more comprehensively researched areas of student learning, and the theory is nothing if not complex. Research supports a nuanced understanding of motivation: students exist within a dynamic ecology; it shapes them, while they also shape it. As shown in figure 7.1, it is important to think of the factors affecting motivation less as linear, input-output models and more as interacting mechanisms. Knowing individual students well enough to see how this web of causality—including engagement and student voice, agency and social context—motivates them to achieve is crucial to teaching that student well. At their core, this is what student-centered approaches to learning are all about.

Motivation and Social Context

Some students enter school motivated and ready to learn, but many do not. A significant body of research traces individual and environmental factors to determine what contributes to the wide variance in levels of motivation.[2] Because social factors typically exert a powerful influence on an individual's desire to make an effort in school, it is an oversimplification to reduce analyses to either individual or environmental factors. One way to think of this dynamic is to consider the many different pathways students take to learning at school. The individual and the environment interact in a complex dynamic as students from different social contexts take different routes toward achievement depending on their social context and their personal proclivities. Family, neighborhood, friends, diet, culture, and social location all influence which way those pathways bend and what is experienced along the way to learning. Each student arrives at a specific lesson on a specific day with a unique perspective and set of experiences informing how she will orient herself toward the activity. To reach each student, educators need to understand what they can about the varied social, economic, and cultural contexts of their students and how these contexts influence students' effort in the classroom.

Students attending schools that have consistently supported academic achievement, instilled the joy of learning, and modeled the benefits of school success possess a clear advantage over peers without these positive experiences. We might think of these young people as being "premotivated" to achieve. These students may have observed that school works well for people they know and trust; have experienced support and encouragement from family, teachers, and school leaders; feel safe when attending school; associate what they learn in class with future success; and feel welcomed and validated by adults and peers at school. More often than not, these students' cultures, beliefs, and backgrounds are represented in their school's staff and in its curricula, behavioral expectations, and institutional values—conditions that reinforce positive associations with school, affirm self-images, and expand their sense of future opportunities.

Other students enter school with a markedly different outlook. Their past school experiences and other social environments create conditions that can marginalize and mark them as different or "other" on account of their race, linguistic heritage, immigration status, socioeconomic status, sexuality, or other cultural factors working alone or in combination. Setting foot in school, such students may confront a context in which faculty and staff rarely look or speak like they do, curricula seldom reflect their ways of knowing or their people's history, behavioral expectations do not respect their ways of interacting, and the espoused or implicit values of the school may conflict with what they have learned at home. For students like these, the predisposition to be unmotivated and to disengage from teacher-directed activity may be strong.

To create truly student-centered learning opportunities—especially for students whose school experiences have been more negative than positive—it is crucial that teachers learn what might be motivating an individual's failure and how that student's context shapes the emergence of that behavior. For students premotivated to achieve, the need for teachers to draw them into lessons, convince them of an activity's value, or inspire them to do their best is low because they are already predisposed to accepting the validity of the curriculum, the authority of the teacher, and the importance of compliance. However, students who start school feeling alienated and marginalized may wait for educators to draw them in—to make them feel invited, needed, interested, and even inspired—before they will be motivated enough to participate in class. For these students, engagement may need to precede motivation.

Fortunately, motivation is malleable. A repeated finding from research on motivation is that context shapes but does not determine academic outcomes.[3] This is why motivation is better understood as an alterable state than a permanent trait. For example, students who are motivated in a particular class because they believe they are successful in it may then use these beliefs to orient themselves to learn in a different class. Such beliefs can be transferable even though the skills learned in the particular subject may not be.[4]

Since motivation emerges as the individual interacts with the environment, when the individual or the environment changes, so too does motivation. This ongoing dynamic highlights a key point for educators: given that achievement motivation is malleable, it is highly problematic to use it as a category to sort or track students. Grouping the so-called unmotivated students together and sequestering them from the supposedly motivated students is likely to exacerbate existing motivational dispositions. A more student-centered approach would be to ascertain what motivates individual students to achieve in a particular class, and then enlist the students' help in identifying other factors that might elevate their motivation. These factors may include changes to the environment and/or changes to the individual's beliefs and behaviors.

For learning to be truly student centered, classroom activities and teacher-student relationships must attend to the cultural and political contexts in which that learning occurs. Instead of trying to teach in a vacuum by shutting out influences from the world outside, teachers can breathe life into lessons and elevate student motivation by integrating individual, neighborhood, regional, and world circumstances that can make the content areas feel real. If this is done in a way that allows each student to recognize that the curriculum (and the teacher) represents him or her, the student's motivation to achieve will align with his motivation to be himself, leading to a truly student-centered learning experience.

Motivation and Individual Beliefs

The relationship between student beliefs and achievement motivation has been a rich topic of investigation in recent decades, and many discoveries hold important implications for classroom educators. To understand how individual beliefs and motivation interact, researchers often examine students' views of intelligence and how they believe it is attained. Contrary to long-held views, researchers now largely agree that intelligence is not a fixed trait determined at birth.[5] Rather, the consensus is "that even though there may be individual differences in biological aptitudes for learning certain kinds of things (music, social skills, and so on), most of functional intelligence is learnable and hence also teachable."[6]

Guided by teachers or parents familiar with this idea, students often come to believe that their intelligence is a dynamic phenomenon, something they can change incrementally depending on how hard they work at something and how well they are supported in doing it. Studies by Stanford psychologist Carol Dweck and others have shown that if a particular student believes intelligence is largely a matter of effort, then that student is likely to be more motivated to attempt difficult academic tasks and to persist despite setbacks, confusion, and even failure.[7] However, if a student believes intelligence is a *fixed* entity (i.e., a stable aptitude determined at birth and resistant to external influence), then difficulty with a particular activity (e.g., math) is more likely to be interpreted as evidence of lack of intelligence in that domain (e.g., "I'm just stupid at math"). Students with these beliefs frequently expect less of themselves, underrate the importance of effort, and overrate how much help they need from others.[8]

This research informs how teachers should and should not use praise to motivate students—a practical problem facing every teacher and affecting every student in every classroom. To be student centered and conversant with research on motivation is to realize that blanket statements about any student's inherent smartness may actually function as a disincentive. Time and again, we have seen that when faced with individual students who seem frustrated or confused, perform below capabilities, or lack confidence, the teacher will tell them that they are "smart." The presumption is that a student who believes this will not be intimidated by new academic challenges.[9] However, if these students' internal appraisals of their own "smartness" do not match the teacher's encouraging label, they may come to a discouraging conclusion: they simply are not smart enough, or the teacher does not understand them and requesting further help will do no good.

What this research on motivation and intelligence beliefs shows us is that a crucial component of being student centered is to help young people learn to persist, to associate their achievement with their effort, not their smartness. This means refraining from the use of hollow praise about intelligence and instead reinforcing the belief that trying will produce increases in proficiency. Accordingly, praise is best applied when it is specific to a skill or talent the student is developing. "Your writing has really improved, Maria. I can see your hard work paying off here." "Abdul, your algebra test scores have gone up quite a bit in the last several weeks. Have you been studying more?" Additionally, asking students to provide their own appraisals of their work will help them formulate their own beliefs about their success and, over time, rely on their own internally generated sense of accomplishment to motivate future work.[10]

Motivation and Expectations of Success

From the activities children play at recess, to the topic a student chooses for a class report, to the careers we select as adults, we decide to participate in arenas about which we care most deeply and in which we believe we will do well. This idea is at the core of a sub-field of motivation research called *expectancy-value theory*, which argues that we are motivated to devote energy to those activities in which we expect to succeed, and we subsequently tend to value those activities over others.

Throughout the school day, students routinely calculate their chances of success by considering a host of variables that they believe will affect their ability to achieve.[11] Some of those are internally assessed (e.g., their skill level), and others are outward looking (e.g., the extent to which circumstances will support their potential to do well). This has enormous implications for the classroom because a teacher's encouragement and management of the learning community greatly influence students' calculations of probable success. Students also routinely conduct a sort of cost-benefit analysis when asked to complete an academic task, by surveying competing demands and desires and then directing attention and energy toward those that offer the greatest return. It is a complex calculation that weighs impulse control and delayed gratification along with the activity's relevance to the student's current and future goals. Once again, there is a lot going on in the mind of the learner!

When it comes to evaluating their own skills in a particular domain (e.g., math, language arts, sports), one thing we know from research is that students' perceived competence is as much a matter of belief as it is of performance. If students believe they will do well at something, they tend to do so and will also tend to choose it over other opportunities where that belief may not be as strong. This is true even when students have experienced difficulty with that activity in the past. Opportunities for success help build students' resiliency, which guards against debilitating frustrations that might otherwise diminish their performance in that domain in the future.

As noted, multiple factors affect students' beliefs about their own intelligence and abilities. The same is true for student expectations of success. One particularly pernicious influence is the impact of racial and ethnic stereotypes. Immersed in cultural stereotypes about which group is expected to do better than others in this domain or that one, students forever confront messages about expectations.[12] When those messages are internalized such that self-evaluations or beliefs about inherent competencies begin to reflect the stereotypes, they can be difficult to undo even in the face of contrary evidence. Additionally, students face the possibility that their individual performance may confirm a collective negative stereotype, which in turn produces performance anxiety. This "stereotype threat" makes it difficult to devote full attention to learning. It affects not only competence beliefs but also motivation levels and identification with school.[13]

Similarly, researchers have identified the prevalence of what University of Texas professor Angela Valenzuela calls *subtractive schooling* in which educators require many youth to check their identities, cultures, languages, and values at the door in order to succeed.[14] In her research and in many other studies that followed it, students reported feeling that to be taken seriously and meet the academic expectations of teachers, administrators, and many of their peers, they had to act "normal" which required them to "subtract" from their identities the very aspects that made them unique—the accent with which they speak English; the clothes, makeup, or hairstyles they wear; or even the way they interact with peers.[15] This practice of subtractive schooling is understood to cause students to lose motivation to achieve, to disengage from school, to diminish expectations for later success in life, and to fracture identities into mutually exclusive academic and authentic halves.

In this sense, educators' cultural expectations can distort students' pathways to learning, which in turn distorts those students' competence beliefs and influence their academic achievement in ways that reinforce stereotypical beliefs about minoritized students' capacities for success in school. While this process may seem like a vicious cycle, it is crucial to recognize that each step is susceptible to interventions that can shift beliefs and assumptions toward more positive and productive ends. Teachers could not be better positioned to affect that process positively, and student centered approaches are ideally suited to the task.

ENGAGEMENT AND STUDENT-CENTERED LEARNING

Student engagement is generally understood to be the primary mechanism that enables motivational processes to contribute to learning and development.[16] Stated another way, students who are not engaged are not going to learn. Engaging is what students do when they move from being motivated to actively learning. We define engagement here as the range of activities a learner employs to generate—sometimes consciously, other times unconsciously—the interest, focus, and attention required to build new knowledge or skills. The concept is generally understood as an umbrella for an array of behaviors, and the research literature is replete with debates about which of engagement's subcomponents possess the most explanatory power. However, there is overall agreement that the key aspects of school engagement are academic, behavioral, cognitive, and psychological engagement. (See "The Subdimensions of School Engagement.") Knowing that engagement behaviors contain each of these elements will be useful when considering how to respond to students in a student-centered way.

As depicted earlier in figure 7.1, engagement plays a critical role in the learner's transition from the thinking and feeling of motivation to the growing and connecting that occurs in all learning. Consequently, researchers have spent decades analyzing the effects of engagement, how it functions, and how best to facilitate it in schools. Engagement consistently has been found to be a robust predictor of student performance and behavior in the classroom,[18] an antidote to student alienation,[19] and a precursor to long-term academic achievement and eventual graduation.[20] Students engaged in school are more likely to earn higher grades[21] and test scores,[22] have better attendance,[23] and have lower dropout rates.[24] And students who decide to engage in one context find it easier, more pleasurable, and more desirable to engage further in that context (and possibly others) at a later time.[25]

In contrast, students who demonstrate low levels of engagement are more likely to suffer long-term adverse consequences that include disruptive

THE SUBDIMENSIONS OF SCHOOL ENGAGEMENT

Researchers have identified multiple subdimensions that combine in various ways to produce behaviors teachers would commonly recognize as engagement:[17]

- *Academic engagement:* Time on task, problems attempted, credits earned toward graduation, homework completion
- *Behavioral engagement:* Attendance, classroom participation, question posing and question answering, extracurricular involvement
- *Cognitive engagement:* Self-regulation, learning goals, perceived relevance of schoolwork to future endeavors, value of the knowledge or skill to be learned
- *Psychological engagement:* Feelings of identification or belonging, relationships with teachers and peers, experiences of autonomy

These four areas are largely accepted as apt descriptors of engagement, although they may be named or subdivided differently.

behavior in class, absenteeism, and withdrawing from school.[26] Because of this, engagement is considered a primary factor in understanding and predicting dropout. In recognition of the contextual factors that compel students to disengage to the extent that they no longer attend school, many researchers are increasingly calling the dropout phenomenon the "push-out" problem.[27] This renaming underscores how important it is to consider engagement as a relational event rather that something that either the teacher or the student controls in isolation.

Student engagement may also serve as a critical social signal that teachers can use to elevate the investment of energy in academic work. Scanning the classroom to see if their efforts are producing success in their students, teachers are ever on the lookout for signs that students are engaging in the activities the teachers have constructed for them. When students demonstrate their engagement through on-task behaviors, questions, or completed work, they elicit reciprocal engaging reactions from teachers. In fact, research has demonstrated that when students are engaged, their teachers tend to provide them with more motivational support and assistance.[28] The more students experience rewards and satisfactions associated with their engagement, and the more their contexts and internal processes support the continuation of that engagement, the more they will tend to choose actions that lead to positive academic, social, and emotional results. Appleton and his colleagues described this cycle as a "rich-get-richer" pattern: those who engage will receive encouraging feedback, which will lead to further increased engagement.[29] This explanation may help to explain some of the racial, socioeconomic, linguistic, sexual, and gender disparities in achievement. This is because those students whose pathways to learning often lead to alienation and marginalization may present a less engaged set of behaviors, and if the teacher is ineffective at recognizing or reversing this trend, opportunities to build ever more engaging interactions may be lost. It is crucial, therefore, that teachers engage students strategically rather than instinctively, that they recognize the varying pathways students take to learning and devote resources to enhancing rather than undermining equity.

Engagement is a decisive turning point in a web of causality, as illustrated in figure 7.1, that links individual students' experiences to their behaviors in schools and beyond. While the social context sets the stage for student decision making and provides unique pathways to learning that depend on family, peers, culture, life events, and teachers, the teacher's engagement of the student and the student's engagement with the activity are where possibilities for learning are most enhanced or squandered. Contexts that combine structure, support, and experiences of autonomy, in which guided exploration and safe experimentation can occur, are likely to promote a balanced sense of independence and rootedness in even the most disengaged students.

These internal and external forces are forever interacting, and the decision to engage occurs within that social/psychological interactivity. If students' experiences preceding engagement are mostly encouraging and positive, they will tend to make the decision to engage. If their experiences have been frustrating or harmful, they may tend to disengage. The more students experience satisfactions associated with engagement, and the more their contexts and internal processes support the continuation of that engagement, the more they will tend to choose actions that lead to positive academic, social, and emotional outcomes.

This cycle of engagement combines social contexts and internal processes in ways that can strengthen or weaken the motivation to achieve depending on the quality of the experiences in that cycle. As we will see, the ability to positively affect a student's decision to engage is an essential aspect of student-centered practices.

Self-Regulation Leads to Engagement

Self-regulation theory provides an especially student-centered perspective on the various dimensions of engagement. Concerned with what students do to generate and sustain their engagement, research into self-regulation processes typically begins with the recognition that students are active participants in their own learning which echoes constructivists' observations that we build rather than absorb knowledge. To be self-regulated is to be goal-directed, to demonstrate control over one's focus, and to take responsibility for one's effort when engaged in learning activity.

Cognitively, "self-regulated learners plan, set goals, organize, self-monitor, and self-evaluate at various points during the process [of building new knowledge or skills]. These processes enable [students] to be self aware, knowledgeable, and decisive in their approach to learning."[30] From the teacher's perspective, self-regulated learners tend to be self-starters who show effort and persistence during learning, who "seek out advice, information, and places where they are most likely to learn."[31]

Self-regulated learners are capable of monitoring the effectiveness of their learning strategies and changing their behavior as needed. For example, a student who is reading a short story realizes he has lost concentration in the last several paragraphs; he asks himself what those paragraphs were about and, coming up with nothing, reminds himself to reread the portions he glossed over. In this case, he has regulated his own learning to better promote his understanding of the content, and he has done so without any interventions from the teacher.

Self-regulation is also a social phenomenon that can shape collective engagement. Group work can be an exercise in considering others' levels of engagement and then taking responsibility for one's own role in influencing the group. Successful groups become "metacognitively aware that they [need] to regroup, monitor carefully what [is] going on in the group, and frequently go back to the instructions so that the focus and structure of the task [are] clear to all the group members."[32] Teachers who are effective at designing and implementing cooperative learning activities are often quite skilled at modeling and reinforcing self-regulation to achieve pro-social outcomes such as these.

Despite all this, the reader might ask: "Why do students need to regulate their engagement at all? Shouldn't they always be ready and eager to learn?" An honest appraisal of our own self-regulating histories will indicate that we all struggle to stay focused, remain on task, and do the hard work of learning new things. For example, have you read this entire chapter in a single sitting, essentially thinking only of what it says and little else for the entire time? If so, that behavior is far more atypical than that of the learner who gets distracted or conjures tangents that are explored for a brief while, then returns to the text and the thinking required to make sense of it later. The point in analyzing self-regulation is not to find new ways of shaming the learner for failing to complete a task unceasingly without distraction; rather, it is to see how that learner regulates her or his attention and manages disruption. Student-centered approaches that target the bolstering of self-regulatory skills can help youth learn how to "stick with it" as they confront challenging material.

What teachers need to recognize is that students have to decide to learn first, then muster the necessary techniques to keep at it until they make progress. Since learning typically requires time, vigilance, and effort, all learners need to find ways to sustain it. Clearly, students learn best when they exercise high degrees of self-regulation. That said, it is important for the teacher to recognize that self-regulation is learned and therefore depends on supportive contexts and proper scaffolding. Seeing how others successfully self-regulate and being shown specific techniques to enhance one's capacity to maintain focus can help the struggling self-regulator develop the skills necessary to succeed, especially in distracting environments or in activities where the learner has little experience.

What might *motivate* the learner to self-regulate? Research suggests that self-regulation flourishes when students are motivated by a sense of competence in a specific domain and perhaps in general.[33] When students feel confident they can succeed, they tend to marshal the techniques they need to get the job done. Conversely, when students imagine they will not be able to accomplish a task or goal, they more easily surrender to distractions, barriers, excuses, and frustration. As we have seen in the self-efficacy research described above, students are constantly rating their chances of success by judging their own level of performance capacity relative to others as well as features of the environment that may affect their odds of succeeding. This analysis produces in students a temporary and malleable verdict about their capacity to do well, and that verdict then shapes their use of the available strategies. Self-regulation is therefore the product of the student's motivations, self-appraisals, environmental evaluations, and level of skill in staying focused.

In any effort to elevate motivation and engagement in student-centered learning contexts, the good news is that self-regulation is among the more teachable skill sets we have. It is learned and developed in relationship to others and to one's environment, so that given the proper supports, some students build an impressive toolbox of self-regulatory strategies that enables them to stay focused and build knowledge and skills in both academic and nonacademic domains. Surveying dozens of studies, the educational psychologist Monique Boekaerts lists an assortment of these self-regulated learning strategies: regulating attention, monitoring content, eliciting content, planning ahead, self-praising, help-seeking, task (re)structuring, self-consequating, and dealing with distracters.[34] And educational researcher Barry Zimmerman presents this list: self-evaluation, organization and transformation, goal-setting and planning, information seeking, record keeping, self-monitoring, environmental structuring, giving self-consequences, rehearsing and memorizing, seeking social assistance, and reviewing.[35] Both lists reinforce the observation that students are the primary agents in their own learning, actively selecting from a host of strategies to best orient their minds toward academic work, sustaining that attention in order to build new knowledge, then reflecting on their learning to see how they might improve the next time.

Sometimes students may not have access to enough teachers, mentors, peers, or family members who can demonstrate the self-regulatory strategies that promote engagement and academic success or their lives are too stressful to allow that calmness that is required for productive focus. A lack of developed self-regulatory skills can severely diminish students' academic performance and make it look as though their intelligence or their knowledge base is somehow deficient (and standardized tests clearly benefit those with highly developed self-regulatory skill sets, while they punish those whose attention-generating and focus-sustaining skills are still developing). Mistaking a lack of self-regulatory skills for a lack of intellectual ability can have tragic and highly problematic consequences, especially for students who may be placed in lower-tracked classes based on such judgments. Zimmerman shows how less-skilled self-regulators will have lower levels of both interest in the activity and beliefs about their self-efficacy, which can translate into lower achievement levels.[36]

In a classroom context, students with low self-regulatory skills are often easily distracted: the goals they have set for themselves are too ambiguous to achieve or too remote from the current moment to fulfill. Consequently, these inexperienced self-regulators may be prone to the immediate gratifications associated with off-task peer socialization, trips to the pencil sharpener, and under-the-desk texting. (See also "Turning Down the (Digital) Noise.") These students typically avoid self-evaluation, but if pressed they are more likely to attribute their lack of achievement to aptitude rather than the choice of strategies or the effort they expended. If the educators in

TURNING DOWN THE (DIGITAL) NOISE

Self-regulation is arguably more important today than ever before. With the daily deluge of media, the glut of information at our fingertips, and the ubiquity of digital devices pumping out music, video, texts, and games, it is no wonder that distractibility is an issue for many youth (and adults).

Recent research has shown that the "noise" of myriad digital distractions threatens productivity and cognitive complexity in learning. Therefore, academic engagement is as much about selective disengagement—unplugging, as it were—as it is about the decision to focus attention and apply effort.

Recent brain research reveals that our brains are indeed capable of doing many things simultaneously, as long as those things do not require much complexity and the costs for making errors are low. However, when the individual attempts to switch rapidly back and forth between competing activities—what we often call *multitasking*—the brain is limited in its capacity to do those activities well. The parts of the prefrontal cortex responsible for controlling impulses, weighing opinions, constructing arguments, making meaning, and solving problems are incredibly complex, but they also are quite slow in comparison with the more primal parts of the brain responsible for quick reactions, unconscious habits, and the "fight or flight" response. When our students (and we) attempt to multitask, we effectively divert cognitive activity from the complex processing regions of the brain to its more reactionary portions, which severely limits the brain's capacity to make nuanced decisions and perceive important details. In short, multitasking hinders the deepest forms of engagement our brains need to learn and express complex things.[37]

If adults do not provide (or enforce) opportunities to reduce distraction in order to help children and adolescents sustain focus, the learner experiences "continuous partial attention," a phenomenon associated with chronic multitasking, which can literally rewire the brain in ways that make higher-order thinking, impulse control, and focus difficult.[38] To access the most sophisticated parts of their brains, students require the elimination of competing disruptions—either through self-generated strategies of regulation or outside restrictions via teacher (and parent) monitoring. For these reasons, the infusion and use of technology in schools need to be monitored judiciously.

When educators and learners can clear away distractions, students' deeper thinking can occur, at which point the ability to concentrate, delve, contrast, question, critique, create, reformulate, and solve can emerge. Helping students to experience their own minds in this way is one of the most powerful contributions we can make to their development and learning.

that student's life too easily believe such evaluations, simple opportunities to enhance self-regulation skills and therefore improve achievement levels can be squandered.

Teaching Students How to Self-regulate

To begin to remedy these discrepancies, teachers may need to know how self-regulation can be developed. Describing Barry Zimmerman's work, Allan Wigfield and Jacquelynne Eccles theorize four developmental steps in building self-regulatory skills:[39]

1. **Observation:** Watching someone who is already skilled at self-regulation
2. **Emulation:** Modeling one's behavior after the expert
3. **Self-control:** Regulating behavior on one's own in relatively simple and structured settings
4. **Self-regulation:** Adapting and controlling one's own behavior under a range of conditions and circumstances

Once learners progress to the fourth stage, they often choose to act in self-regulated ways rather than respond to the demands from others. As a consequence, they are likely to be more easily and more consistently engaged when proper motivations exist. It is important to remember what we noted earlier: no number of available strategies will compensate for the lack of motivation: a person has to want it in order to stick with it.

Given the social nature of teaching and learning, it may be helpful to think of the motivation to self-regulate as *co-regulation*. Teachers, coaches, mentors, and counselors all help students self-regulate in subtle and not-so-subtle ways: "Damian, do you need to sit somewhere else to complete this worksheet so you're not distracted by your friends?" "Sara, how do you plan to organize your time over the next three weeks to make sure you are ready to present your best work?" In these examples, the educator is guiding the student into the development and use of a self-regulatory strategy, one that suggests the *self* in self-regulation may be too individualistic in the classroom context. Students are usually quite receptive to expert guidance when they are motivated to succeed in a domain within the expert's purview.

Similar to our concept of *co-authoring*, in which educators participate in the construction of adolescent identities, co-regulation underscores the necessity to see the learning moment as relational.[40] Applied in a student-centered classroom, collaborative activities are likely to achieve greater benefits than more didactic ones. Modeling followed by joint teacher-student lessons in problem solving rather than individual practice will likely provide greater opportunities for students to observe the teacher's experienced ways of regulating engagement.

Few people have all or even most self-regulation strategies at their disposal. Many students have difficulty engaging even when they want to. For those students especially, it may be necessary to teach self-regulation skills explicitly—to show them how we all manage our engagement in learning activity and to give them a greater assortment of tools the next time they try. To that end, what if middle school educators taught an "Introduction to Your Mind, Part 1" class that is revisited in high school with the companion "Part 2"? What if those classes incorporated insights and activities from learning theory, cognitive science, brain research, and educational psychology to acquaint students with their own brains and the supports and strategies necessary to help them develop? Such an intervention would be pointedly student centered in that it would arm students with the knowledge they need to self-regulate, advocate for themselves, and educate their teachers about the ways they learn best.

THE POWER OF STUDENT VOICE

One of the most powerful tools available to schools to increase motivation, engagement, and academic achievement is helping students feel that they have a stake in their learning. Fostering *student voice*—empowering youth to express their opinions and influence their educational experiences—has been shown repeatedly to play this crucial role. To feel motivated to do something and to become engaged in the activity, youth (like adults) generally need to feel they have a say in how that activity is conducted and an impact on how it concludes. Time and again, research has shown that the more educators give their students choice, control, challenge, and opportunities for collaboration, the more their motivation and engagement are likely to rise. Student voice is profoundly student centered, as it begins and ends with the thoughts, feelings, visions, and actions of students themselves.

It is particularly important for adolescents, who are developing a sense of identity and the ability for complex thinking, to have the chance to impact decision making, particularly those decisions that affect them directly. Research shows that increasing levels of self-determination promote greater integration of students' own sense of purpose, interest, and desire with what may be required of them from outside forces.

Student-centered classrooms that capitalize on the power of self-determination by encouraging student-voice-oriented activity can substantially increase motivation and achievement. Promoting student voice also has been linked to other important educational outcomes, including higher achievement in marginalized student populations, greater classroom participation, decreased behavior problems, better self-reflection in struggling students, and enhanced school reform efforts.

Student Voice Activities

Student voice is a broad term describing a range of activities that can occur in and out of school. It can be understood as expression, performance, and creativity and as co-constructing the teaching/learning dynamic. Paraphrasing Dana Mitra, we use the term *student voice activities* to refer to pedagogies that give youth the opportunity to influence decisions shaping their lives and those of their peers, either in or outside of school settings.[41]

Whereas most curricula and pedagogy seek to change the student in some way, either through the accumulation of new knowledge, the shifting of perspectives, or the alteration of behaviors, student voice activities position students as the agents of change. As described above, agency can be understood as the capacity to act in a way that produces meaningful change in oneself or the environment. Thus, promoting student agency goes hand in hand with fostering student voice, as it does with promoting motivation and engagement (see figure 7.1).

In research and in practice, student voice-oriented activities in classrooms may be represented along a spectrum (see figure 7.2). As one moves across the figure from left to right, students' roles, responsibilities, and decision-making authority grow. On the left side, student voice activity is limited to youth speaking their minds; on the right, students may be directing collective actions of both peers and adults. Activities in the middle areas blend these orientations in ways that recognize students as stakeholders, while providing opportunities for them to collaborate with, but not yet lead others to achieve specific goals. The headings (e.g., *Expression, Consultation*) signify the bulk of what students do at each level. Moving from left to right, student voices are more included, formalized, and empowered. This corresponds to the movement across the bottom ramp of the figure, showing how the expectations and roles of adults gradually change in accordance with students' changing roles on the spectrum.

At the left side of the student voice spectrum, students have opportunities to express themselves, whether sharing opinions, creating art, performing theater, signing petitions, or even publishing op-ed pieces in the local paper. The point is that students get public outlets for their

FIGURE 7-2   The spectrum of student voice oriented activity

Students articulating their perspectives		Students involved as stakeholders		Students directing collective activities
Students as data sources		Students as collaborators		Students as leaders of change

Expression	Consultation	Participation	Partnership	Activism	Leadership
Volunteering opinions, creating art, celebrating, complaining, praising, objecting	Being asked for opinion, providing feedback, serving on a focus group, completing a survey	Attending meetings or events in which decisions are made, frequent inclusion when issues are framed and actions planned	Formalized role in decision making, standard operations require (not just invite) student involvement, adults are trained in how to work collaboratively with youth partners	Identifying problems, generating solutions, organizing responses, agitating and/or educating for change both in and outside of school contexts	(Co-)planning, making decisions and accepting significant responsibility for outcomes, (co-) guiding group processes, (co-) conducting activities

Most student voice activity in schools/classrooms resides at this end of the spectrum.

The need for adults to share authority, demonstrate trust, protect against co-optation, learn from students, and handle disagreement increases from left to right.

Students' influence, responsibility, and decision-making roles increase from left to right.

perspectives. When students are invited to provide feedback on some aspect of their school or community, they are understood to be functioning as consultants. When adults want to know what youth think in order to inform later decision making, they may use surveys, focus groups, or informal conversations to gauge adolescents' views. For example, teachers may ask students to fill out anonymous course evaluations; schools may ask students to participate in surveys or focus group interviews to assess the school climate or seek students' views on a particular aspect of the way things are (or might be) done.

Although students do not exercise decision-making power in these cases, the power to be heard is in itself a departure from normal operating procedures and can help a great deal in making classrooms and schools more student centered. For example, these activities may help lead students to feel they are valued as members of the community. In fact, educational researchers Dana Mitra and Stephen Gross have found, "when students believe that they are valued for their perspectives and respected, they begin to develop a sense of ownership and attachment to the organization in which they are involved."[42] Other researchers have found that when students can talk about their experiences of learning in school and have their accounts taken seriously, they gain not only a stronger sense of membership but also a stronger sense of respect, self-worth, self-as-learner, and agency.[43]

Educators who openly discuss teaching and learning with students and invite them to provide critical feedback on instruction, curricula, assessments, classroom management, and school climate are tapping those students as a resource. As Mitra points out, "Students possess unique knowledge and perspectives about their schools that adults cannot fully replicate [and they] have access to information and relationships that teachers and administrators do not, such as providing a bridge between the school and families reluctant to interact with school personnel, including first-generation immigrant families."[44] In this sense, allowing for youth expression and eliciting their consultation increases student-centered learning because the development of individualized instruction depends on knowing each student's context, needs, interests, and perspectives.

Participation and partnership emerge in the middle of the student voice spectrum as students' influence and responsibility increase. Student voice activities become partnerships when youth have formal and regular opportunities to advocate for changes they desire and then collaborate with adults during implementation. Many studies of successful student voice programs have uncovered a common misconception that an increase in youth leadership means that adults must simply "get out of the way."[45] This is neither true nor desirable. Effective adult-youth partnerships consist of activities in which participants develop a collective vision for their work and distribute meaningful roles for each youth and adult member, with shared responsibility for decisions and shared accountability for group outcomes.[46] Adults still guide and coach these partnerships, but youth are understood to be indispensible rather than auxiliary to the work.

Whether youth serve as researchers,[47] evaluators,[48] or program designers,[49] numerous studies make it clear that partnering with students can greatly enhance the success of school reform efforts and lead to gains in youth development.[50] In fact, one study found that when students are involved in evaluating programs, conducting research as part of school reform efforts, or investigating issues in their communities, they experience growth in identity exploration, self-confidence, social capital, social competencies, civic competencies, research skills, critical thinking skills, and problem-solving skills.[51] It is hard to envision a more positive set of outcomes for a single educational activity.

At the far right of figure 7.2, youth are understood as leaders. Programs that prepare students to lead tend to view youth as problem solvers, with the skills and insights communities require in order to move forward.[52] Appropriate supports and growth opportunities are integrated with incremental increases in influence, responsibility, and decision-making authority as adults and youth work alongside one another to effect change.

When students are leaders, they gain important skills: they convene meetings, direct actions, write proposals, design Web sites, and recruit peers. As with the other forms of student voice, adults are often highly involved as mentors, guides, and resource providers, but the students (eventually) take charge when it comes to making most decisions.

Community-based programs in which students and adults shared governance responsibilities have been found to be effective.[53] When students help lead, youth show deeper commitment to their communities, greater self-confidence, increased ability to take on governance roles and responsibilities, a strengthened sense of organizational commitment, and greater connections to the community. In one study of a school-based program with student voice at its foundation, the skills and community connections the youth formed yielded college recommendations, internship offers, job opportunities, college application advice, speaking engagements, references for employment applications, and financial consultations, leading one youth participant to remark: "Doors I didn't even know existed are now open."[54]

From a developmental perspective, adolescent identity and cognitive development depend on experiences of imitation, experimentation, adaptation, and invention. By trying on different identities in a complex process that integrates messages from family, peers, other adults, culture, and any number of influences, youth construct possibilities for themselves, projections of who they are and believe they will become. Being given opportunities to do constructive work among similarly experimenting peers and caring adults can help adolescents fully appreciate the range of possibilities in front of them, especially when they can shape the environment in which that growth occurs. After all, it is difficult to feel responsible when you have no agency. To have a voice in how an activity is carried out or in how the meaning specific to that activity is constructed can greatly enhance students' motivation to engage precisely because they are allowed to invent their environment as they simultaneously invent themselves.

Educators committed to student-centered learning recognize this by looking for ways to incorporate choice, expression, and self-determination in classroom activity. One objective in doing this is to elevate academic achievement, of course, but another is to immerse students in the possibilities of their own minds, to let them see and feel what they can do with their own thinking when they become motivated and get engaged. This immersion is an end in itself. To be captured by their work—driven if not thrilled by it—can be life-altering for adolescents in search of meaning, identity, and trajectories toward fulfilling adulthood.

Conditions for Success

Currently, most student voice activities in schools consist of less-intensive involvement, in the forms of expression, consultation, and some participation. Increasing partnership, activism, and leadership would motivate more students to make an effort and ultimately succeed.

As clear as the benefits are, implementing effective student voice activities is no easy task. The research is replete with challenges, pitfalls, and ill-conceived strategies too numerous to cover in detail here. Suffice it to say that difficulties can emerge from a variety of situations, among them: the need to alter traditional structures, practices, beliefs, and values to allow student voice to flourish;[55] the dangers of co-opting student voices rather than learning from them;[56] the tricky business of cultivating respectful disagreement between youth and adults;[57] and concerns about time limits, levels of administrative support, teachers losing power, and whether full inclusion of all voices is being achieved.[58]

In each of these cases, the threat of relegating student voice activity to mere tokenism is ever present, which is why, as in all good teaching, a clear set of objectives and a coordinated plan that outlines roles, responsibilities, and re-sources is paramount. To that end, researchers Margaret Libby, Matt Rosen, and Maureen Sedonaen highlight the importance of providing organi-zational pathways for leadership development, the necessity of advance preparation by youth and adults, the need to moderate program intensity depending on the skill level of participants, and the difficulty of sustaining youth-adult partnerships in a resource-scarce environment.[59] Studies like these highlight the extent to which effective student-centered learning is de-pendent on paying attention to structural issues as well as staff preparation.

To learn something deeply, students need to internalize it and make it their own. To be able to use that learning and influence issues that matter to them, students need to participate substantively: they need to practice leading in contexts that provide autonomy, agency, and the personalized attention of caring adults. Therefore, student voice activities revolve around the development and application of individual students' skills, ideas, and connections to others, which make the learning inspired in such programs profoundly student centered.

TEACHER-CENTERED SCHOOLS FOR STUDENT-CENTERED LEARNING

Motivation, engagement, and voice are the trifecta of student-centered learning, but they cannot happen unless three things are deeply understood. First, no single motivational pathway or type of engagement guarantees academic achievement. Each student is a unique blend of individual stories and needs, each differently positioned to have his or her story heard and needs expressed.[60] Second, motivation and engagement vary depending on the student and his or her situation. Some students need engagement to be motivated, while others are motivated regardless of whether the teacher individually engages them. Third, students' psychological connection to school affects motivation levels and participatory behaviors. Feeling welcomed into, included in, and validated by school can profoundly affect a students' capacity to engage, as well as their efforts to achieve.

If we believe that schools too often make students feel anonymous and powerless, disengaged and alienated, then it is crucial that reform efforts seek to ameliorate rather than exacerbate these conditions. Practically speaking, this may mean that those familiar with the research on motivation, engagement, and student voice use their own agency to promote the following simple but powerful lesson: without motivation, there is no push to learn; without engagement there is no way to learn; and without voice, there is no authenticity in the learning. For students to create new knowledge, succeed academically, and develop into healthy adults, they require each of these experiences.

The same may be said for teachers. Student-centered learning is sometimes misunderstood either as pandering to students or as a practice that makes the teacher irrelevant. These notions could not be further from the truth. In many ways, student-centered approaches to learning make the classroom far more rigorous and the teacher all the more indispensible. The practice of recognizing each student's unique set of social pathways and academic abilities and then individualizing classroom activities to match them—even approximately—depends on healthy, well-adjusted, skilled educators who integrate key findings from research into their practices. To teach student-centered learning well, teachers need experiences that mirror those that research suggests they provide for their students. Consequently, to build student-centered classrooms, we need to build schools and school cultures that are teacher centered.

In the end, if we understand teaching to be a creative profession and the classroom to be a learning community invested in building knowledge, then we might best understand teachers as the "chief learners" in classrooms. Experimentation, exploration, investigation—these are the activities the student-centered teacher can share with students. Thus student-centered approaches will open opportunities for teachers to show how they learn, demonstrate how they self-regulate, explain how they are motivated, and illustrate how they make meaning of content. When students gain access to the chief learner's way of motivating, engaging, and expressing him- or herself, they can begin to see how their own thinking, emotions, and experiences shape their learning. Thus, student-centered practices become wholly inclusive because everyone is a student. The rewards of learning and teaching in such an environment are hard to overestimate.

Notes

Introduction

1. We use both the terms *black* and *African American* here, as authors use each in the book, depending on the particular chapter's content focus. *Black* is a more general term to denote people living in the United States who have ancestry in the Caribbean, South America, and Asia, among other places; whereas African American is specific to people of African descent. In addition, the chapter 5 authors use an alternate notation—*Latin@*—to refer to people who are Latino/a. In each case, chapter authors explain their choice of terms.

Chapter 1

1. It is impossible to estimate how many U.S. high schools embrace student-centered learning—and execute it well. Few school districts, including those ranked by some measures as high-performing, appear to have any philosophical bent that could be classified as student-centered approaches at the district level. See B. Levin, A. Datnow, and N. Carrier, *Changing School District Practices: The Students at the Center Series* (Boston: Jobs for the Future, 2012).

2. For more information, see: http://www.bigpicture.org/, www.earlycolleges.org; and http://www.internationalsnps.org/, and http://www.essentialschools.org/.

3. C. Howley, M. Strange, and R. Bickel, "Research About School Size and School Performance in Impoverished Communities," *ERIC Digest* (ED 448 968) (Charleston, WV: ERIC Clearinghouse on Rural Education and Small Schools, 2000).

4. A. Steinberg and L. Allen, *From Large to Small: Strategies for Personalizing the High School* (Boston: Jobs for the Future, for the Northeast and Islands Regional Educational Laboratory at Brown University and the Carnegie Corporation of New York, 2002).

5. Web site Audio and video clips of students and teachers describing their

experiences in student-centered schools and what these elements mean to them can be found at the Students at the Center Web site on the resources page: www .studentsatthecenter.org.

6. D. J. Stipek, "Relationships Matter," *Educational Leadership* 64, no. 1 (2006): 46–49.

7. Quotes from staff and administrators are from interviews conducted by contributors from March 2011 to May 2011.

8. K. Cushman, *Fires in the Bathroom* (New York: New Press, 2003).

9. D. J. Stipek, *Motivation to Learn: From Theory to Practice*, 3rd ed. (Boston: Allyn & Bacon, 1998); J. Passe, *When Students Choose Content: A Guide to Increasing Motivation, Autonomy, and Achievement* (Thousand Oaks, CA: Corwin Press, Inc., 1996); E. L. Deci and R. M. Ryan, *Intrinsic Motivation and Self-determination in Human Behavior* (New York, NY: Plenum, 1985).

10. For more information on the campaign, see: http://www.thinkbeforeyoufrack .org/.

11. M. Davis, "Elaborated Socio-cultural Model of Learning" (paper presented at the Arkansas Symposium for Student Success, Conway, AR, March 30, 2011).

12. P. Alexander, "The Development of Expertise: The Journey from Acclimation to Proficiency," *Educational Researcher* 32, no. 8 (2003): 10–14.

13. In chapter 3, David H. Rose and Jenna W. Gravel explore the potential for technology to facilitate student-centered classrooms in greater detail. Here we focus on how the schools in our study embrace the digital age and use it to deepen their models.

14. T. R. Sizer, *Horace's Compromise* (Boston: Houghton Mifflin, 1984).

15. R. E. Slavin, *Educational Psychology: Theory and Practice*, 7th ed. (Boston: Pearson Education, Inc., 2003).

Chapter 2

1. G. J. Cizek, "An Introduction to Formative Assessment: History, Characteristics, and Challenges," in *Handbook of Formative Assessment*, ed. H. L. Andrade and G. J. Cizek (New York: Routledge, 2010).

2. Ibid.

3. R. Butler and M. Nisan, "Effects of No Feedback, Task-related Comments, and Grades on Intrinsic Motivation and Performance," *Journal of Educational Psychology* 78, no. 3 (1986): 210–216; A. Lipnevich and J. Smith, "Response to Assessment Feedback: The Effects of Grades, Praise, and Source of Information," Research report RR-08-30 (Princeton, NJ: Educational Testing Service, 2008).

4. A. Cimpian et al., "Subtle Linguistic Cues Affect Children's Motivation,"

Psychological Science 18, no. 4 (2007): 314–316.

5. Lipnevich and Smith, "Response to Assessment Feedback."

6. Cizek, "An Introduction to Formative Assessment."

7. M. Perie, S. Marion, and B. Gong, "Moving Toward a Comprehensive Assessment System: A Framework for Considering Interim Assessments," *Educational Measurement* 28, no. 3 (2009): 5–13.

8. H. L. Andrade and A. Valtcheva, "Promoting Learning and Achievement Through Self-assessment," *Theory into Practice* 48, no. 1 (2009): 12–19.

9. B. Zimmerman and D. Schunk, *Handbook of Self-regulation of Learning and Performances* (New York: Routledge, 2011).

10. H. Andrade, Y. Du, and K. Mycek, "Rubric-referenced Self-assessment and Middle School Students' Writing," *Assessment in Education* 17, no. 2 (2010): 199–214.

11. J. A. Ross, A. Hogaboam-Gray, and C. Rolheiser, "Student Self-evaluation in Grade 5–6 Mathematics Effects on Problem-solving Achievement," *Educational Assessment* 8, no. 1 (2002): 43–59.

12. S. R. Lewbel and K. M. Hibbard, "Are Standards and True Learning Compatible?" *Principal Leadership (High School Ed.)* 1, no. 5 (2001): 16–20.

13. N. Duffrin et al., "Transforming Large Introductory Classes into Active Learning Environments," *Journal of Educational Technology Systems* 27, no. 2 (1998): 169–178.

14. B. MacDonald and D. Boud, "The Impact of Self-assessment on Achievement: The Effects of Self-assessment Training on Performance in External Examinations," *Assessment in Education* 10, no. 2 (2003): 343–345.

15. H. L. Andrade and Y. Du, "Student Responses to Criteria-referenced Self-assessment," *Assessment and Evaluation in Higher Education* 32, no. 2 (2007): 159–181.

16. K. L. Topping, "Peers as a Source of Formative Assessment," in *Handbook of Formative Assessment*, ed. H. L. Andrade and G. J. Cizek (New York: Routledge, 2010).

17. Ibid.

18. J. C. Yang, H. W. Ko, and I. L. Chung, "Web-based Interactive Writing Environment: Development and Evaluation," *Educational Technology & Society* 8, no. 2 (2005): 214–229.

19. Topping, "Peers as a Source of Formative Assessment."

20. Ibid.

21. S. Brookhart, "Portfolio Assessment," in *Twenty-First Century Education: A Reference Handbook*, vol. 1, ed. T. L. Good (Thousand Oaks, CA: SAGE, 2008); J. Herman and L. Winters, "Portfolio Research: A Slim Collection," *Educational*

Leadership 52, no. 2 (1994): 48–55.

22. C. Chang and K. Tseng, "Use and Performances of Web-based Portfolio Assessment," *British Journal of Educational Technology* 40, no. 2 (1998): 358–370.

23. http://newtechhigh.org/?page_id=969.

24. http://newtechhigh.org/sean/.

25. C. C. Kulik, J. A. Kulik, and R. L. Bangert-Drowns, "Effectiveness of Mastery Learning Programs: A Meta-analysis," *Review of Educational Research* 60, no. 2 (1990): 265–299.

26. Ibid.

27. M. K. Russell, "Technology-aided Formative Assessment of Learning: New Developments and Applications," in *Handbook of Formative Assessment*, ed. H. L. Andrade and G. J. Cizek (New York: Routledge, 2010).

28. T. Landauer, K. Lochbaum, and S. Dooley, "A New Formative Assessment Technology for Reading and Writing," *Theory into Practice* 48, no. 1 (2009): 44–52.

29. D. Wade-Stein and E. Kintsch, "Summary Street: Interactive Computer Support for Writing," *Cognition and Instruction* 22, no. 3 (2004): 233–262.

30. M. Franzke, E. Kintsch, D. Caccamise, N. Johnson, and S. Dooley, "Summary Street: Computer Support for Comprehension and Writing," *Journal of Educational Computing Research* 33, no. 1 (2005): 53–80.

31. P. Bambrick-Santoyo, "Data in the Driver's Seat," *Educational Leadership* 65, no. 4 (2007): 43–46.

32. J. Davidson, "Exhibitions: Connecting Classroom Assessment with Culminating Demonstrations of Mastery," *Theory into Practice* 48, no. 1 (2009): 36–43.

33. For a video example of an exhibition, see: http://www.edutopia.org/urban-academy.

34. Coalition of Essential Schools, *Measuring Up: Demonstrating the Effectiveness of the Coalition of Essential Schools* (Oakland, CA: Author, 2006).

35. For a more detailed discussion of large-scale assessment improvements through evidence-centered design, instructionally relevant score reports, and context, see H. Andrade, K. Huff, and G. Brooke, *Assessing Learning: The Students at the Center Series* (Boston: Jobs for the Future, 2012).

36. P. Nichols, *A Framework for Developing Assessments that Aid Instructional Decisions*, ACT Research Report 93-1 (Iowa City, IA: American College Testing, 1993); P. Nichols, "A Framework for Developing Cognitively Diagnostic Assessments," *Review of Educational Research* 64, no. 4 (1994): 575–603; National Research Council, *Knowing What Students Know: The Science and Design of Educational Assessment* (Washington, DC: National Academy Press, 2001); J. Pellegrino, "Understanding How Students Learn and Inferring What They Know:

Implications for the Design of Curriculum, Instruction, and Assessment," in *NSF K–12 Mathematics and Science Curriculum and Implementation Centers Conference Proceedings*, ed. M. J. Smith (Washington, DC: National Science Foundation and American Geological Institute, 2002).

37. K. Huff and D. Goodman, "The Demand for Cognitive Diagnostic Assessment," in *Cognitive Diagnostic Assessment for Education*, ed. J. Leighton and M. Gierl (Cambridge, UK: Cambridge University Press, 2007); A. VanderVeen et al., "Developing and Validating Instructionally Relevant Reading Competency Profiles Measured by the Critical Reading Section of the SAT," in *Reading Comprehension Strategies: Theory, Interventions, and Technologies*, ed. D. S. McNamara (Mahwah, NJ: Erlbaum, 2007).

38. A. Beaton and N. Allen, "Chapter 6: Interpreting Scales Through Scale Anchoring," *Journal of Educational and Behavioral Statistics* 17, no. 2 (1992): 191–204.

39. A. Rupp, J. Templin, and R. Henson, *Diagnostic Measurement: Theory, Methods, and Applications* (New York: Guilford Press, 2010).

40. J. Popham, *Transformative Assessment* (Alexandria, VA: Association for Supervision and Curriculum Development, 2008).

41. T. Corcoran, F. A. Mosher, and A. Rogat, *Learning Progressions in Science: An Evidence-based Approach to Reform* (New York: Center on Continuous Instructional Improvement, Teachers College, Columbia University, 2009).

42. M. Heritage et al., "From Evidence to Action: A Seamless Process in Formative Assessment?" *Educational Measurement Issues and Practice* 28, no. 3 (2009): 24–31.

43. A. C. Alonzo, T. Neidorf, and C. W. Anderson, "Using Learning Progressions to Inform Large-Scale Assessment," in *Learning Progressions in Science*, ed. A. C. Alonzo and A. W. Gotwals (Rotterdam, The Netherlands: Sense Publishers, 2012).

44. C. Wylie and D. Wiliam, "Analyzing Diagnostic Items: What Makes a Student Response Interpretable?" (paper presented at the annual meeting of the American Educational Research Association and the National Council on Measurement in Education, Chicago, IL, April 9–13, 2007).

45. Alonzo et al., "Using Learning Progressions."

46. R. Luecht, "From Design to Delivery: Engineering the Mass Production of Complex Performance Assessments" (paper presented at the annual meeting of the National Council on Measurement in Education, New Orleans, LA, April 15, 2002).

Chapter 3

1. Many additional resources including rich video, descriptive models, examples

of learning environments enabled by new technologies, curriculum, and high tech public schools can be found in the original version of this paper on the studentsatthecenter.org website, and on the websites of organizations such as the National Center on Universal Design for Learning (http://www.udlcenter .org/); Edutopia (http://www.edutopia.org/); and the International Association for K–12 Online Learning (http://www.inacol.org/).

2. In chapter 6, Christina Hinton, Kurt W. Fischer, and Catherine Glennon further discuss advances in our understanding of how the brain learns and the applicability to student-centered approaches.

3. C. L. Lopez and H. J. Sullivan, "Effect of Personalization of Instruction Context on the Achievement and Attitudes of Hispanic Students," *Education Technology Research and Development* 40, no. 4 (1992): 5––13; D. C. Miller and R. W. Kulhavy, "Personalizing Sentences and Text," *Contemporary Educational Psychology* 16 (1991): 287–292; K. A. Renninger, L. Ewen, and A. K. Lassher, "Individual Interest as Context in Expository Text and Mathematical Word Problems," *Learning and Instruction* 12 (2002): 467–491.

4. E. T. Bates and L. R. Wiest, "Impact of Personalisation of Mathematical Word Problems on Student Performance," *Mathematics Educator* 14, no. 2 (2004): 17–26; J. P. Wright and C. D. Wright, "Personalised Verbal Problems: An Application of the Language Experience Approach," *Journal of Educational Research* 79, no. 6 (1986): 358–362.

5. It is difficult to demonstrate in print all that the UDL framework offers. In the Web-based version, clicking on a checkpoint brings up an elaboration of its meaning and importance. The Web also has links to practical examples of recommended options and research evidence for their efficacy. Moreover, many examples and resources cannot even be demonstrated in print because they are inherently multimedia, interactive, and "digital." For an interactive version of the guidelines, the research behind each guideline, and multimedia examples of its practice, see: http://www.udlcenter.org/aboutudl/udlguidelines.

6. Access this online at: http://www.udlcenter.org/aboutudl/udlguidelines/ principle2#principle2_g6_c1.

7. Access this online at: http://www.udlcenter.org/research/researchevidence/ checkpoint6_1.

8. The National Council of Teachers of Mathematics' Illuminations is a free online tool that offers a range of virtual manipulatives (objects designed so that a learner can perceive some mathematical concept by manipulating them) that facilitate students' understanding of a variety of math concepts. These virtual manipulatives offer novel ways to present students with new information. See:

http://illuminations.nctm.org/ActivitySearch.aspx.

9. See: http://www.samanimation.com/.

10. See: http://voicethread.com/.

11. See: http://bookbuilder.cast.org/.

12. J. Roschelle et al., *Scaling Up SimCalc Project: Can a Technology Enhanced Curriculum Improve Student Learning of Important Mathematics? (Technical Report 01)* (Menlo Park, CA: SRI International, 2007), 2.

13. Ibid.

14. Ibid., 6.

15. See chapter 6.

16. L. Vygotsky, *Mind in Society: The Development of Higher Psychological Processes* (Cambridge, MA: Harvard University, 1978).

17. C. P. Proctor et al., "Improving Comprehension Online: Effects of Deep Vocabulary Instruction with Bilingual and Monolingual Fifth Graders," *Reading and Writing: An Interdisciplinary Journal 22, no.* 10 (2009): 993–1019.

18. P. Coyne et al., "Literacy by Design: A Universal Design for Learning Approach for Students with Significant Intellectual Disabilities," *Remedial and Special Education* 33, no. 3 (2010): 162–172.

19. Ibid.

20. Additional discussion of technology's role in student-centered assessment can be found in chapter 2.

21. J. P. Gee, "Learning by Design: Good Video Games as Learning Machines," *E-Learning and Digital Media* 2, no. 1 (2005): 5–16.

22. OpenLearningInitiative,"OpenLearningInitiative,"http://oli.web.cmu.edu/openlearning/initiative.

23. M. Lovett, O. Meyer, and C. Thille, "The Open Learning Initiative: Measuring the Effectiveness of the OLI Statistics Course in Accelerating Student Learning," *Journal of Interactive Media in Education,* May 2008, http://jime.open.ac.uk/2008/14.

24. Ibid.

25. Ibid.

26. D. H. Rose, J. W. Gravel, and Y. Domings, *UDL Unplugged: The Role of Technology in UDL.* (Wakefield, MA: CAST, Guilford Press, 2010); CAST, *Universal Design for Learning Guidelines Version 2.0* (Wakefield, MA: Author, 2011).

27. CAST, *Universal Design for Learning Guidelines.*

28. See:http://www.udlcenter.org/aboutudl/udlguidelines/principle3#principle 3_g7.

29. See: http://kids.sandiegozoo.org/animal-cams-videos.

30. M. Prensky, "Digital Natives, Digital Immigrants," *On the Horizon (MCB University Press)* 9, no. 5 (2001): 1–6.

31. See: http://www.epals.com/groups/about/pages/epals-overview.aspx; http://edu .glogster.com/; and http://www.blogger.com.

32. See: http://www.crunchbase.com/company/hoot.

33. J. Jansen, "Use of the Internet in Higher-Income Households," http:// pewinternet.org/Reports/2010/Better-off-households.aspx.

34. L. Robinson, "A Taste for the Necessary: A Bourdieuian Approach to Digital Inequality," *Information, Communication, & Society* 12, no. 4 (2009): 488–507.

35. D. H. Rose and G. Vue, "2020's Learning Landscape: A Retrospective on Dyslexia." *Perspectives on Language and Literacy* 36, no. 1 (2010): 33–37.

36. See: http://www.udlcenter.org/advocacy/referencestoUDL/HEOA.

37. See: U.S. Department of Education, "U.S. Department of Education Funded Centers that Support UDL, " http://www.osepideasthatwork.org/udl/support.asp.

38. See: http://www.bcsc.k12.in.us/site/default.aspx?PageID=1.

39. See: http://www.pearsonschool.com/.

40. See: http://www.7x7.com/tech-gadgets/inkling-reinvents-textbooks-interactive-multimedia-learning-tools-tablet.

41. M. Minow, "Designing Learning for All Learners," in *A Policy Reader in Universal Design for Learning*, ed. D. T. Gordon, J. W. Gravel, and L. A. Shifter (Cambridge, MA: Harvard Education Press, 2009), 5–18.

Chapter 4

1. A. W. Tatum, *Reading for Their Life: (Re)building the Textual Lineages of Black Adolescent Males* (Portsmouth, NH: Heinemann, 2009).

2. S. Neuman, *Educating the Other America: Top Experts Tackle Poverty, Literacy, and Achievement in Our Schools* (Baltimore, MD: Brookes, 2008).

3. D. Hall, E. Cassidy, and H. Stevenson, "Acting 'Tough' in a 'Tough' World: An Examination of Fear Among Urban African American Adolescents," *Journal of African American Psychology* 34, no. 3 (2008): 381–398; D. Swanson, M. Cunningham, and M. B. Spencer, "Black Males' Structural Conditions, Achievement Patterns, Normative Needs, and 'Opportunities,'" *Urban Education* 38, no. 5 (2003): 608–633.

4. N. Duke, P. D. Pearson, L. Strachan, and A. K. Billman, "Essential Elements of Fostering and Teaching Reading Comprehension," in *What Research Has to Say About Reading Instruction, 4th ed.*, ed. S. Samuels and A. Farstrup (Newark, DE: International Reading Association, 2011); S. Graham, "Motivation in African Americans," *Review of Educational Research*, 1994, no. 64: 55–117; J. Guthrie

and A. McRae, "Reading Engagement Among African American and European American Students," in *What Research Has to Say About Reading Instruction*, 4th ed., Samuels and Farstrup.

5. R. Ceballo, V. C. McLoyd, and T. Toyokawa, "The Influence of Neighborhood Quality on Adolescents' Educational Values and School Effort," *Journal of Adolescent Research* 19, no. 6 (2004): 716–739; J. Davis, "Early Schooling and Academic Achievement of African American Males," *Urban Education* 38, no. 5 (2003): 515–537. R. Mickelson and A. Greene, "Connecting Pieces of the Puzzle: Gender Differences in Black Middle School Students' Achievement," *Journal of Negro Education* 75, no. 1 (2006): 34–48.

6. A. Graham and K. Anderson, "'I Have to Be Three Steps Ahead': Academically Gifted African American Male Students in an Urban High School on the Tension Between an Ethnic and Academic Identity," *Urban Review* 40, no. 5 (2008): 472–499; C. Smalls, R. White, T. Chavous, and R. Sellers, "Racial Ideological Beliefs and Racial Discrimination Experiences as Predictors of Academic Engagement Among African American Adolescents," *Journal of African American Psychology* 33, no. 3 (2007): 299–330.

7. N. Henderson and M. Milstein, *Resiliency in Schools: Making It Happen for Students and Educators* (Thousand Oaks, CA: Corwin Press, Inc., 2003); R. Stanton-Salazar and S. Spina, "The Network Orientations of Highly Resilient Urban Minority Youth: A Network-analytic Account of Minority Socialization and its Educational Implications," *Urban Review* 32, no. 3 (2000): 227.

8. E. McHenry, *Forgotten Readers: Recovering the Lost History of African American Literary Societies* (Durham, NC: Duke University Press, 2002).

9. A. W. Randolph, "To Gain and to Lose: The Loving School and the African American Struggle for Education in Columbus, Ohio, 1831–1882," in *The Sage Handbook of African American Education*, ed. L. Tillman (Los Angeles: Sage, 2009).

10. K. Holloway, *Bookmarks: Reading in Black and White* (New Brunswick, NJ: Rutgers University Press, 2006).

11. P. M. Belt-Beyan, *The Emergence of African American Literacy Traditions: Family and Community Efforts in the Nineteenth Century* (Westport, CT: Praeger Publishers, 2004).

12. Tatum, *Reading for Their Life*.

13. M. T. Fisher, *Black Literate Lives* (New York: Routledge, 2009).

14. T. Perry, "Freedom for Literacy and Literacy for Freedom: The African American Philosophy of Education" in *Young, Gifted, and Black: Promoting High Achievement Among African American Students*, ed. T. Perry, C. Steele, and A. Hilliard (Boston: Beacon Press, 2003).

15. L. Hogue, *The African American Male, Writing, and Difference* (New York: State University of New York Press, 2003); D. Mullane, *Crossing the Danger Water: Three Hundred Years of African American Writing* (New York: Anchor Books, 1993); C. Wall, *Worrying the Line: Black Women Writers, Lineage, and Literary Tradition* (Chapel Hill, NC: The University of North Carolina Press, 2005).

16. Mullane, *Crossing the Danger Water.*

17. Tatum, *Reading for Their Life.*

18. A. W. Tatum, "Toward a More Anatomically Complete Model of Literacy Instruction: A Focus on Black Male Adolescents and Texts," *Harvard Educational Review* 78, no. 1 (2008): 155–180.

19. Ibid.

20. This material is adapted from Tatum, "Toward a More Anatomically Complete Model."

21. Tatum, *Reading for Their Life.*

22. A. W. Tatum, "Building the Textual Lineages of African American Male Adolescents," in *Adolescent Literacy*, ed. K. Beers, R. Probst, and L. Rief (Portsmouth, NH: Heinemann, 2007), 81–85.

Chapter 5

1. We use the @ sign to indicate both an "a" and "o" ending (Latina and Latino). The presence of both endings de-centers the patriarchal nature of the Spanish language, where is it customary for groups of males (Latinos) and females (Latinas) to be written in the form that denotes only males (Latinos). We write the term Latin@ with the "a" and "o" intertwined (as opposed to the more commonly used Latina/o), as a sign of solidarity with individuals who identify as lesbian, gay, bisexual, transgender, questioning, and queer (LGBTQ).

We use the term *black*, as opposed to *African American*, to highlight the fact that many blacks living in the United States have ancestry in the Caribbean, South America, and Asia, among other places. As blacks living and attending schools in the United States, they are racialized in similar ways, regardless of country of origin.

2. K. Devlin, *The Math Gene: How Mathematical Thinking Evolved and How Numbers Are Like Gossip* (New York: Basic Books, 2001).

3. J. S. Lipton and E. S. Spelke, "Origins of Number Sense: Large Number Discrimination in Human Infants," *Psychological Science* 14, no. 5 (2003): 396–401.

4. Clearly, there is not a single or universal Latin@ or black experience in mathematics, or in anything else. However, we believe the major forms of marginalization that Latin@ and black youth experience during school in the United

States are similar—related to their being seen as intellectually inferior to white students—and warrant joint examination.

5. R. Baron, D. Tom, and H. M. Cooper, "Social Class, Race and Teacher Expectations," in *Teacher Expectancies,* ed. J.B. Dusek, (Hillsdale, NJ: Lawrence Erlbaum, 1985).

6. L. Bol and R. Q. Berry III, "Secondary Mathematics Teachers' Perceptions of the Achievement Gap," *High School Journal* 88, no. 4 (2005): 32–45.

7. C. M. Steele and J. Aronson, "Stereotype Threat and the Test Performance of Academically Successful African Americans," in *The Black-White Test Score Gap*, ed. C. Jencks and M. Phillips (Washington, DC: Brookings Institution Press, 1998).

8. R. E. Ferguson, "Teachers' Perceptions and Expectations and the Black-White Test Score Gap," *Urban Education* 38, no. 4 (2003): 460–507.

9. D. W. Stinson, "Negotiating the 'White Male Math Myth': African American Male Students and Success in School Mathematics," *Journal for Research in Mathematics Education* 44, no. 1 (2013): 69-99; D. W. Stinson, "Negotiating Sociocultural Discourses: The Counter-storytelling of Academically (and Mathematically) Successful African American Male Students," *American Educational Research Journal* 45, no. 4 (2008): 975–1010; E. O. McGee, "A Model of Mathematical Resilience: Black College Students Negotiating Success in Mathematics and Engineering" (paper presented at the pre-session of the annual meeting of the National Council of Teachers of Mathematics, Washington, DC, 2009); D. T. Rambane and M. C. Mashige, "The Role of Mathematics and Scientific Thought in Africa: A Renaissance Perspective," *International Journal of African Renaissance Studies, Multi-, Inter- and Transdisciplinarity* 2, no. 2 (2007): 183–199.

10. D. B. Martin, "Mathematics Learning and Participation as Racialized Forms of Experience: African American Parents Speak on the Struggle for Mathematics Literacy," *Mathematical Thinking and Learning* 8, no. 3 (2006a): 197–229; D. B. Martin, "Mathematics Learning and Participation in African American Context: The Co-construction of Identity in Two Intersecting Realms of Experience," in *Diversity, Equity, and Access to Mathematical Ideas,* ed. N.S. Nasir and P. Cobb (New York: Teachers College Press, 2006b), 146–158.

11. L. Darling-Hammond et al., *Preparing Teachers for a Changing World: What Teachers Should Learn and Be Able to Do* (San Francisco: John Wiley and Sons, 2005).

12. R. Gutiérrez, "A 'Gap Gazing' Fetish in Mathematics Education? Problematizing Research on the Achievement Gap," *Journal for Research in Mathematics Education* 39, no. 4 (2008): 357–364.

13. P. Daro, "Common Core State Standards in Mathematics" (presentation to the Chicago Lesson Study conference, Chicago, IL, 2011), http://www.mathed leadership.org/docs/events/IN/NCSM11-301_Daro.pdf, 26.

14. Ibid., 23.

15. National Council of Teachers of Mathematics (NCTM), "Equity in Mathematics Education," www.nctm.org/positionstatements.aspx?id=13490.

16. S. Lerman, "The Social Turn in Mathematics Education Research," in *Multiple Perspectives on Mathematics Teaching and Learning,* ed. J. Boaler (Westport, CT: Ablex, 2000).

17. S. Restivo, "Theory of Mind, Social Science, and Mathematical Practice," in *Perspectives on Mathematical Practices: Bringing Together Philosophy of Mathematics, Sociology of Mathematics, and Mathematics Education,* ed. B. van Kerkhove and J. P. van Bendegem (Dordrecht, Netherlands: Springer, 2007), 74.

18. P. Cobb, M. Gresalfi, and L. L. Hodge, "An Interpretive Scheme for Analyzing the Identities that Students Develop in Mathematics Classrooms," *Journal for Research in Mathematics Education* 40, no. 1 (2009): 40–68; Martin, "Mathematics Learning and Participation as Racialized Forms of Experience"; I. Esmonde and J. M. Langer-Osuna, "Power in Numbers: Student Participation in Mathematical Discussions in Heterogeneous Spaces," *Journal for Research in Mathematics Education,* 44, no. 1 (2013): 288–315.

19. M. Bazin, M. Tamez, and Exploratorium Teacher Institute, *Math and Science Across Cultures: Activities and Investigations from the Exploratorium* (New York: The New Press, 2002).

20. R. Eglash, *African Fractals: Modern Computing and Indigenous Design* (New Brunswick, NJ: Rutgers University Press, 1999); R. Eglash, "Transformational Geometry and Iteration in Cornrow Hairstyles," *Culturally Situated Design Tools,* http://csdt.rpi.edu/african/CORNROW_CURVES/index.htm; R. Eglash et al., "Culturally Situated Design Tools: Ethnocomputing from Field Site to Classroom," *Anthropology and Education* 108, no. 2 (2010): 347–362.

21. National Research Council, *Engaging Schools: Fostering High School Students' Motivation to Learn* (Washington, DC: National Academies Press, 2004).

22. M. Civil, "Building on Community Knowledge: An Avenue to Equity in Mathematics Education," in *Improving Access to Mathematics: Diversity and Equity in the Classroom,* ed. N. S. Nasir and P. Cobb (New York: Teachers College Press, 2007); M. Civil, "Everyday Mathematics, Mathematicians' Mathematics, and School Mathematics: Can We Bring Them Together?" in *Everyday and Academic Mathematics in the Classroom, Monograph, No. 11, Journal of Research in Mathematics Education,* ed. M. E. Brenner and J. N. Moschkovich (Reston, VA:

National Council of Teachers of Mathematics, 2002); N. González et al., "Bridging Funds of Distributed Knowledge: Creating Zones of Practices in Mathematics," *Journal of Education for Students Placed at Risk* 6, no. 1–2 (2001): 115–132; L. Moll et al., "Funds of Knowledge for Teaching: A Qualitative Approach to Developing Strategic Connections Between Homes and Classrooms," *Theory into Practice* 31, no. 2 (1992): 132–141.

23. A few examples include: C. Briggs-Hale et al., *After School Mathematics Practices: A Review of Supporting Literature* (Austin, TX: SEDL, 2006); R. E. Fullilove and P. U. Treisman, "Mathematics Achievement Among African American Undergraduates at the University of California, Berkeley: An Evaluation of the Mathematics Workshop Program," *Journal of Negro Education* 59, no. 30 (1990): 463–478.

24. G. G. Joseph, *Crest of the Peacock: Non-European Roots of Mathematics* (Princeton, NJ: Princeton University Press, 2010).

25. B. Barton, "Making Sense in Ethnomathematics: Ethnomathematics Is Making Sense," *Educational Studies in Mathematics* 31, no. 1–2 (1996): 201–233; A. J. Bishop, *Mathematical Enculturation: A Cultural Perspective on Mathematics Education* (Dordrecht, Netherlands: Kluwer Academic Publishers, 1988); G. Knijnik, "Mathematics Education and the Brazilian Landless Movement: Three Different Mathematics in the Context of the Struggle for Social Justice," *Philosophy of Mathematics Education Journal*, 2007, no. 21; Rambane and Mashige, "Mathematics and Scientific Thought in Africa."

26. P. Gerdes, "On Culture, Geometrical Thinking and Mathematics Education," in *Ethnomathematics: Challenging Eurocentrism in Mathematics Education*, ed. A. B. Powell and M. Frankenstein (Albany, NY: State University of New York Press, 1997).

27. C. Zaslavsky, *Math Games & Activities from Around the World* (Chicago, IL: Chicago Review Press, 1998); L. Crane, "African Games of Strategy, a Teaching Manual," in *African Outreach Series 2* (Urbana-Champaign, IL: University of Illinois, 1982), 1–63.

28. G. Knijnik, "'Regimes of Truth' on Adult Peasant Mathematics Education: An Ethno-mathematics Study" (paper presented to the Rome Symposium on the Occasion of the 100th Anniversary of ICMI, 2008); G. Knijnik, "An Ethnomathematics Perspective on Mathematics Education," (paper presented in the Mathematics Education in Contemporary Society Conference, Manchester, UK, 2011).

29. Bishop, *Mathematical Enculturation*.

30. M. Fantinato, "Teachers' Practice Under the Ethnomathematical Perspective: A Study Case in Young and Adult Education" (proceedings of the Fifth

International Mathematics Education and Society Conference, Lisbon, Portugal: Centro de Investigação em Educação/Aalborg, Department of Education, Learning and Philosophy, 2008).

31. A. Begg, "Ethnomathematics: Why, and What Else?" *ZDM* 33, no. 3 (2001): 71–74.

32. J. P. Smith III, "Everyday Mathematical Activity in Automobile Production Work." *Journal for Research in Mathematics Education: Everyday and Academic Mathematics in the Classroom, Monograph 11* (Reston, VA: NCTM, 2002).

33. T. Nunes, A. D. Schliemann, and D. W. Carraher, *Street Mathematics and School Mathematics* (Cambridge, UK: Cambridge University Press, 1993).

34. W. L. Millroy, "An Ethnographic Study of the Mathematical Ideas of a Group of Carpenters." *Journal for Research in Mathematics Education. Monograph No. 5* (Reston, VA: NCTM, 1992); G. B. Saxe, "Candy Selling and Math Learning," *Educational Researcher* 17, no. 6 (1998); G. B. Saxe, *Culture and Cognitive Development: Studies in Mathematical Understanding* (Hillsdale, NJ: Lawrence Erlbaum, 1991); J. Lave, *Cognition in Practice: Mind, Mathematics, and Culture in Everyday Life* (Cambridge, UK: Cambridge University Press, 1988); J. Lave and E. Wenger, *Situated Learning: Legitimate Peripheral Participation* (Cambridge, UK: Cambridge University Press, 1991); J. O. Masingila, "Mathematical Practice in Carpet Laying," *Anthropology and Education Quarterly* 25, No. 4 (1994): 430–462; T. N. Carraher, D. W. Carraher, A. D. Schliemann, "Mathematics in the Streets and in Schools." *British Journal of Developmental Psychology*, 1985, no. 3: 259–268; A. D. Schliemann, "Mathematics Among Carpenters and Carpenters' Apprentices: Implications for School Teaching," in *Mathematics for All (Science and Technology Education Document Series No. 20)*, ed. P. Damerow, M. Dunckley, B. Nebres, and B. Werry (Paris: UNESCO, 1985).

35. D. Carraher and A. Schliemann, "Is Everyday Mathematics Truly Relevant to Mathematics Education?" *Journal for Research in Mathematics Education*, 2002, no. 11: 87–115.

36. L. Resnick, "Learning In and Out of School," *Educational Researcher* 16, no. 9 (1987): 13–20.

37. A. Lesgold et al., "Expertise in a Complex Skill: Diagnosing X-rays," in *The Nature of Expertise*, ed. M. T. H. Chi, R. Glaser, and M. J. Farr (Mahwah, NJ: Lawrence Erlbaum, 1988); C. Hoyles, R. Noss, and S. Pozzi, "Proportional Reasoning in Nursing Practice," *Journal for Research in Mathematics Education* 32, no. 1 (2001): 4–27.

38. Lave, *Cognition in Practice*; Lave and Wenger, *Situated Learning*; Masingila, "Carpet Laying."

39. J. O. Masingila, "Examining Students' Perceptions of their Everyday Mathematics Practice," *Everyday and Academic Mathematics in the Classroom, Monograph*, vol. 11, *Journal for Research in Mathematics Education* (Reston, VA: NCTM, 2002); N. S. Nasir, "Identity, Goals, and Learning," *Mathematical Thinking and Learning* 4, no. 2–3 (2002): 211–245; N. S. Nasir, "'Points Ain't Everything': Emergent Goals and Average and Percent Understandings in the Play of Basketball Among African-American Students," *Anthropology and Education Quarterly* 31, no. 3 (2000): 283–305; N. S. Nasir, V. Hand, and E. Taylor, "Culture and Mathematics in School: Boundaries between 'Cultural' and 'Domain' Knowledge in the Mathematics Classroom and Beyond," *Review of Research in Education* 32, no. 1 (2008): 187–240; N. S. Nasir and M. M. de Royston, "Power, Identity, and Mathematical Practices Outside and Inside of School," *Journal for Research in Mathematics Education* 44, no. 1 (2013): 264–287.

40. G. de Abreu, "Learning Mathematics in and outside School: Two Views on Situated Learning," in *Learning Sites: Social and Technological Resources for Learning*, ed. J. Bliss, R. Salio, and P. Light (Oxford: Elsevier Science, 1999); G. de Abreu and T. Cline, "Parents' Representations of their Children's Mathematics Learning in Multi-ethnic Primary Schools," *British Educational Research Journal* 31, no. 3 (2005): 697–722; G. de Abreu and T. Cline, "Social Valorisation of Mathematical Practices: The Implications for Learners in Multicultural Schools," in *Improving Access to Mathematics: Diversity and Equity in the Classroom*, ed. N. S. Nasir and P. Cobb (New York: Teachers College Press, 2007); G. de Abreu, T. Cline, and T. Shamsi, "Exploring Ways Parents Participate in their Children's School Mathematical Learning: Case Studies in a Multi-ethnic Primary School," in *Transitions Between Contexts of Mathematical Practices*, ed. G. de Abreu, A. Bishop, and N. C. Presmeg (Dordrecht, The Netherlands: Kluwer, 2002); J. Adler, "The Dilemma of Transparency: Seeing and Seeing Through Talk in the Mathematics Classroom," *Journal for Research in Mathematics Education* 30, no. 1 (1999): 47–64; M. Setati and J. N. Moschkovich, "Mathematics Education and Language Diversity: A Dialogue Across Settings," *Journal for Research in Mathematics Education*, forthcoming; M. Setati, J. Adler, Y. Reed, and A. Bapoo, "Incomplete Journeys: Code-Switching and Other Language Practices in Mathematics, Science and English," *Language and Education* 16, no. 2 (2002): 2–22.

41. R. E. Honey, "A Conversation with Megan Bang about 'Indigenizing' the Design of Learning Environments and the Challenge of Context and Diversity in Education," *InformalScience*, accessed on November 8, 2011. http://informal science.org/member/interview/bang.

42. Briggs-Hale et al., *After School Mathematics Practices*; R. Halpern, "After

School Programs for Low-income Children: Promises and Challenges," *Future of Children* 9, no. 2 (1999): 81–95; S. P. Klein and R. Bolus, *Improvements in Math and Reading Scores of Students Who Did and Did Not Participate in Foundations After School Enrichment Program during the 2001–2002 School Year* (Santa Monica, CA: Gansk and Associates, 2002); P. A. Lauer et al., "Out-of-School-Time Programs: A Meta-analysis of Effects for At-risk Students," *Review of Educational Research* 76, no. 2 (2006): 273–313; J. Mokros, M. Kliman, and H. Freeman, *Time to Enhance Math in After-school* (Cambridge, MA: TERC, 2005); T. Rothman and M. Henderson, "Do School-based Tutoring Programs Significantly Improve Students Performance on Standardized Tests?" *Research in Middle Level Education* 34, no. 6 (2011): 1–10; M. E. Welsh et al., "Promoting Learning and School Attendance through After-school Programs: Student-Level Changes in Educational Performance Across TASC's First Three Years" (report prepared for the After School Corporation, 2002).

43. Lauer et al., "Out-of-School-Time Programs."

44. Ibid.

45. Ibid.

46. J. S. Eccles and J. Templeton, "Extracurricular and Other After-school Activities for Youth," *Review of Research in Education* 26, no. 1 (2002): 113–180.

47. M. F. Mueller, "The Co-construction of Arguments by Middle-school Students," *Journal of Mathematical Behavior* 28, no. 2–3 (2009): 138–149; M. F. Mueller and C. Maher, "Learning to Reason in an Informal Math After-school Program," *Mathematics Education Research Journal* 21, no. 3 (2009): 7–35.

48. Briggs-Hale et al., *After School Mathematics Practices.*

49. Mueller, "The Co-construction of Arguments by Middle-school Students"; Mueller and Maher, "Learning to Reason in an Informal Math After-school Program."

50. L. L. Khisty and C. Willey, "After-school: An Innovative Model to Better Understand the Mathematics Learning of Latinas/os," in *Learning in Out-of-School Time*, ed. P. Bell, B. Bevan, A. Razfar, and R. Stevens (New York: Springer, 2011).

51. H. Dominguez, "Creating a Possible World with Actual Minds: Bilingual Students and El Maga, a Teacher-like Cyber Figure in a Mathematics After-school Program," *Educational Studies in Mathematics* 76, no. 3 (2011).

52. O. S. Fashola, *Building Effective Afterschool Programs* (Thousand Oaks, CA: Corwin Press, 2002).

53. Halpern, "After School Programs for Low-income Children"; Mokros, Kliman, and Freeman, *Time to Enhance Math.*

54. M. Frankenstein, "Understanding the Politics of Mathematical Knowledge

as an Integral Part of Becoming Critically Numerate," *Radical Statistics*, 1994, no. 56: 22–40; M. Frankenstein, "Reading the World with Math: Goals for a Critical Mathematical Literacy Curriculum," in *Rethinking Mathematics: Teaching Social Justice by the Numbers*, ed. E. Gutstein and B. Peterson (Milwaukee, WI: Rethinking Schools, 2005); P. Freire, *Pedagogy of the Oppressed* (New York: Continuum, 1970); E. Gutstein, "Teaching and Learning Mathematics for Social Justice in an Urban, Latino School," *Journal for Research in Mathematics Education* 34, no. 1 (2003): 37–73; E. Gutstein, *Reading and Writing the World with Mathematics: Toward a Pedagogy for Social Justice* (New York: Routledge, 2006).

55. E. Gutstein, "Math, Maps, and Misrepresentation," *Rethinking Schools* 15, no. 3 (2001): 6–7.

56. Gutstein, *Reading and Writing*.

57. E. E. Turner and B. T. F. Strawhun, "'With Math, It's Like You Have More Defense': Students Investigate Overcrowding at their School," in *Rethinking Mathematics: Teaching Social Justice by the Numbers*, ed. E. Gutstein and B. Peterson (Milwaukee, WI: Rethinking Schools, 2005), 84.

58. M. E. Staples, "Integrals and Equity: A Math Lesson Prompts New Awareness for Prep School Students—and their Teacher," in *Rethinking Mathematics: Teaching Social Justice by the Numbers*, ed. E. Gutstein and B. Peterson (Milwaukee, WI: Rethinking Schools, 2005).

59. A. Brantlinger, "The Geometry of Inequality," in *Rethinking Mathematics: Teaching Social Justice by the Numbers*, ed. E. Gutstein and B. Peterson (Milwaukee, WI: Rethinking Schools, 2005); Turner and Strawhun, "'With Math, It's Like You Have More Defense;'" Gutstein, "Mathematics for Social Justice"; Gutstein, *Reading and Writing*.

60. Brantlinger, "Geometry of Inequality"; Gutstein, "Mathematics for Social Justice."

61. Brantlinger, "Geometry of Inequality"; Turner and Strawhun, "'With Math, It's Like You Have More Defense'"; Gutstein, "Mathematics for Social Justice."

62. Brantlinger, "Geometry of Inequality."

63. J. Diez-Palomar, M. Varley, and K. Simic, "Children and Adults Talking and Doing Mathematics: A Study of an After-school Math Club," in *Proceedings of the 28th Annual Meeting of the North American Chapter of the International Group for the Psychology of Mathematics Education*, ed. S. Alatorre, J. L. Cortina, M. Sáiz, and A. Méndez (Mérida, México: Universidad Pedagógica Nacional, 2006); M. Frankenstein, "Incorporating Race, Gender, and Class Issues into a Critical Mathematical Literacy Curriculum," *Journal of Negro Education* 59, no. 3 (1990): 337–347; M. Frankenstein, "Equity in Mathematics Education: Class in

the World Outside the Class," in *New Directions for Equity in Mathematics Education,* ed. W. G. Secada, E. Fennema, and L. B. Adajian (Cambridge, UK: Cambridge University Press, 1995).

64. Turner and Strawhun, "'With Math, It's Like You Have More Defense.'"

65. Gutstein, "Mathematics for Social Justice"; Gutstein, *Reading and Writing.*

66. M. Frankenstein, *Relearning Mathematics: A Different Third R—Radical Math* (London, UK: Free Association Books, 1989); Frankenstein, "Incorporating Race, Gender, and Class Issues"; M. Borba and O. Skovsmose, "The Ideology of Certainty in Mathematics Education," *For the Learning of Mathematics* 17, no. 3 (1997): 39–43.

67. R. Gutiérrez, "The Sociopolitical Turn in Mathematics Education," *Journal for Research in Mathematics Education* 44, no. 1 (2013): 37–68.

68. T. G. Bartell, "Learning to Teach Mathematics for Social Justice: Negotiating Social Justice and Mathematical Goals," *Journal for Research in Mathematics Education*, 44, no. 1 (2013): 129–163.

69. J. Osler, "A Guide for Integrating Issues of Social and Economic Justice into Mathematics Curriculum," *Radical Math*, accessed on December 14, 2011. http://radicalmath.org/main. php?id=resources.

70. Gutstein, *Reading and Writing.*

71. Gutstein, *Reading and Writing*; Turner and Strawhun, "'With Math, It's Like You Have More Defense.'"

72. E. Gutstein, *Reading and Writing.*

73. Bartell, "Learning to Teach Mathematics for Social Justice"; Frankenstein, "Equity in Mathematics Education"; E. B. Freedman, "Is Teaching for Social Justice Undemocratic?" *Harvard Educational Review* 77, no. 4 (2007): 442–473; S. A. Gregson, "Negotiating Social Justice Teaching: One Full Time Teacher's Practice Viewed from the Trenches," *Journal for Research in Mathematics Education,* 44, no. 1 (2013): 164–198; Gutstein, *Reading and Writing.*

74. See: http://utopiadream.info/ca.

Chapter 6

1. W. Singer, "Development and Plasticity of Cortical Processing Architectures," *Science* 270, no. 5237 (1995): 758–764; L. R. Squire and E. R. Kandel, *Memory: From Mind to Molecules* (New York: Scientific American Library, 2009).

2. D. O. Hebb, *The Organization of Behavior* (New York: Wiley & Sons, 1949); Squire and Kandel, *Memory.*

3. For an excellent, brief video about how experiences shape brain architecture from the Center on the Developing Child at Harvard, see: http://developing

child.harvard.edu/resources/multimedia/videos/three_core_concepts/brain_architecture/

4. T. Elbert et al., "Increased Cortical Representation of the Fingers of the Left Hand in String Players," *Science* 270, no. 5234 (1995): 305–307; C. Pantev et al., "Increased Auditory Cortical Representation in Musicians," *Nature* 23, no. 392 (1998): 811–814.

5. Elbert et al., "Cortical Representation in String Players."

6. Pantev et al., "Auditory Cortical Representation in Musicians."

7. C. Pantev et al., "Music and Learning-induced Cortical Plasticity," *Annals of the New York Academy of Sciences*, no. 999 (2003): 438–450.

8. L. G. Ungerleider, J. Doyon, and A. Karni, "Imaging Brain Plasticity During Motor Skill Learning," *Neurobiology of Learning and Memory* 78, no. 3 (2002): 553–564.

9. P. Li Voti et al., "Correlation Between Cortical Plasticity, Motor Learning and BDNF Genotype in Healthy Subjects," *Experimental Brain Research* 212, no. 1 (2011): 91–99; B. D. McCandliss, M. I. Posner, and T. Givo'n, "Brain Plasticity in Learning Visual Words," *Cognitive Psychology*, no. 33 (1997): 88–110; D. J. Ostry et al., "Somatosensory Plasticity and Motor Learning," *Journal of Neuroscience* 30, no. 15 (2010): 5384–5393; Y. Shtyrovl, V. Nikulin, and F. Pulvermüller, "Rapid Cortical Plasticity Underlying Novel Word Learning," *Journal of Neuroscience* 30, no. 50 (2010): 16864–16867.

10. R. H. Hamilton and A. Pascual-Leone, "Cortical Plasticity Associated with Braille Learning," *Trends in Cognitive Sciences* 2, no. 5 (1998): 168–174.

11. Squire and Kandel, *Memory*.

12. S. E. Shaywitz, *Overcoming Dyslexia* (New York: Random House, Inc., 2003).

13. G. H. Recanzone et al., "Topographic Reorganization of the Hand Representation in Cortical Area 3b of Owl Monkeys Trained in a Frequency-discrimination Task," *Journal of Neurophysiology* 67, no. 5 (1992): 1031–1055.

14. G. H. Recanzone, C. E. Schreiner, and M. M. Nerzenich, "Plasticity in the Frequency Representation of Primary Auditory Cortex Following Discrimination Training in Adult Owl Monkeys," *Journal of Neuroscience* 13, no. 1 (1993): 87–103.

15. L. Ruytjens et al., "Neural Responses to Silent Lipreading in Normal Hearing Male and Female Subjects," *European Journal of Neuroscience* 24, no. 6 (2006): 1835–1844; N. M. Weinberger, "Cortical Plasticity in Associative Learning and Memory," in *Learning and Memory: A Comprehensive Reference*, ed. J.H. Byrne (Oxford, UK: Elsevier Ltd., 2008); J. A. Winer and C. E. Schreiner, ed., *The Auditory Cortex* (New York: Springer, 2011).

16. K. W. Fischer and T. R. Bidell, "Dynamic Development of Action and

Thought," in *Handbook of Child Psychology*, ed. W. Damon and R. M. Lerner (New York: John Wiley & Sons, Inc., 2006); C. Hinton and K. W. Fischer, "Learning from a Developmental and Biological Perspective," in *The Nature of Learning: Using Research to Inspire Practice*, ed. H. Dumont, D. Istance, and F. Benavides (Paris: OECD, 2011); J. P. Shonkoff and D. A. Phillips, ed., *From Neurons to Neighborhoods: The Science of Early Childhood Development* (Washington, DC: National Academy Press, 2000); M. Ridley, *Nature via Nurture: Genes, Experience and What Makes Us Human* (New York: HarperCollins, 2003).

17. S. Arbelle et al., "Relation of Shyness in Grade School Children to the Genotype for the Long Form of the Serotonin Transporter Promoter Region Polymorphism," *American Journal of Psychiatry* 160, no. 4 (2003): 671–676.

18. C. E. Snow, M. S. Burns, and P. Griffin, *Preventing Reading Difficulties in Young Children* (Washington, DC: National Academy Press, 1998); C. E. Snow, P. Griffin, and M. S. Burns, *Knowledge to Support the Teaching of Reading: Preparing Teachers for a Changing World* (San Francisco: Jossey-Bass, 2005).

19. Fischer and Bidell, "Action and Thought"; K. W. Fischer, J. H. Bernstein, and M. H. Immordino-Yang, *Mind, Brain, and Education in Reading Disorders* (Cambridge, UK: Cambridge University Press, 2007); C. C. Knight and K. W. Fischer, "Learning to Read Words: Individual Differences in Developmental Sequences," *Journal of Applied Developmental Psychology*, 1992, no. 13: 377–404.

20. Fischer and Bidell, "Action and Thought"; R. P. Fink and J. Samuels, *Inspiring Success: Reading Interest and Motivation in an Age of High-stakes Testing* (Newark, DE: International Reading Association, 2007).

21. C. Kegel, A. G. Bus, and M. H. van IJzendoorn, "Differential Susceptibility in Early Literacy Instruction through Computer Games: The Role of the Dopamine D4 Receptor Gene (DRD4)," *Mind, Brain and Education* 5, no. 2 (2011): 71–78.

22. Shonkoff and Phillips, ed., *From Neurons to Neighborhoods*.

23. J. Henrich, S. J. Heine, and A. Norenzayan, "The Weirdest People in the World?" *Behavioral and Brain Sciences*, 2010, no. 33: 61–135.

24. E. Turkheimer et al., "Socioeconomic Status Modifies Heritability of IQ in Young Children," *Psychological Science* 14, no. 6 (2003): 623–628.

25. N. Chomsky, "Review of B. F. Skinner's *Verbal Behavior*," *Language*, no. 35 (1959): 26–58.

26. H. J. Neville and J. T. Bruer, "Language Processing: How Experience Affects Brain Organization," in *Critical Thinking About Critical Periods*, ed. D. B. Bailer, J. T. Bruer, F. J. Symons, and J. W. Lichtman (Baltimore, MD: Paul H. Brookes Publishing, 2001): 151–172.

27. S. Y. Bookheimer, "Functional MRI of Language: New Approaches to

Understanding the Cortical Organization of Semantic Processing," *Annual Review of Neuroscience*, 2002, no. 25 (151–188).

28. S. Y. Bookheimer et al., "Regional Cerebral Blood Flow During Auditory Responsive Naming: Evidence for Cross-modality Neural Activation," *NeuroReport* 9, no. 10 (1998): 2409–2413; S. L. Thompson-Schill, G. Aguirre, M. D'Esposito, and M. J. Farah, "A Neural Basis for Category and Modality Specifics of Semantic Knowledge," *Neuropsychologia*, no. 37 (1999): 371–376.

29. Bruer, "Second Language Learning"; Neville and Bruer, "Language Processing"; P. K. Kuhl, "Brain Mechanisms in Early Language Acquisition," *Neuron* 67, no. 5 (2010): 713–737.

30. Neville and Bruer, "Language Processing."

31. Ibid.

32. J. Fledge and K. Fletcher, "Talker and Listener Effects on Degree of Perceived Foreign Accent," *Journal of the Acoustical Society of America* 91, no. 1 (1992): 370–389.

33. J. Worden, C. Hinton, and K. W. Fischer, "What Does the Brain Have to Do with Learning?" *Phi Beta Kappan* 92, no. 8 (2011): 8–13.

34. C. Hinton, K. Miyamoto, and B. della-Chiesa, "Brain Research, Learning and Emotions: Implications for Education Research, Policy, and Practice," *European Journal of Education* 43, no. 1 (2008): 87–103; OECD, *Understanding the Brain: The Birth of a Learning Science* (Paris: Author, 2007).

35. M. Tomasello, *The Cultural Origins of Human Cognition* (Cambridge, MA: Harvard University Press, 1999).

36. Hinton and Fischer, "Learning from a Developmental and Biological Perspective."

37. S. Dehaene, *Reading in the Brain: The Science and Evolution of a Human Invention* (New York: Penguin, 2009).

38. G. Jobard, F. Crivello, and N. Tzourio-Mazoyer, "Evaluation of the Dual Route Theory of Reading: A Metanalysis of 35 Neuroimaging Studies," *NeuroImage* 20, no. 2 (2003); J. Levy et al., "Testing for the Dual-route Cascade Reading Model in the Brain: An fMRI Effective Connectivity Account of an Efficient Reading Style," *PLoS One* 4, no. 8 (2009): 6675–6687.

39. Levy et al., "Dual-route Cascade Reading Model"; R. Gaillard et al., "Direct Intracranial, fMRI, and Lesion Evidence for the Causal Role of Left Inferotemporal Cortex in Reading," *Neuron* 50, no. 2 (2006): 191–204.

40. Dehaene, *Reading in the Brain*.

41. E. Paulesu et al., "Dyslexia: Cultural Diversity and Biological Unity," *Science* 291, no. 5511 (2001): 2165–2167.

42. OECD, *Where Immigrant Students Succeed: A Comparative Review of Performance and Engagement in PISA* (Paris: Author, 2003).

43. Bruer, "Second Language Learning"; Neville and Bruer, "Language Processing"; Kuhl, "Early Language Acquisition."

44. S. Dehaene, *The Number Sense: How the Mind Creates Mathematics* (Oxford: Oxford University Press, 2011); Hinton et al., "Brain Research, Learning and Emotions"; OECD, *Understanding the Brain*.

45. K. Wynn, "Numerical Competence in Infants," in *The Development of Mathematical Skills,* ed. C. D. Donlan (East Sussex, UK: Psychology Press, 1998); L. Ferigenson, S. Dehaene, and E. S. Spelke, "Core Systems of Number," *Trends in Cognitive Neuroscience* 8, no. 7 (2004): 1–8.

46. V. Izard et al., "Newborn Infants Perceive Abstract Numbers," *Proceedings of the National Academy of Sciences* 106, no. 25 (2009): 10382–10385; P. Starkey, E. S. Spelke, and R. Gelman, "Numerical Abstraction by Human Infants," *Cognition,* no. 36 (1990): 97–127.

47. K. Wynn, "Addition and Subtraction by Human Infants," *Nature,* no. 358 (1992): 749–750.

48. Dehaene, *The Number Sense.*

49. H. Gardner, *Frames of Mind: The Theory of Multiple Intelligences* (New York: Basic Books, 1983).

50. M. Hittmair-Delazer, U. Sailer, and T. Benke, "Impaired Arithmetic Facts but Intact Conceptual Knowledge–a Single Case Study of Dyscalculia," *Cortex* 31, no. 1 (1995): 139–147.

51. Dehaene, *The Number Sense.*

52. Hittmair-Delazer et al., "Case Study of Dyscalculia."

53. M. H. Immordino-Yang and A. R. Damasio, "We Feel, Therefore We Learn: The Relevance of Affective and Social Neuroscience to Education," *Mind, Brain, and Education* 1, no. 1 (2007): 3–10, 3.

54. N. H. Frijda, *The Laws of Emotions* (New York: Erlbaum, 2006).

55. R. J. Davidson and N. A. Fox, "Frontal Brain Asymmetry Predicts Infants' Response to Maternal Separation," *Journal of Abnormal Psychology* 98, no. 2 (1989): 127–131.

56. J. M. Fuster, *The Prefrontal Cortex* (London: Academic Press, 2008).

57. B. Luna and J. A. Sweeney, "The Emergence of Collaborative Brain Function: fMRI Studies of the Development of Response Inhibition," *Annals of the New York Academy of Science,* no. 1021 (2004): 296–309.

58. K. Luan Phan et al., "Neural Substrates for Voluntary Suppression of Negative Affect: A Functional Magnetic Resonance Imaging Study," *Biology Psychiatry,* no.

57 (2005): 210–219; K. N. Ochsner et al., "Rethinking Feelings: An fMRI Study of the Cognitive Regulation of Emotion," *Journal of Cognitive Neuroscience* 14, no. 8 (2002): 1215–1299; K. N. Ochsner et al., "For Better or For Worse: Neural Systems Supporting the Cognitive Down- and Up-Regulation of Negative Emotion," *NeuroImage*, no. 23 (2004): 483–499; M. L. Phillips et al., "The Neurobiology of Emotion Perception: The Neural Basis of Normal Emotion Perception," *Biological Psychiatry*, no. 54 (2003): 504–514.

59. Ochsner et al., "For Better or For Worse."

60. J. D. E. Gabrieli, *Development of Emotions and Learning: A Cognitive Neuroscience Perspective* (Cambridge, MA: Building Usable Knowledge in Mind, Brain, and Education, 2004); Luna and Sweeney, "Collaborative Brain Function."

61. Gabrieli, *Development of Emotions and Learning.*

62. Hinton et al., "Brain Research, Learning and Emotions"; OECD, *Understanding the Brain.*

63. OECD, *Against the Odds: Disadvantaged Students who Succeed in School* (Paris: Author, 2011).

64. Hinton et al., "Brain Research, Learning and Emotions."

65. C. K. Cain and J. E. LeDoux, "Emotional Processing and Motivation: In Search of Brain Mechanisms," in *Handbook of Approach and Avoidance Motivation,* ed. A. J. Elliot (New York: Taylor and Francis Group, 2008); P. J. Lang, "Emotion and Motivation: Toward Consensus Definitions and a Common Research Purpose," *Emotion Review* 2, no. 3 (2010): 229–233; P. J. Lang and M. Davis, "Emotion, Motivation and the Brain: Reflex Foundations in Animal and Human Research," *Progress in Brain Research*, no. 156 (2006): 3–29; OECD, *Understanding the Brain.*

66. T. W. Robbins and B. J. Everitt, "Neurobehavioural Mechanisms of Reward and Motivation," *Current Opinion in Neurobiology* 6, no. 2 (1996): 228–236.

67. Cain and LeDoux, "Emotional Processing and Motivation"; Robbins and Everitt, "Neurobehavioural Mechanisms of Reward and Motivation."

68. C. S. Dweck, *Mindset* (New York: Random House, 2006).

69. Ibid.

70. Ibid.

71. T. Grindal, C. Hinton, and J. Shonkoff, "The Science of Early Childhood Development: Lessons for Teachers and Caregivers," in *In Defense of Childhood,* ed. B. Falk (New York: Teachers College Press, 2011); B. S. McEwen and R. M. Sapolsky, "Stress and Cognitive Function," *Current Opinion Neurobiology*, 1995, no. 5: 205–216; Shonkoff and Phillips, ed., *From Neurons to Neighborhoods.*

72. For an excellent, brief video on the impact of toxic stress on the brain, from

the Center on the Developing Child at Harvard, see: http://developingchild.harvard.edu/resources/multimedia/videos/three_core_concepts/toxic_stress/
73. McEwen and Sapolsky, "Stress and Cognitive Function"; Shonkoff and Phillips, ed., *From Neurons to Neighborhoods.*
74. Shonkoff and Phillips, ed., *From Neurons to Neighborhoods.*
75. G. Rappolt-Schlichtmann, C. C. Ayoub, and J. W. Gravel, "Examining the 'Whole Child' to Generate Usable Knowledge," *Mind, Brain, and Education* 3, no. 4 (2009): 209–217; G. Rappolt-Schlichtmann et al., "Poverty, Relationship Conflict, and the Regulation of Cortisol in Small and Large Group Contexts at Child Care," *Mind, Brain, and Education* 3, no. 3 (2009): 131–142; G. Rappolt-Schlichtmann and S. E. Watamura, "Inter- and Transdisciplinary Research on Hormones with Problems of Educational Practice," *Mind, Brain, and Education* 4, no. 4 (2010): 156–158.
76. Rappolt-Schlichtmann et al., "Poverty, Relationship Conflict."
77. J. A. Mangels et al., "Emotion Blocks the Path to Learning Under Stereotype Threat," *Social Cognitive and Affective Neuroscience,* 2011, no. 6; Shonkoff and Phillips, ed., *From Neurons to Neighborhoods*; OECD, *Understanding the Brain.*
78. Shonkoff and Phillips, ed., *From Neurons to Neighborhoods*; Rappolt-Schlichtmann et al., "Poverty, Relationship Conflict."
79. Hinton and Fischer, "Learning from a Developmental and Biological Perspective"; M. H. Immordino-Yang, "The Stories of Nico and Brooke Revisited: Toward a Cross-disciplinary Dialogue about Teaching and Learning in Mind, Brain, and Education," *Mind, Brain, and Education* 2, no. 2 (2008): 49–51; National Scientific Council on the Developing Child, "Young Children Develop in an Environment of Relationships" (working paper no. 1, Center on the Developing Child, Harvard University, Cambridge, 2004).
80. L. S. Vygotsky, *Mind in Society* (Cambridge, MA: Harvard University Press, 1978)
81. C. Hinton and K. W. Fischer, "Research Schools: Ground Research in Practice," *Mind Brain, and Education* 2, no. 4 (2008): 157–160; C. Hinton and K. W. Fischer, "Research Schools: Connecting Research and Practice at Ross School" in *Educating the Whole Child for the Whole World: Ross Schools and the Promise of Education for the Global Era*, ed. M. Suarez-Orozco and C. Sattin-Bajaj (Berkeley, CA: University of California Press, 2010).
82. H. Gardner, "How Education Changes," in *Globalization, Culture, and Education in the New Millennium*, ed. M. Suárez-Orozco and D. B. Qin-Hilliard (Berkeley, CA: University of California Press, 2004), 21.

Chapter 7

1. Our review and analysis of the literature on motivation, engagement, and student voice occurs in an educational context marked by a focus on reform and standardization. From a research perspective, the current reliance on high-stakes standardized tests as the primary assessment of student achievement and teacher efficacy and, ostensibly, as a primary motivator of individual and institutional performance has come under fire. See, for example, A. L. Amrein and D. C. Berliner, *An Analysis of Some Unintended and Negative Consequences of High-stakes Testing* (Tempe, AZ: Arizona State University, Education Policy Studies Laboratory, 2002); C. P. Brown, "Children of Reform: The Impact of High-stakes Education Reform on Preservice Teachers," *Journal of Teacher Education* 61, no. 5 (2010): 477–491; M. S. Crocco and A. T. Costigan, "High-stakes Teaching: What's at Stake for Teachers (and Students) in the Age of Accountability," *New Educator*, no. 2 (2006): 1–13; M. S. Crocco and A. T. Costigan, "The Narrowing of Curriculum and Pedagogy in the Age of Accountability: Urban Educators Speak Out," *Urban Education* 42, no. 6: 512–535; M. W. Ellis, "Leaving No Child Behind Yet Allowing None Too Far Ahead: Ensuring (In)equity in Mathematics Education through the Science of Measurement and Instruction," *Teachers College Record* 110, no. 6 (2008): 1330–1356; G. Gay, "The Rhetoric and Reality of NCLB," *Race Ethnicity and Education* 10, no. 3 (2007): 279–293; H. Mintrop and G. L. Sunderman, *Why High Stakes Accountability Sounds Good but Doesn't Work—and Why We Keep on Doing It Anyway* (Los Angeles: The Civil Rights Project, the Regents of the University of California, 2009); E. G. Murillo and S. Y. Flores, "Reform by Shame: Managing the Stigma of Labels in High Stakes Testing," *Educational Foundations* 16, no. 2 (2002): 93–108; D. Selwyn, "Highly Quantified Teachers: NCLB and Teacher Education," *Journal of Teacher Education* 58, no. 2 (2007): 124–137; D. G. Smith and G. Garrison, "The Impending Loss of Talent: An Exploratory Study Challenging Assumptions about Testing and Merit," *Teachers College Record* 107, no. 4 (2005): 629–653; M. Watanabe, "Tracking in the Era of High Stakes State Accountability Reform: Case Studies of Classroom Instruction in North Carolina," *Teachers College Record* 110, no. 3 (2008): 489–534.

2. See, for example, J. S. Eccles et al., "Development during Adolescence: The Impact of Stage-environment Fit on Young Adolescents' Experiences in Schools and in Families," *American Psychologist* 48, no. 2. (1993): 90–101; A. M. Ryan, P. R. Pintrich, and C. Midgley, "Avoiding Seeking Help in the Classroom: Who and Why?" *Educational Psychology Review* 13, no. 2 (2001): 93–114; S. Fordham and J. U. Ogbu, "Black Students' School Success: Coping with the Burden of 'Acting

White,'" *Urban Review* 18, no. 3 (1986): 176-206; J. U. Ogbu, *Minority Status, Oppositional Culture, and Schooling* (New York: Routledge, 2008).

3. P. K. Murphy and P. A. Alexander, "A Motivated Exploration of Motivation Terminology." *Contemporary Educational Psychology*, no. 25 (2000): 3–53.

4. K. W. Fischer, "A Theory of Cognitive Development: The Control and Construction of Hierarchies of Skills," *Psychological Review* 87, no. 6 (1980): 477–531; K. W. Fischer and S. P. Rose, "Growth Cycles of Brain and Mind," *Educational Leadership* 56, no. 3 (1998): 56–60.

5. See chapter 6 for a more detailed discussion of the development of intelligence.

6. J. Bransford et al., "Theories of Learning and their Roles in Teaching," in *Preparing Teachers for a Changing World,* ed. L. Darling-Hammond and J. Bransford (San Francisco: Wiley & Sons, 2005), 62.

7. C. S. Dweck, *Self-theories: Their Role in Motivation, Personality, and Development (Essays in Social Psychology)* (Philadelphia: Psychology Press, 1999); H. Grant and C. S. Dweck, "Clarifying Achievement Goals and Their Impact," *Journal of Personality and Social Psychology* 85, no. 3 (2003): 541–553; M. L. Kamins and C. S. Dweck, "Person Versus Process Praise and Criticism: Implications for Contingent Self-worth and Coping," *Developmental Psychology* 35, no. 3 (1999): 75–86; J. A. Mangels et al., "Why Do Beliefs About Intelligence Influence Learning Success? A Social Cognitive Neuroscience Model," *Social Cognitive and Affective Neuroscience*, no. 1 (2006): 75–86.

8. Summarizing this research in *NurtureShock: New Thinking About Children*, Po Bronson and Ashley Merryman note that even very capable and high-functioning students give up when they encounter a difficult task if they believe it is a function of ability rather than effort (New York: Twelve, 2009). As Carol Dweck puts it in *Self-theories* (p. 1), "You might think that students who were highly skilled would be the ones who relish a challenge and persevere in the face of setbacks. Instead, many of these students are the most worried about failure, and the most likely to question their ability and to wilt when they hit obstacles."

9. For insights into how smartness claims function culturally, see B. Hatt, "Street Smarts vs. Book Smarts: The Figured World of Smartness in the Lives of Marginalized, Urban Youth," *Urban Review* 39, no. 2 (2007): 145–166 and B. Hatt-Echeverria, "Beyond Biology and Ability: Understanding Smartness as Cultural Practice" (proceedings from annual meeting of the American Educational Research Association, San Francisco, 2006).

10. For a detailed description of student self-assessment, its uses, and its impact on learning, see chapter 2.

11. J. S. Eccles et al., "Expectancies, Values, and Academic Behaviors," in

Achievement and Achievement Motives: Psychological and Sociological Approaches, ed. J. T. Spence (San Francisco: W. H. Freeman, 1983); J. S. Eccles and A. Wigfield, "In the Mind of the Achiever: The Structure of Adolescents' Academic Achievement Related Beliefs and Self-perceptions," *Personality and Social Psychology Bulletin,* no. 21 (1995): 109–132.

12. C. Smith and L. C. Hung, "Stereotype Threat: Effects on Education," *Social Psychology of Education* 11, no. 3 (2008): 243–257.

13. J. Aronson et al., "The Effects of Stereotype Threat on the Standardized Test Performance of College Students," in *Readings about the Social Animal,* 9th ed., ed. E. Aronson (New York: Worth Publishers, 2004); J. W. Osborne, "Linking Stereotype Threat and Anxiety," *Educational Psychology* 27, no. 1 (2007): 135–154; Smith and Hung, "Stereotype Threat"; C. M. Steele, "A Threat in the Air: How Stereotypes Shape Intellectual Identity and Performance," *American Psychologist* 52, no. 6 (1997): 613–629.

14. The practice of subtractive schooling was later researched and further developed by: A. V. Garza and L. Crawford, "Hegemonic Multiculturalism: English Immersion, Ideology, and Subtractive Schooling," *Bilingual Research Journal* 29, no 3. (2005): 599–619; Hatt-Echeverria, "Beyond Biology and Ability"; K. Menken and T. Kleyn, "The Long-term Impact of Subtractive Schooling in the Educational Experiences of Secondary English Language Learners," *International Journal of Bilingual Education & Bilingualism* 13, no. 4 (2010): 399–417; A. Valenzuela, "Reflections on the Subtractive Underpinnings of Education Research and Policy," *Journal of Teacher Education* 53, no. 3 (2002): 235–241; A. Valenzuela, *Subtractive Schooling: U.S.-Mexican Youth and the Politics of Caring* (Albany, NY: SUNY Press, 1999); J. Worthy et al., "Fifth-grade Bilingual Students and Precursors to 'Subtractive Schooling,'" *Bilingual Research Journal* 27, no. 2 (2003): 275–294.

15. A. Borjian and A. Padilla, "Voices from Mexico: How American Teachers Can Meet the Needs of Mexican Immigrant Students," *Urban Review* 42, no. 4 (2010): 316–328; H. Chun and G. Dickson, "A Psychoecological Model of Academic Performance Among Hispanic Adolescents," *Journal of Youth and Adolescence* 40, no. 12 (2011): 1581–1594; G. Conchas, L. Oseguera, and J. Vigil, "Acculturation and School Success: Understanding the Variability of Mexican American Youth Adaptation Across Urban and Suburban Contexts," *Urban Review* 44, no. 4 (2012): 401–422; L. F. Rodríguez, and G. Q. Conchas, "Preventing Truancy and Dropout Among Urban Middle School Youth," *Education and Urban Society Education* 41, no. 2 (2009): 216–247; C. Suárez-Orozco and M. Suárez-Orozco, "Educating Latino Immigrant Students in the Twenty-First Century: Principles for the Obama

Administration," *Harvard Educational Review* 79, no. 2 (2009): 327–401.

16. C. Furrer and E. Skinner, "Sense of Relatedness as a Factor in Children's Academic Engagement and Performance," *Journal of Educational Psychology* 95, no. 1 (2003): 148–162.

17. For an exhaustive survey of the subdimensions identified in research, see J. J. Appleton, S. L. Christenson, and M. J. Furlong, "Student Engagement with School: Critical Conceptual and Methodological Issues of the Construct," *Psychology in the Schools* 45, no. 5 (2008): 369–386, 378.

18. Klem and Connell, "Relationships Matter."

19. J. A. Fredericks, P. C. Blumenfeld, and A. H. Paris, "School Engagement: Potential of the Concept, State of the Evidence," *Review of Educational Research* 74, no. 1 (2004): 59–109.

20. J. P. Connell, M. B. Spencer, and J. L. Aber, "Educational Risk and Resilience in African-American Youth: Context, Self, Action, and Outcomes in School," *Child Development* 65, no. 2 (1994): 496–503.

21. C. Goodenow, "Classroom Belonging Among Early Adolescent Students: Relationships to Motivation and Achievement," *Journal of Early Adolescence* 13, no. 1 (1993): 21–43.

22. W. W. Willingham, J. M. Pollack, and C. Lewis, "Grades and Test Scores: Accounting for Observed Differences," *Journal of Educational Measurement* 39, no. 1 (2002): 1–37.

23. Klem and Connell, "Relationships Matter."

24. B. B. Ekstrom et al., "Who Drops Out of High School and Why? Findings from a National Study," *Teachers College Record* 87, no. 3 (1986): 356–373.

25. Ibid.

26. J. Archambault et al., "Student Engagement and Its Relationship with Early High School Dropout," *Journal of Adolescence* 32, no. 3 (2009): 651–670; L. F. Rodríguez and G. Q. Conchas, "Preventing Truancy and Dropout among Urban Middle School Youth," *Education and Urban Society Education* 41, no. 2 (2009): 216–247; R. W. Rumberger, "The Economics of High School Dropouts," in *International Encyclopedia of Education*, 3rd ed., ed. P. Peterson, E. Baker, and B. McGraw (Oxford: Elsevier, 2010).

27. Appleton, Christenson, and Furlong, "Student Engagement with School."

28. Furrer and Skinner, "Sense of Relatedness"; E. A. Skinner and M. J. Belmont, "Motivation in the Classroom: Reciprocal Effects of Teacher Behavior and Student Engagement Across the School Year," *Journal of Educational Psychology* 85, no. 4 (1993): 571–581; E. A. Skinner, T. A. Kindermann, and C. J. Furrer, "A Motivational Perspective on Engagement and Disaffection: Conceptualization and

Assessment of Children's Behavioral and Emotional Participation in Academic Activities in the Classroom," *Educational and Psychological Measurement* 69, no. 3 (2009): 493–525.

29. Appleton, Christenson, and Furlong, "Student Engagement with School."

30. B. J. Zimmerman, "Self-regulated Learning and Academic Achievement: An Overview," *Educational Psychologist* 25, no. 1 (1990): 3–17.

31. Zimmerman, "Self-regulated Learning," 5.

32. M. Boekaerts, "What Have We Learned About the Social Context-Student Engagement Link?" *Teachers College Record* 113, no. 2 (2011): 375–393.

33. See, for example, Boekaerts, "Social Context-Student Engagement Link"; P. H. Winne, "Key Issues in Modeling and Applying Research on Self-regulated Learning," *Applied Psychology: An International Review* 54, no. 2 (2005): 232–238; Zimmerman, "Self-regulated Learning."

34. Boekaerts, "Social Context-Student Engagement Link."

35. Zimmerman, "Self-regulated Learning."

36. B. J. Zimmerman, "Developing Self-fulfilling Cycles of Academic Regulation: An Analysis of Exemplary Instructional Models," in *Self-regulated Learning: From Teaching to Self-reflective Practice*, ed. D. H. Schunk and B. J. Zimmerman (New York: Guilford Press, 1998).

37. P. E. Dux et al., "Isolation of a Central Bottleneck of Information Processing with Time-resolved fMRI," *Neuron* 52, no. 6 (2006): 1109–1120.

38. L. Stone, "Living with Continuous Partial Attention," *Harvard Business Review*, February 2007, 28–29.

39. A. Wigfield and J. S. Eccles, "The Development of Competence Beliefs, Expectancies for Success, and Achievement Values from Childhood through Adolescence," in *Development of Achievement Motivation*, ed. A. Wigfield and J. S. Eccles (San Diego, CA: Academic Press, 2002).

40. M. J. Nakkula and E. Toshalis, *Understanding Youth: Adolescent Development for Educators* (Cambridge, MA: Harvard Education Press, 2006).

41. D. L. Mitra and S. J. Gross, "Increasing Student Voice in High School Reform: Building Partnerships, Improving Outcomes," *Educational Management Administration & Leadership* 37, no. 4 (2009): 819–830.

42. Ibid, 4.

43. J. Rudduck, H. Demetriou, and D. Pedder, "Student Perspectives and Teacher Practices: The Transformative Potential," *McGill Journal of Education* 38, no. 2 (2003): 274–288.

44. Mitra and Gross, "Increasing Student Voice in High School Reform," 4.

45. D. L. Mitra, "Student Voice and Student Roles in Education Policy Reform,"

in *AERA Handbook on Education Policy Research*, ed. D. Plank, G. Sykes, and B. Schneider (London: Routledge, 2009), 20.

46. D. L. Mitra, "Adults Advising Youth: Leading While Getting Out of the Way," *Educational Administration Quarterly* 41, no. 3 (2005): 520–553.

47. L. A. Camino, "Youth-adult Partnerships: Entering New Territory in Community Work and Research," *Applied Developmental* Science 4, supp. 1 (2000): 11–20; A. M. Colatos and E. Morrell, "Apprenticing Urban Youth as Critical Researchers: Implications for Increasing Equity and Access in Diverse Urban Schools," in *Critical Voices in School Reform: Students Living through Change*, 1st ed., ed. B. Rubin and E. Silva (London, UK: Routledge, 2003); J. L. Kincheloe, "Clarifying the Purpose of Engaging Students as Researchers," in *International Handbook of Student Experience in Elementary and Secondary School*, ed. D. Thiessen and A. Cook-Sather (Dordrecht, The Netherlands: Springer, 2007).

48. Rudduck, Demetriou, and Pedder, "Student Perspectives and Teacher Practices"; S. Yonezawa and M. Jones, "Using Students' Voices to Inform and Evaluate Secondary School Reform," in *International Handbook of Student Experience in Elementary and Secondary School*, ed. D. Thiessen and A. Cook-Sather (Dordrecht, The Netherlands: Springer, 2007); S. Zeldin, C. O'Connor, and L. Camino, "Youth as Evaluators: What's an Adult to Do?" *Practice Matters* (Ithaca, NY: Cornell University, Family Life Development Center, 2006).

49. A. Cook-Sather, "'Change Based on What Students Say': Preparing Teachers for a Paradoxical Model of Leadership," *International Journal of Leadership in Education* 9, no. 4 (2006): 345–358; J. Rudduck and J. Flutter, *How to Improve Your School: Giving Pupils a Voice* (New York: Continuum, 2004); E. M. Silva, "Struggling for Inclusion: A Case Study of Students as Reform Partners," in *Critical Voices in School Reform: Students Living through Change, 1st ed.*, ed. B. Rubin and E.M. Silva, (London: Routledge, 2003).

50. Mitra and Gross, "Increasing Student Voice in High School Reform"; D. L. Mitra, "The Significance of Students: Can Increasing 'Student Voice' in Schools Lead to Gains in Youth Development?" *Teachers College Record* 106, no. 4 (2004): 651–688.

51. Zeldin, O'Connor, and Camino, "Youth as Evaluators."

52. L. Camino and S. Zeldin, "From Periphery to Center: Pathways for Youth Civic Engagement in the Day-to-day Life of Communities," *Applied Developmental Science* 6, no. 4 (2002): 213–220; J. U. Osberg, D. Pope, and M. Galloway, "Students Matter in School Reform: Leaving Fingerprints and Becoming Leaders," *International Journal of Leadership in Education* 9, no. 4 (2006): 329–343.

53. S. Zeldin, "Youth as Agents of Adult and Community Development," *Applied*

Developmental Science 8, no. 2 (2004): 75-90.

54. Ibid.

55. P. J. McQuillan, "Possibilities and Pitfalls: A Comparative Analysis of Student Empowerment," *American Educational Research Journal* 42, no. 4 (2005): 639–670.

56. M. Fielding, "Transformative Approaches to Student Voice: Theoretical Underpinnings, Recalcitrant Realities," *British Educational Research Journal* 30, no. 2 (2004): 295–311; M. Fielding, "Beyond 'Voice': New Roles, Relations, and Contexts in Researching with Young People," *Discourse* 28, no. 3 (2007): 301–310.

57. J. Denner, B. Meyer, and S. Bean, "Young Women's Leadership Alliance: Youth-adult Partnerships in an All-female After-school Program," *Journal of Community Psychology* 33, no. 1 (2005): 87–100.

58. J. Ruddock, "Student Voice, Student Engagement, and School Reform," in *International Handbook of Student Experience in Elementary and Secondary School*, ed. D. Thiessen and A. Cook-Sather (Dordrecht, Netherlands: Springer, 2007).

59. M. Libby, M. Rosen, and M. Sedonaen, "Building Youth-adult Partnerships for Community Change: Lessons from the Youth Leadership Institute," *Journal of Community Psychology* 33, no. 1 (2005): 111–120. To help educators overcome these pitfalls, Michael Fielding has developed a list of principles and values necessary to conduct teacher-student partnerships in charting school reform and has created a checklist of questions adults need to be able to answer to effectively collaborate with youth in "Students as Radical Agents of Change," *Journal of Educational Change* 2, no. 2 (2001): 123–141.

60. D. Lawrence-Brown, "Differentiated Instruction: Inclusive Strategies for Standards-based Learning that Benefit the Whole Class," *American Secondary Education* 32, no. 3 (2004): 34–62; L. J. Santamaria, "Culturally Responsive Differentiated Instruction: Narrowing Gaps between Best Pedagogical Practices Benefiting All Learners," *Teachers College Record* 111, no. 1 (2009): 214–247; M. Sapon-Shevin, N. Zigmond, and J. M. Baker, "Is Full Inclusion Always the Best Option for Children with Disabilities?" in *Taking Sides: Clashing Views on Controversial Issues in Educational Psychology*, 2nd ed., ed. L. Abbeduto (Guilford, CT: McGraw-Hill/Dushkin, 2002).

About the Editors

Rebecca E. Wolfe, PhD, the Students at the Center project director, is a senior program manager on *Jobs for the Future*'s Pathways Through Postsecondary team, focused on improving the educational options of young people who have disengaged or disconnected altogether from the educational system. She works with local and state leaders to improve graduation rates and create and scale up high-quality pathways that lead to college and career success. She is the author or coauthor of *Developing Rigorous Competencies for Off-track Youth* and *Back on Track to College: A Texas School District Leverages State Policy to Put Dropouts on the Path to Success*.

Adria Steinberg, EdM, vice president at *Jobs for the Future*, leads its program and policy efforts to improve educational options of young people who have disengaged or disconnected altogether from the educational system. Ms. Steinberg and her Pathways Through Postsecondary team work with state and federal policymakers to improve graduation rates and create and scale up high-quality pathways that lead to college and career success. She is the author or coauthor of *Pathway to Recovery: Implementing a Back on Track Through College Model*; and *Reinventing Alternative Education: An Assessment of Current State Policy and How to Improve It*.

Nancy Hoffman, PhD, vice president and senior adviser at *Jobs for the Future*, works on state policy, higher education, and transitions to postsecondary education. She has coedited two JFF books: *Double the Numbers:*

Increasing Postsecondary Credentials for Underrepresented Youth; and *Minding the Gap: Why Integrating High School with College Makes Sense and How to Do It*. Dr. Hoffman has worked as a consultant for the Organisation for Economic Co-operation and Development (OECD). Her most recent book, *Schooling in the Workplace: How Six of the World's Best Vocational Education Systems Prepare Young People for Jobs and Life*, is based on that work. She serves on the Massachusetts Board of Higher Education. (All three books are published by Harvard Education Press.)

About the Contributors

Heidi Andrade, EdD, is an associate professor of educational psychology and the Associate Dean for Academic Affairs at the School of Education, University at Albany-State University of New York. Her research and teaching focus on the relationships between thinking, learning, and assessment, with emphases on classroom assessment, student self-assessment, and self-regulated learning.

Georgia Brooke is an advanced doctoral student at the School of Education, University at Albany-State University of New York. Her interests include formative assessment, gifted education, and the interplay between psychological and biological forces, including the impact of environmental pollution on cognitive functioning.

Barbara Cervone, EdD, is founder and president of What Kids Can Do, Inc., an international nonprofit organization that promotes the value of young people tackling projects that combine powerful learning with public purpose. From 1994 to 2001 she directed Walter H. Annenberg's "Challenge to the Nation," then the largest private investment in public education in the nation's history. Dr. Cervone is a 2008 Purpose Prize Winner.

Kathleen Cushman is an educator and writer who has specialized in the lives and learning of youth for over two decades. In 2001 she cofounded What Kids Can Do, Inc., with Barbara Cervone. Her work there has resulted in nine book collaborations with students, most recently *Fires in the Mind: What Kids Can Tell Us About Motivation and Mastery* (Jossey-Bass 2010).

Kurt W. Fischer, PhD, Charles Bigelow Professor of Education and the director of the Mind, Brain, and Education Program at the Harvard Graduate School of Education, studies cognitive and emotional development and learning from birth through adulthood, combining analysis of the commonalities across people with the diversity of pathways of learning and development. He is the author of "Dynamic Development of Action, Thought, and Emotion" in the *Handbook of Child Psychology* (Volume 1); *Human Behavior and the Developing Brain*; *Mind, Brain, and Education in Reading Disorders*; and a dozen other books, as well as over two hundred scientific articles.

Catherine Glennon, EdM, is a doctoral candidate at Teachers College Columbia University, where her research focuses on music cognition and learning. She is also building an international network of Research Schools that carry out practical research. She previously earned a master's degree from the Harvard Graduate School of Education.

Jenna W. Gravel, EdM, is a doctoral student at the Harvard Graduate School of Education whose research interests focus on effective implementation of Universal Design for Learning (UDL) and the impact that this framework has on student learning. Prior to attending HGSE, she worked as a project manager and research associate at CAST, an education research and development organization. Before joining CAST, she worked as a middle school inclusion specialist as well as a staff assistant for an advocacy group for parents of children with disabilities.

Rochelle Gutiérrez, PhD, is a professor in the Department of Curriculum and Instruction and Latina/Latino Studies at the University of Illinois at Urbana-Champaign. Her research focuses on equity in mathematics education, race/class/language issues in teaching and learning mathematics, effective teacher communities, and social justice. She has written several articles and book chapters that address the achievement gap, English learners, mathematics teaching in Mexico, and sociopolitical trends in mathematics education. She is working on a book entitled *Developing Academic Excellence and Identity in Mathematics Students: Windows into Urban Teaching.*

Christina Hinton, EdD, is a faculty member at the Harvard Graduate School of Education and a research fellow at Sesame Workshop. Her research focuses on implications of neuroscience research for education, educational media, and global education. At HGSE, she is leading an international network of Research Schools that carry out practical research. She completed her doctorate and master's at Harvard in mind, brain, and education. Prior to this, she worked in multilateral diplomacy and international policy making at the Organization for Economic Cooperation and Development's Center for Educational Research and Innovation in Paris. Dr. Hinton lectures internationally on education and neuroscience, and has presented at numerous international, governmental, and academic institutions across the Americas, Asia, Australia, Europe, and the Middle East.

Kristen Huff, EdD, is the Senior Fellow for Assessment at the Regents Research Fund. Her main research interest is integrating evidence-centered design theory and practice into large-scale assessment to ensure that what is valued in student learning is measured on exams and communicated through instructionally relevant score reports.

Sonya E. Irving, EdM, is a doctoral candidate in the Department of Curriculum and Instruction at the University of Illinois. Her expertise is in evaluative research as a means to support teachers for instructional improvement, especially as it relates to equity in mathematics education. She has worked for several years as a mathematics teacher. She holds a bachelor's degree from Howard University and a master's degree from the Harvard Graduate School of Education.

Michael J. Nakkula, EdD, is a practice professor and chair of the Division of Applied Psychology and Human Development at the University of Pennsylvania's Graduate School of Education. He teaches courses on adolescent development and the intersection of counseling, mentoring, and education within urban public schools. He is the lead author of *Building Healthy Communities for Positive Youth Development* (Springer 2010).

David H. Rose, EdD, is a developmental neuropsychologist and educator whose primary focus is on the development of new technologies for learning. In 1984, Dr. Rose cofounded CAST, a nonprofit research and development organization whose mission is to improve education for all learners through innovative uses of modern multimedia technology and contemporary research in the cognitive neurosciences. He also teaches at the Harvard Graduate School of Education, where he has been on the faculty for nearly thirty years.

Alfred W. Tatum, PhD, is an associate professor at the University of Illinois at Chicago. He also serves as the director of the UIC Reading Clinic, where he hosts an annual African American Adolescent Male Summer Literacy Institute. He authored the award-winning book, *Teaching Reading to Black Adolescent Males: Closing the Achievement Gap* (Stenhouse Publishers, 2005). His second book, *Reading for Their Life: Re(Building) the Textual Lineages of African American Adolescent Males*, was published by Heinemann in August 2009.

Eric Toshalis, EdD, is an assistant professor at the Graduate School of Education and Counseling at Lewis & Clark College in Portland, Oregon, where he directs the Summer Middle and High School Level Program and teaches adolescent development and classroom management. Dr. Toshalis is the coauthor, with Michael J. Nakkula, of *Understanding Youth: Adolescent Development for Educators* (Harvard Education Press, 2006).

Index